LifeBlood

LifeBlood

Gill Fyffe

FREIGHT BOOKS

First published 2015

Freight Books
49-53 Virginia Street
Glasgow, G1 1TS
www.freightbooks.co.uk

A CIP catalogue reference for this book is available from the British Library

ISBN 978-1-910449-16-5
eISBN 978-1-910449-17-2

Typeset by Freight in Plantin Std

the publisher acknowledges investment from
Creative Scotland toward the publication of this book

Gill Fyffe read English at the University of St Andrews and was awarded an MLitt with distinction for a verse biography of Rose de Beauharnais, the empress Josephine. Gill's life has been affected by the consequences of a contaminated blood transfusion. She taught at the University of St Andrews and Fettes College, Edinburgh, before side-effects forced her to resign. She is immensely proud of her son and daughter who, educated at Fettes College, went on to study at Imperial and RADA, Oxford and LARA. Gill now lives in Soho. *LifeBlood* is her first book.

LifeBlood

The ward sister decides to move me into the room reserved for medical complications.

'Which you may well be,' she jokes, tilting the Venetian blind, 'but we wouldn't know, because your notes haven't turned up. If they still haven't turned up by the time the doctor does his round, I'll have to have a chat with you about that.'

I sink onto the pillow.

'Now I won't ignore you altogether,' she promises and rams home a plastic door wedge.

The plastic wedge makes a camera of the door. Figures flit back and forth within its frame. My eyelids flicker, slowing them to an animated cartoon. At the end of the show, the door slams shut.

My eyes snap open.

'So the head's engaged!' the ward sister has returned to encourage. 'Doctor thinks we may as well go for induction while we've got the chance. What do you think?'

I don't know. Are they asking me? I stare at the sister, and then together we stare at her clipboard. She turns a clean page and re-clips it.

'Your first child was born in – ?'

'1985.'

'A normal birth?'

'Section.'

'Any idea why?'

'Childbed fever.'

'Wait a minute.'

She crosses back to the door, opens it and checks that the doctor is still on the ward. When he acknowledges her wave, she stoops to ram back the plastic wedge.

In the labour suite, my pre-programmed contractions are interspersed with the spontaneous shouts of a healthy teenage delivery next door.

'Fuck's sake!'

I meet the midwife's eyes. She rolls hers. She is young and pretty with a gentle courtesy. She tells me that the doctor on duty is the same one I saw on the ward.

'He's the best,' she explains bending towards me in a stage whisper. 'He's such a stickler. We're all terrified of him.'

The midwife doesn't seem terrified, more like a house-proud young bride as she moves around her labour room, wiping down a sink and straightening the blanket over my feet. Her lips are closed in a small smile. She might be humming, but so is the monitor attached to my unborn baby's head. Beyond it, in preparation for events to come, my husband is sleeping in an armchair brought from the post-natal ward at his special request.

I concentrate on the steady green blip blip of our baby's heartbeat as long as I can.

'Actually,' says the midwife, 'I don't mind if you swear. Breathe,' she continues. 'Breathe. Breathe.'

I double up. We breathe again in unison. The midwife opens a new packet of latex gloves, and puts its cardboard lid in a pedal bin. She turns the heartbeat monitor so that I can see it better.

A telephone buzzes.

'Well, technically at two o'clock,' she replies, glancing up at a wall clock whose hands stand at half past. 'But I'll stay on if we're short-staffed.'

She turns to wave away my gasps of gratitude.

By the time my baby starts to arrive I am beyond gratitude. The room has grown hot and smaller. The hands on the wall clock no longer make sense. The doctor is telling me I am not to worry. He is only next door. He stops on his way out to tell the pretty midwife to report simultaneous deliveries. Telephones ring after him. My husband wakens up.

The midwife grows harassed. She tries to telephone, but the doctor reappears so she has to stop telephoning to strip off his latex gloves and pull a clean pair over his upturned wrists. The doctor gives me pain relief. He has grown expressionless. He is telling the midwife to report that I am weakening, and so are my induced contractions. A monitor on his belt beeps to report another admission.

The doctor calls for forceps. Sweat is visibly running into his eyes. Our daughter is born, and laid upon my stomach. The doctor dashes out.

'Thank God!' chokes my husband, and holds my hand.

But the room is spinning with the clock so I lose sight of him. There is only the top of our baby's head, and her tiny shoulder beneath the palm of my right hand. I can't tell if the midwife is still there either until the doctor dashes back in to scream at her. He screams so loudly that the spinning stops.

The doctor and the midwife are stopped too. I gaze at them over the baby's head. The midwife bursts into tears. The room has returned to its proper size, but the doctor towers over us.

'You can't repeat the injection.'

The midwife looks devastated. I smile to reassure her. The pain of contraction has stopped, and my baby lies warm beneath my hand. As though he thinks I have not understood the situation, the doctor sits by my bed to explain it.

'The injection was meant to boost your final contractions, to deliver the placenta. I'm afraid it was administered too soon. The only option now is that I remove the placenta myself.'

My husband is asked to leave. Another doctor arrives, and a different nurse. The nurse lifts our daughter, cradling her into a cotton blanket.

'Don't worry,' she says, so that I realise I've stopped smiling.

The room seems to be filling up with people. An anaesthetist is reading the midwife's notes. The midwife is still refusing to go home. I am shocked to discover, when she glances up at the wall clock, that her shift finished seven hours ago. A third doctor looks in and raises his eyebrows in interrogation.

'Manual extraction,' explains the anaesthetist.

The nurse who took our daughter has gone. An older one is opening sterile packets and talking to the midwife in a comforting undertone.

'Can we get on?' asks the doctor, no longer sitting by my bed but standing beyond its foot, his hands upturned in waiting.

First one latex glove and then another is unrolled over them. The older nurse crosses to my side. When he is sure he has located the placenta, the doctor clenches his remaining hand into a fist and beats it upon my stomach.

Thanks to the anaesthetist, there is no pain. There is, therefore, no emergency. The placenta is eventually loosened and removed.

The doctor straightens, and wipes the sweat from his eyes with his upper arm.

'Thank you,' I whisper.

There is blood everywhere.

'There will be pain,' he apologises.

But pain means not dead from septicaemia. Our eyes meet in a sad shared smile.

'You don't want a transfusion?'

'I don't want AIDS.'

The doctor smiles.

'We'll take a blood sample and if your haemoglobin count is more than six then I'll reconsider.' He nods to a nurse. 'But a transfusion is a painless procedure and totally safe. Don't be alarmed by scare stories on television. There is no risk of infection from blood.'

The nurse's latex gloves snap around her wrists in contradiction. The doctor meets my pointed stare and looks away.

I am decided. The doctor could be wrong about the blood transfusion. He was wrong about the pain. There isn't any. I feel nothing. My mind is clear. I can't move, but my mind is clear. I know that it is Friday. I know that it is October 1988.

Beyond the hospital walls, the world is going crazy about AIDS. No-one HIV positive dare reveal their condition. Homosexuals are demonised. Special mouthpieces have been manufactured so that paramedics can avoid contact during mouth-to-mouth resuscitation. Children with grazed knees may not swim in public swimming pools. Classroom packs of latex gloves ensure teachers need never touch their pupils. You are not only sleeping with your lover, but with all his previous lovers. The advice is clear. If you don't want to die of AIDS, avoid contact with blood.

'And a transfusion is a whole pint, isn't it?' I ask the doctor.

'Four,' he says, reading the laboratory's haemoglobin count. 'Four pints.'

He writes the order on a requisition form.

'No!'

The doctor sighs.

'Your haemoglobin count is much too low. That's why—'

'What is it?'

He looks impatient.

'Three point nine.'

'What should it be?'

'Ten.'

I change tack.

'I don't want to put my baby at risk—'

'But there *is* no risk!'

'I want to *know* my baby will be safe. I want a second opinion.'

The doctor runs his hands through his hair. Deep shadows darken his eye sockets. He drops his hands to his knees with a slap and stands up.

'All right. A second opinion.'

An older nurse appears near my head and takes me by surprise. She cups my face in her hands.

'Are you listening? I'm going to turn you onto your side. It's time to feed your baby.'

Our daughter has to lie on the bed, instead of in my arms. I hold her shoulders with the palm of one hand and whenever she stops feeding the nurse helps her to start again. A dark red paper wad is eased from under me, and a white sterile one is slipped in its place. We turn onto the other side. Then the nurse changes our daughter's nappy and pushes her plastic crib nearer to my bed, so that I can watch her sleep.

'There is a risk but it is negligible,' confirms the second opinion.

His lapel badge says that he is one of the ward's consultants. His expression says he had not expected to make a further round of it.

'Do I need a transfusion? Isn't that a matter of opinion?'

'An infinitesimally small risk, but you are perfectly sensible to check. And since you seek my opinion,' his tone hardens, 'it is that you should take the transfusion.'

I try not to match his impatience.

'What will happen if I don't?'

'Well, your body will gradually manufacture red blood cells to replace those you have lost. But it will take three, four, six months. You will remain weakened for a long time.'

I don't feel weakened. I feel strong. I am not going to take their transfusion.

'I can feed my baby, can't I?'

'Course you can!' comforts the older nurse, swapping another sterile wad into place in preparation for the night-feed. 'Ups-a-daisy. There you go. And here comes Baby.'

She has brought a younger nurse to help her. The younger nurse's lapel badge says she is a graduate trainee. She lays our daughter on the bed beside me. She is already *au fait* with the situation.

'The whole canteen is talking about it. You shouldn't feel pressured. It's just doctors being doctors. They always think they know best. Lots of nurses say they would refuse a transfusion too.'

'Would you?'

'Well, personally I would accept, but I'm just saying that not everyone—'

'Personally,' interrupts the older nurse, 'I wouldn't touch a transfusion with a tarry barge pole.'

Our daughter is failing to feed. The older nurse takes her out of the trainee's hands and expertly manoeuvres her tiny form into place on the bed.

'And it's not only HIV you have got to worry about,' she tells me cheerfully. 'There's hepatitis, and God knows what.'

I ask the older nurse to bring the telephone trolley so that I can tell my husband what is happening.

'What shall I do?' he asks.

'Get over here fast?'

'What – leave the office?'

I close my eyes. After the trauma of our daughter's birth, he has retreated into his appointments diary. With excruciating slowness, he gets back up to speed.

'You mean you're *still* bleeding?'

'I think so.'

'God. How much blood have you *lost?*'

'Four units, apparently.'

'Four – isn't that a hell of a lot?'

'I don't know. I can't get them to talk to me. I mean, the consultant came, but he wouldn't listen to what I was saying. They think I'm panicking.'

'But if the risk is negligible—'

'Now you're not listening to me. I don't *care* whether it's negligible. It's still a *risk*. I don't want to take it. I want to keep us all safe.'

'You should ask them straight how ill you are—'

'I would like you to ask. I'm too weak now. They are patronising me.'

There is a silence, then a new note of panic in his voice.

'How weak?'

'The nurse is holding the telephone receiver so that I can talk to you.'

My telephone call has been allowed by the ward sister, who is of the doctor's opinion. She is watching from the nursing station. The older nurse hangs up. She lets go my elbow to push the telephone trolley back up the ward.

For one second of triumph I stand unaided. There is time to lock glances with the ward sister. I have fed my baby and telephoned my husband. I am well.

The look the ward sister gives me in return, when I open my eyes a minute later and discover the ceiling, is one of irritation. I can't hear what she is saying for the hooting of an electronic emergency alarm. She rolls me into the recovery position, so that a doctor appears and disappears from view. The alarm stops.

'Turn it off!' the ward sister is shouting.

I hear the doctor murmur that a consultant from the Blood Transfusion Service has been called in to talk to me. The ward sister gets me back into bed and relays this information again. A tear runs across my temple and into my ear.

'I was strong enough to telephone.'

The ward sister brushes away the tear.

'Oh, we're not in any doubt about your willpower,' she snaps.

The consultant from the Blood Transfusion Service arrives with my husband.

'Thank you for coming,' says the ward sister to the consultant, 'but I'm not sure this is the right moment. We've just had a faint.'

The doctor who delivered our daughter has also returned and is hovering at the nursing station, his face as haggard as mine. The fight has gone out of us both.

'What will happen,' I hear my husband ask him, 'if she isn't transfused?'

'If the haemorrhaging has stopped, nothing will happen. We'll put her on iron tablets. You will need to help to care for the baby but she is strong so –' the doctor purses his lips '– maybe for as little as a month?'

I close my eyes in relief.

'What will happen,' persists my husband, 'if she haemorrhages again?'

I open my eyes. They are standing face to face. Each seems sorry for the other.

'If she haemorrhages again,' says the doctor, 'we won't be able to transfuse fast enough.'

My husband comes to sit by my bed. He is crying.

'Please,' he says. 'Please.'

'Am I not strong enough?'

'You can hardly lift your head off the pillow,' he chokes.

The doctor steps into view. He is difficult to see because I am crying too.

The bloodpacks arrive with their own nurse. She puts on latex gloves for her own protection to set up a drip-stand by my bed. The nurse checks and doublechecks my blood type. The plastic tubing which connects the bloodpack to the needle in my hand is very long. The first scarlet drops begin to inch their way along it.

I spend every inch not ripping out the needle. The transfusion is saving my life. Three times the nurse returns to pull on latex gloves and swap bloodpacks. Three times I watch the latex gloves snap around her wrists, and I don't rip out the needle.

I love the older nurse. It is not the morphine talking. I love her. My husband comes. I make him say he loves her too.

When the morphine wears off, I waken into a nightmare.

'Still in pain?' asks the older nurse. 'We'll try to hold off for now, but let me know if you need another shot.'

But no-one is released from postnatal care on morphine. We walk behind the nurse, who carries our daughter. My husband has one hand under my elbow and the other under my armpit, with covert instructions that he is not to let me take my own weight.

'Have you a christening planned?' asks the nurse.

I promise our son a picnic.

'You deserve it,' I tell him, 'looking after Baby all day. *And* me.'

'He deserves a picnic,' I yell at my husband once he has returned from the office, an hour later than he promised, and exhausted, so he says. '*You're* exhausted? *He's* only three years old, and he's run around all day fetching nappies, and yoghurt from the fridge—'

'I've got to get up in the morning—'

'I won't be *able* to get up in the morning. And I'm bored rigid lying here—'

'They ought to be in bed—'

'Don't you dare!' I rage from my sofa. 'Don't you *dare* put anyone to bed. We've waited all day. I took the transfusion. We want a *picnic!*'

My husband takes time to hang up his jacket, to reassert normality.

'But it's *dark* outside. We can't eat a picnic in the dark. Maybe you're depressed or something?'

I catch my breath, then re-engage in a higher gear.

'– *bullying* me with crap about depression –'

'– it's a well-known *fact* –'

I make it onto an elbow. Pain floods my body with inhuman energy. He looks round and is startled.

'Think very carefully,' I promise him, 'whether you want this conversation. Because if you do, I'll call a taxi and show up in your office tomorrow to hold it in front of your staff.'

His expression falters.

'Or,' I snarl, 'you can pick up some fish and chips and carry me into the garden for a *picnic.*'

'In the name of the Father and of the Son and of the Holy Ghost,' finishes the priest.

'Where did you get your hat?' whispers my sister.

'Laura Ashley.'

She looks at my husband, who is grim-faced on one side of the altar my father designed for the cathedral. It is a private christening after Mass, very stylish, but fraught with religious and family tensions.

'Have you two had a row?'

'Yes.'

'Have you had a row with dad too?'

'No, he got caught in the cross-fire.'

'Ooops,' grins my sister, and then, after a minute, 'would you mind if I had one like it?'

'What, a row?'
'No, stupid. A Laura Ashley hat.'

My sister buys a Laura Ashley interior to match her hat. Her windows are hung with the finest linen. Her walls are papered with stripes and fleur de lys. Her chairs groan beneath cotton ticking cushions.

'Wow, it's beautiful. I'm jealous.'
'How are things going?'
'Not well. We row all the time.'
'You're putting your marriage at risk.'
I am surprised I do not care.
'Maybe I want to put it at risk?'
'Maybe you're over-tired?'

The nurse at the baby clinic is more definite. Her eyes skim over my notes, pausing over the blood transfusion, then look up in a swift appraising glance.

'You look very thin. And you've been in a lot of pain. Would you say you were over-tired?'

The nurse has taken our daughter's temperature and taken off her nappy. She puts her on a blanket in the stainless steel basin of a set of scales, and stands up to take my temperature. The scales' digital reading flashes scarlet.

'Your baby has lost weight.'

I recall the stylish christening, the rows with my husband, the expedition to Laura Ashley to buy the hat, and sicken with guilt.

'And your temperature is high.'
'High?'
'On the high side. How long has your baby been crying?'
'Three, four days?'
You must feed her now.'
'But I just fed her—'
'Your baby is failing to thrive.'

I hear my own gasp. The nurse brings me a cup of tea, to facilitate the extra feed. My heart is racing. As I hold our daughter, she quivers to its beat.

'Is she sleepy after her feeds?'

'Yes, always. She goes straight to sleep after them.'

'For how long?'

'Well, that's the problem. Up until now she's been sleeping well.'

'How long has she slept after her feeds this week?'

'Well – well, this week – only half an hour.'

'She is exhausting herself trying to feed,' says the nurse. 'Then after half an hour, hunger wakens her again. Are you still taking pain-killers?'

'Not for a month now.'

'Well then,' says the nurse, coming round her desk. 'Let's see what the scales say.'

Our daughter's eyes have closed. Her open mouth falls off my nipple. It is late afternoon, and the nurse's window has darkened behind a Christmas tree. The tree lights and the digital reading of the stainless steel scales sparkle in synchrony.

'How much should she have gained?'

'Six ounces would be ideal. But given all you've been through, we probably can't hope for more than four.'

The blanket slips. Our daughter shivers and frets in her basin. The digital reading dances up and down its scale.

'Sssh, sssh,' comforts the nurse, replacing the blanket.

We watch the reading settle. It is the same as it was before the feed. The nurse lifts our daughter to her shoulder. She dials an internal telephone with the other hand.

'One of the doctors, please,' and then, 'a baby has been accidentally starved.'

I have starved our daughter. I have starved her for a week.

'For three days,' comforts the nurse, calming me down while a doctor carries out an examination on a plastic mat. 'I saw you on Tuesday, remember? And your temperature wasn't high then. You were fine on Tuesday.'

The doctor interrupts.

'The baby is fine too. But she must be fed as soon as possible. Do you have a feeding bottle at home?'

I can't believe it.

'No, I've nothing—'

'The nurse will tell you what you need to feed your baby.' The doctor rises to leave, patting my shoulder, but speaking to the nurse. 'As soon as possible.'

'As soon as possible,' I repeat to my husband.

We are standing in the kitchen amid a welter of brand-new feeding apparatus. I am holding our daughter and he is reading the instructions on a packet of sterilising tablets. Our daughter is wailing.

'Wait a minute, give me a minute,' shouts my husband. 'And stop that bloody crying.'

He means mine.

'Like this?' he continues, upending the bottle and letting the warm milk drip onto the back of my hand.

'I don't know. The nurse says it will be difficult to persuade her to feed from a plastic teat.'

'Well, does it feel too hot?'

'Sort of lukewarm.'

The warm milk splashes onto my hand again. Our daughter goes rigid in my arms and screams with rage. We hold the bottle as the diagram in the instructions indicates. Without hesitation she clenches the teat between her gums. There is an unfamiliar silence.

'Baby happy now,' says our son.

'And why the hell is your temperature up?' demands my husband.

'One of those things I suppose.'

'I told you the christening was too much for you.'

'I'm sure the christening has nothing to do with this.'

'God, you're not sickening for something are you? You're not coming down with something, are you?'

'No.'

'Because I'm up to my eyes at the office,' he complains, going out the back door.

Through the window, I watch his tail-lights recede.

When I tire of the rows, I turn to our son for advice.

'Shall we leave, or shall we stay with Daddy?'

'Stay with Daddy.'

'But if he's cross again and starts shouting?'

'Stay with Daddy.'

'If he makes you cry, like last time?'

'Uh—'

There is a sizeable pause. Our son considers. His expression clears.

'Stay with Daddy.'

I serve breakfast in the garden, where our daughter is sleeping. It is Saturday morning.

'Are you playing home or away?'

'Away. St Andrews.'

I sit up. St Andrews is my alma mater.

'Why didn't you say? We can meet you after the match for tea.'

Our son stops digging for treasure and takes off a pirate hat. My husband's expression grows to a mild regret.

'I'm afraid you can't come. A couple of the younger lads in the team don't have any transport so I've offered them a lift in my car.'

There is a moment of silence. Our son replaces his pirate hat and picks up his spade. I hear a rushing noise, and have time to wonder what it is.

'*Your* car?'

The rushing noise is a wave of anger so great that in a second the garden is engulfed in it.

'When you say *your* car, do you mean the car my salary helped to buy before I had *your* children?'

'Yeah, but obviously I meant—'

'The car my salary used to fill with petrol?'

'I didn't mean to suggest—'

'*Your bloody car!*' I scream, so that our daughter wakes to scream with me, and I have to take a deep breath, stop screaming and pick her up.

The wave of anger passes over the garden. In its wake, my husband exchanges a quick glance with our son.

'Look, of course I didn't mean *my* car. That was a slip of the tongue. It's *our* car, of course it is. It's just that I've already offered these young lads a lift—'

'I'm afraid they can't come,' I mimic him, 'because if you won't take us I'll find someone else to drive *my car*, to St Andrews, for tea. You and your friends will have to take the bus.'

'But—'

'As I've been doing,' I continue 'in the mistaken belief that without my salary I can't afford driving lessons. Only it occurs to me now, if I cancel your hockey club subscription, I can probably afford quite a few.'

In St Andrews, the team is waiting to play with eight men. My husband clambers out of my car and lifts the carrycot wheels out of the boot.

'You're welcome to stay and watch the match?' he offers in further appeasement.

I do not dignify this suggestion with an answer. For this reason, when we meet for tea, he does not even ask *where to?* He loads the carrycot wheels back in the boot, the carrycot onto the backseat, the pirate hat in the glove compartment and drives the lot a mile out of town to the most expensive afternoon tea we know.

In the quiet of the late afternoon, the garden of the inn contemplates a mile of fields, which break and fall away, down to the ruins of the medieval cathedral, and the sea. I spend half an hour in the ladies' lavatory playing with bottles of perfumes, emerging into the garden scented with Guerlain and regret.

'I thought you'd left me,' jokes my husband.

'Without a salary?'

There is an awkward pause.

'Look I know life's been tough, with the transfusion and not being able to stand up for a month –'

I narrow my eyes. He fails to notice.

'– but take a joke, yeah? You're still not well enough to earn a salary. I wish I could get home from the office more often to help you but I can't.'

'You could work from home.'

He looks up, startled.

'No I couldn't. There isn't space.'

'Well, we could move to a bigger house. You could build one. And then you could open a design practice of your own.'

'Spend my time building a house and risk the only income we've got?' he scoffs.

My teacup rattles into its saucer.

'*Risk?*'

I am on my feet.

'*Risk!*'

He stumbles to his.

'It's only *money*!' I am shouting. 'It's not *blood!*'

He buckles as I push our daughter into his arms.

'Not *blood!* Not flesh and *blood!*'

'Christ, take a joke,' he complains as he struggles to hold her. 'I said I thought you'd left me as a *joke.*'

The ruins of St Andrews cathedral dissolve in my tears of frustration.

'*We already decided not to leave you!*' I shout.

'I told you this would happen,' my husband frets. 'I warned you. Don't say I didn't warn you.'

He indicates to slow at the kerb where a broken wall still provides the only access to our newly built house. In the streetlight, its chimney piece stands sentinel between two elms.

'They've finished the chimney!' I whisper. 'It's got tiles round the top.'

He switches off the ignition.

'Great. We've got a chimney. We haven't got a fireplace, because we've run out of money. I warned you. Don't say—'

His voice is rising again. I point towards the car's back seat.

'Sssh!'

He looks over his shoulder. The children are wrapped in blankets and asleep in their car-seats. He turns back to run his hands through his hair in the rear-view mirror.

'You realise this will take all night?'

'At least you haven't an office to go to.'

'Christ,' seethes my husband.

Between us we untie a chest of drawers from the roof rack and heave it through our newly hung front door.

'Leave it here?'

'We can't,' he puffs. 'We have to take it up.'

'But if the building inspector does come,' I argue, 'he could just as easily inspect upstairs. He'll see our beds for a start.'

'No he won't. We can't put up beds. If he suspects we've had to move in without a certificate, he'll change the locks.'

It is the first time my husband has impressed me.

'How will we sleep then?' I whisper.

'In a heap on the floor until we get that certificate. Which won't happen until they've finished the stairs. Which won't happen for another two weeks. Don't say I didn't warn you.'

I recognise my son's classroom at once. It is exactly as he has described it. His teacher is exactly as he has described her. I am careful to close the door behind me, in case she makes me go back out and come in again. She looks at her register and tells me there has been good progress.

'Yeah, we're pretty happy too,' I smile.

'I'm sorry?'

'Well,' I laugh. 'You know. We sort of worked out everything was all right. I mean, he's in the yellow group.'

'The yellow group.'

We are sitting at a hexagon of undersized desks. I point to their bowl of plastic daffodils, and try not to gloat.

'This is it, isn't it? The top group.'

The teacher's expression hardens.

'No, certainly not. Our educational policy is founded on a mixed-ability approach which does not acknowledge outdated concepts of attainment—'

'Yes but –' I persist, '– between you and me? Considering that the pink group haven't learned any times tables yet?'

'We absolutely do not acknowledge, nor do our teaching methods, outdated concepts of attainment.'

'Oh.'

The teacher snaps shut her register.

'I don't know where you got the idea that the yellow group was the top group but I do assure you that our teaching methods do not acknowledge—'

'Well, the clever boy who got the top mark is in the yellow group,' I defend myself.

The clever boy's father is an architect. The clever boy comes top in everything, has a mother who is French and walks to school in a waxed jacket. None of these cut any ice with the teacher.

'—our strong assertion is that outdated concepts of attainment have no place in a modern educational policy—'

'Yes you said that, but the facts are that everyone in the yellow group is on page thirty-five, whereas no-one in the green group, who are clearly second top, has got beyond page twenty-eight—'

I am aggrieved. It has been quite an effort to keep up with the clever boy.

'I don't mean to labour the point, but—'

'You are mistaken. There is nothing special about the yellow group. In fact,' the teacher opens her register again, 'in fact, I have drawn up the groups for the autumn term and your child has been reallocated to the blue group. We reallocate on a regular basis,' she goes on, without a smile, 'in order to promote a strict educational policy based on a mixed ability approach—'

'And what group is the boy who got the top mark in for the autumn term?'

She looks shocked.

'We do not discuss the educational progress of any pupil in inappropriate adult company.'

'Has he been reallocated to the blue group?'

'—wholly inappropriate for me to discuss the academic record of a pupil with anyone save—'

She sees that I am reading the register upside down and snaps it shut again.

'Well, thank you for coming in. We look forward to welcoming you, next month, at our annual sports day.'

She glances towards the door. Through its pane of glass, the clever boy's mother is chatting, no doubt in French. There is no option but to rise. The teacher already has.

'You understand we have a schedule to keep.'

'Will you acknowledge outdated concepts of attainment,' I defy the schedule enough to ask, 'at your annual sports day? I mean, what will you do if somebody wins a race?'

The teacher's eyes close. She shudders at the thought.

'What?' frowns my husband, once the conversation is relayed to this point.

'No winners or losers. Apart from their being an outdated concept, competitive behaviour increases the risk to children of physical injury. So then we had a row about risk—'

'*Oh God,*' says my husband, and puts his head in his hands.

I hold up mine in protest.

'No, it's fine. Well, the teacher's not too happy. But the clever boy's mother agreed with every word I said.'

'You even wallpapered the loo!' grins our neighbour, returning to my dinner table.

My husband has a mouthful of pie, and holds up four fingers.

'Four?'

He swallows.

'I wallpapered four.'

'You have four lavatories?' the neighbour asks me.

'Well, how many have you got?'

He laughs.

'One, of course.'

His pretty wife, who is not drunk because she is nursing their first child, pushes his shoulder out of the way.

'Three,' she confirms.

Her husband is astonished. The other side of the table stop talking to follow this exchange.

'Go on!' they tease. 'Go on! Count them.'

'Well, there's a lavatory next to the bath—'

'ONE!' roars the other side of the table.

'Shall we go through to the fire?' I ask hurriedly.

I lead the way. My husband brings up the rear.

'How many Victorian grates have you got?' I hear him say.

'You're awake?'

I open my eyes.

'The moment they left you went out like a light against the radiator.'

'Did I?'

'Don't you remember? I had to drag you off it. How's the arm?'

I am too tired to find out how is my arm. It is underneath my head.

'Fine.'

'Let me take a look at it.'

'No.'

'We'd better. Come on.'

'What time is it?'

'Just after three.'

'Did you load the dishwasher?'

'Yeah. Sit up.'

'Too tired.'

'You must.'

In the firelight, the full extent of the damage is revealed.

'God, what a mess,' grimaces my husband, holding up my sleeve.

The blister is about three inches long, and swollen into a taut bubble.

'You'll have to lance it.'

'I know.'

'You should ring the doctor.'

'I can't.'

'Why not?'

'You know why not. He'll think I'm doing it deliberately.'

My husband frowns. Above the blister, scar after scar disfigures my skin.

'I'm beginning to wonder myself.'

I pull down my sleeve, too tired to argue.

He sits back on his heels.

'Well, why do you do it then? You *know* radiators can raise blisters. Why do you *do* it?'

'I don't mean to do it. I'm just tired. Cold and really really tired.'

To prove the point I slide back down on the sofa.

'No, sit up.'

'Make coffee,' I negotiate. 'Make coffee and then I'll sit up.'

A wonderful thing happens. I open my eyes. The cafetière of coffee I didn't drink still stands next to me. On either side of it, tall figures wait.

I roll over. Through the window dawn lights the crowns of the firs behind the house. It is the edge of dawn. I am on the edge.

I roll back, trembling with excitement.

'Come with us,' offer the tall figures.

'With the children?'

'Yes.'

The cafetière's silver stand catches the dawn and reflects it.

'Shall I come without my husband?'

The tall figures are not disconcerted by the question, but they shake their heads.

'He will save you,' they warn.

'You want to sell the *house?*'

My husband is incredulous. He is looking at the bandage on my arm.

'I'm not delusional, if that's what you're suggesting.'

'How is the blister?'

'Better.'

'Did you lance it?'

'Yeah.'

He shudders.

'Something's wrong. Last night I couldn't wake you. You were practically unconscious. Something's not right. And now you want to sell the *house?*'

He sits down at the table.

'Everything we have is invested in this house. If we wait ten years, we'll make a profit. If we wait five we might break even. If we sell now, we'll lose money.'

'I know.'

'Well, is there a reason to sell now?'

I tell him about the tall figures. I don't tell him he will save me, because I don't think I need saved.

'But we can't just sell the house,' he argues. 'Not without a proper reason. There has to be a reason we can understand. There's something going on that we don't understand.'

On the road to St Andrews, our car is second in a line of cars. Dusk has fallen with the temperature. Shops will close in an hour. The line of cars' headlights come on. Ours do not.

I am asleep at the wheel.

Our car drives on, long enough to cross the central line of unbroken white paint, not long enough to hit the oncoming vehicle racing towards us.

I open my eyes.

On my nearside is the gap in the line of cars which I have left. There is nothing to stop me sliding back into it. But I understand that if I hit the oncoming car I will kill the driver. In a panic, I spin the steering wheel hard to the left.

We race through the gap and off the road.

I only understand the car is in the air when it nosedives back towards the ground. A fence post looms, filling the windscreen. We crash-land into it, and topple slightly onto the car's nearside.

Inside the car there is shock and silence. I put my shoulder to the door. It is jammed shut. In my imagination a terrifying conflagration ignites with a roar.

No! I scream.

I pull up my legs, spin in my chair and punch both heels at the jammed door. It bounces wide against its hinges. My heels kick against the dashboard as I reach into the back of the car.

Our son is grabbed by the collar, our daughter by her hair. He has freed himself from his safely buckle. She is torn from her car-seat straps with one vicious tug. Together with my screams, we tumble from the car.

There is undergrowth, not the manicured golfing green I expected. *Run!* I scream to our son, pulling him off his feet. We stumble and scramble through thirty metres of gorse along the edge of a culvert.

The road sits high on its banking above our heads. There are lights, and one great headlit glow where somebody has pulled over. A dark figure appears within the glow, peering down in silhouette.

Save us! I shout up towards it.

Figures scramble down the bank and cross the culvert another thirty metres further on. They race back to our car, which has not ignited, and trip over us in the dark. There are shouts, and a blanket. Somehow we are all got up the bank onto the road.

Lit by headlights, the dark figures are revealed in uniform. Their car has POLICE painted over its bonnet. They are by coincidence those I would have killed.

Their radios crackle. I sit with our children in the back of the police car. There is a request for a recovery vehicle.

They'll need a crane to get it out of the field. It's a twelve foot drop. And then, to my chagrin, *write-off by the look of it.*

The journey to St Andrews is made in silence. I haven't been arrested, but it feels like it. At the police station, we are shown into an interview room and I am breathalysed. When it is negative they offer tea.

The policeman whom I nearly killed reappears with a chargesheet on a clipboard. The same question is repeated over and over. We are agreed on road conditions, the line of cars, my estimated speed. We are agreed I have fallen asleep at the wheel.

'But why turn off the road?' he repeats, his pen hovering over the chargesheet, as bewildered as I feel. 'But why turn off the road?'

I am at a loss. There are no words to satisfy the chargesheet's demand for a specific level of negligence.

'All I can remember is thinking that if I hit you, I would kill you.'

On a whim, the policeman tears the chargesheet from the clipboard and crumples it into the wastepaper basket. He leaves without comment. A younger uniformed colleague enters to indicate the telephone, closing the door behind his exit.

My husband answers on the third ring.

'Hello?'

'I crashed the car,' I manage.

'Are you all right?' he is shouting. 'Are the children all right?'

His panic subsides as my sobbing goes out of control.

'It doesn't matter, so long as you and the children are safe.'

'Oh God!' I sob. 'You won't say that when you see the car.'

The door to the interview room re-opens and a policewoman puts her head around it. She hands me a box of tissues.

'You forgot to dial nine for a line out. Which is fine, except the duty sergeant copped that through his earphones. No, don't be sorry. There's a bit of a party getting up next door. It's not every day we don't wind up one of our own statistics. Here, shall I take the wee chap through and give you a minute to yourself?'

Later, once we all are safely strapped into my husband's, and now our only, car, we turn onto an unfamiliar route.

'Where are you going?'

'I'm not sure at the moment.'

He slows at a fork in a back road out of town.

'You're trying to avoid my car?'

'Yes.'

'You've seen it?'

'I stopped on the way in.'

'How did you know where to stop?'

'You took a good bit of the verge down with you.'

My hands start to tremble.

'Was it – was it—'

'It's written off. What happened? Was it ice?'

'No, no—'

'You just drove off the road?'

'No – I—'

Our eyes meet. I don't want to admit I fell asleep at the wheel. I am young and fit. Shame descends like a curtain.

'I – I fell asleep. Then I panicked. There was no need. I came out of lane a bit, panicked, and thought I could drive onto the golf course.'

My husband frowns.

'Why didn't they charge you? It doesn't make sense. Something's not right.'

He signals left, to make a three point turn in a convenient entrance. The entrance has stone gateposts, and high wooden gates fixed back against them. Beyond the gatepost is a large stone house, with Gothic turrets, a playing field, and perimeter of trees. From the branches of the nearest, children are waving.

We stop at a grand hotel. A pinafored waiter studiously ignores my bruises, and the bloodied scratches on our son's legs. When I lift our daughter into the highchair he proffers, a large quantity of her blond hair remains stuck to my coat.

'Coffee thank you,' my husband intervenes. 'And cakes.'

Our son's traumatised expression brightens.

'Cakes?'

'Just this once.'

'Cakes *and* juice?'

'Just this once.'

The cakes arrive on a silver cakestand. The children are transfixed. I am transfixed. My husband's eyes narrow.

'Listen, before you get carried away, sufficient unto the day and all that. You just wrote off your car—'

'It's a reason.'

'What?'

'You said there had to be a proper reason. This is it. If we sell the house, we can build another one here, in St Andrews, near that school.'

'We know nothing about a school—'

'All those children climbing trees! Remember I told you – in my dream, remember? – they told me to bring the children.'

'It was just a silly dream.'

'And today was just a silly traffic accident?'

My husband's head is in his hands.

'You think someone *made* you crash off the road?'

'We didn't crash. We *flew!*'

He looks up, then laughs.

'I thought you were serious for a minute!'

'Not about the divine intervention,' I allow. 'Only about the school.'

At their new school, where our children are allowed to climb trees, home-made wooden stilts are also available.

'These are my friends,' says my son.

They teeter above him. The darker-haired is impressively Elastoplast-free.

'I won't shake hands,' he grins. 'But mum would love to meet you. She's in the boot room.'

'Same,' manages the fair-haired boy, and falls off.

The bootroom is a narrow ante-chamber to the reception hall. It is of a plain concrete construction, but marked out by the warm sweaty smell of junior trainers and the warm sweaty taste of adult gossip. Within it, three tall figures wait.

'Are you the new boy's mother?' askes the tallest.

She mentions an aristocratic Scottish lineage. I make an awkward introduction, apologising that I don't know anyone.

'You soon will,' observe the second tallest, with a wry glance towards the first.

The aristocrat introduces her.

'She's an historian. You've probably read her?'

'Unlikely,' says the historian, 'since I'm only published in America.'

Up close, the historian is not physically tall, but her eyes flash fire.

'Where are you living?'

I take a deep breath.

'Actually, we just sold our house. So we're living in an attic on Argyle Street.'

'On Argyle Street? Where is that?' asks the historian.

'Is it the Mansard attic up the pend which leads past the pan-tiled cottage? Thought that might be you,' smiles the aristocrat.

My jaw drops.

'Where is that?' repeats the historian.

'The house I was telling you about. New family, he's an engineer, she doesn't look well.'

They raise their eyebrows interrogatively.

'I'm fine!' I protest.

'Hm,' says the aristocrat. 'Where are your parents?'

'My parents?'

'Where do they live? North of the Forth?'

I clutch a bootrack for support.

'North of the Tay.'

'Pictish,' she nods. 'Pale skin. Though you do look tired.'

I hold out my hand to the silent third. She is beautiful, with the olive skin and almond eyes of a Japanese plutocracy.

'Married a millionaire,' explains the aristocrat. 'Lives in the castle. Are you free for lunch on Saturday?'

In this new world we inhabit, multiple lavatories count for nothing. The lunch is a political one. My table companion is the son of a lord, who can trace his stretch of coastline back to a squire who fought for William the Conqueror.

'I've heard about you,' he politely recalls. 'You're the Mansard attic up the pend behind the pan-tiled cottage? Allow me to make your introductions. This lady has escaped from Sarajevo to look for her son. And this is the party spokesman for Foreign Affairs.'

'Welcome back,' says my old tutor.

We shake hands.

'It's lovely to be back,' I tell him.

'It must be ten years?'

I look at the Victorian townhouse behind him. *School of English* reads the brass plaque at its door.

'I suppose there have been a lot of changes?' I ask him.

He looks at the ruins of the twelfth century castle behind me.

'Not as many as you'd think,' he grins. 'You've met the new professor?'

'He interviewed me.'

We turn into the School of English together. On a wooden board in the entrance hall, against his painted surname, the tutor flicks a shutter from OUT to IN. At the top of the column of names, in a mismatched font, dazzles the name of the new professor.

'We were lucky to get him,' nods my old tutor, 'considering the eye-watering award for poetry. He's a good chap. As you will discover.'

My new friends come to lunch. I do my best at a local auction, acquiring a wooden nursing chair with brocade hangings for two pounds, and an earthenware urn painted with bluebells for twenty.

'Haven't your new carpets arrived?' grins the historian.

'God,' complains the aristocrat, 'who can afford rugs? Though I do think,' she adds as I take her coat, 'with school fees so expensive, we ought to get a headmaster we can lust after.'

Without turning a hair, she sits on one end of the garden bench we have brought inside for a sofa.

'Now,' she continues to the millionaire's wife. 'I've found you a housekeeper.'

'Thank you,' returns the millionaire's wife. 'I have told you before. I do not like a housekeeper. I do not need one.'

The aristocrat shoots her a look.

'I call that a very selfish attitude. The poor woman is desperate for a job. She can't go back to Sarajevo. Good soup,' she interrupts herself to tell me.

I wonder whether the soup will recommend me as the housekeeper.

'Yes,' says the aristocrat, turning back to me, 'you could do with a job yourself. Not just that fiddly university tutoring. Why don't you teach at the girls' school?'

'Yes,' says the historian. 'Why are you not teaching at the girls' school? When she could so easily arrange it for you?'

'Well, I'd like to—'

'Do you know the headmistress?' asks the aristocrat.

'No, I—'

'No matter. I expect she'll call tomorrow.'

'Did you give her my number?'

'Of course.'

'Why don't you invite the headmistress to lunch?' beams the historian. 'No, wait.' She turns to the millionaire's wife. 'Why don't you, now that you have a housekeeper to cook it?'

'Is this for your husband?' the millionaire's wife asks me, picking up a fifth bowl of soup. 'Shall I take it to the coal cellar?'

'You see the problem?' mutters the historian, sotto voce, after her. 'And why didn't she say design office, instead of coal cellar? After all, your husband has scrubbed it out and has got geraniums and everything.'

The headmistress puts down her pen and comes around her desk to pour tea from a silver service.

'You look as though you need a cup. Are you quite well?'

I take the chair she offers.

'Yes, very well,' I smile.

She pushes a cup and saucer across the tea table. When I reach for it, my fingers tremble. Our eyes meet.

'Just a little tired,' I concede.

'There has been some concern, among your new colleagues, that you are over-tired?'

'Oh no, not *over*-tired,' I reassure her. 'Not since I gave up my tutoring commitment at the university.'

We drink our tea in silence. The headmistress replaces her cup in her saucer.

'The trouble is, we do require you to make a full commitment here.'

There is a different silence. She lifts the silver teapot as though to fill it up.

'Do you mean, with duties in the evenings?' I ask.

'We are a boarding school,' she has to point out.

The silver teapot tilts out of my vision, and back into it again. In its polished lid, my reflection is hollow-eyed.

'I don't think I can manage evenings,' I confess.

'No,' agrees the headmistress. 'I don't think you can.'

She reaches across the table for my saucer, to save me getting up.

The pend off Argyle Street is narrow, scarcely wide enough for two people to pass. It widens at our gate. Beyond the gate stone steps climb one wall of the coal cellar to form part of its roof. Beneath the steps my husband's voice advises truss lengths. I push the vine aside and unlock the door. At the top of the steps stands the bluebell urn, planted with Russian vine from the historian's garden.

Every day the Russian vine meets me sooner than it did the day before. The ironwork around the stone steps is draped in it. Great hoops of leaves are wound around a telephone wire and set to make a coppice of a telegraph pole. To the right the kitchen, where a letter lies waiting on the table. To the left a sitting room in antique wallpapered roses, with an empty fireplace, the brocade nursing chair and the garden bench.

'Shall I put the oven on, to warm the bread?' I call back down.

I open my eyes. An hour has passed. I pull myself up on beech slats. Through the window, the Russian vine leaves are silhouetted in the light of a street lamp.

'Is it time to collect the children?'

'I'll go. Here, there's a letter for you.'

I close my eyes.

'Come on, open it. You ought to.'

I take the letter. It has a window pane, in which my name and the correct address for the Mansard attic are blurred.

My husband picks up his car-keys from the kitchen. I hear him switch on the oven to warm the bread. The envelope with the windowpane opens, and a folded letter falls out.

East of Scotland Blood Transfusion Service…

'Back in ten minutes,' yells my husband.

Which I think must be right. Just as he was right to switch on the oven. And it is right that I get up from the garden bench, to beat some eggs for scrambling. After supper there will be prep to be got right. A dozen French verbs. The nine times table. So if anything is wrong, it must be this letter.

East of Scotland Blood Transfusion Service…

My husband sticks his head round the door.

'Did you hear me? Back in ten minutes. I put the oven on. If you feel up to it, you could beat the eggs.'

The world is turning upside down too fast for me to turn with it.

'Wait. Wait! Something's not right…'

But it isn't the letter. The letter is unequivocal, making everything else wrong.

'What's the matter?' my husband frowns.

I push the letter away from me, into his hand.

'What is it?'

He glances over it. It is a cursory glance, because he has already turned on the oven.

'What's the matter? It's just some clinic appointment—'

I have to listen to my own voice for information.

'No. It's bad.'

'What are you getting upset about? It's nothing—'

'It's bad news.'

'What?'

'The blood was contaminated.'

He stares at the letter, puts down his car-keys and reads it again. My voice interrupts him.

'I'm contaminated.'

He looks up in confusion.

'You can't be – let me read it.'

'I must be—'

'No, you're not. This is advisory – they want you to get a test—'

'—for AIDS?'

'For Hepatitis C.' He catches his breath. 'Let's not panic. It only says – here it is – *strongly advise that you seek medical help*—'

'Hepatitis C?'

'You're *fine*. It just says *seek medical help*. It's just a scare—'

I sink onto the brocade nursing chair.

'I'm always exhausted.'

'Oh don't be ridiculous. You've got two kids, for God's sake.'

'All those blisters—'

'That was last year—'

He stops. There are no radiators in the Mansard attic. He looks back at the letter. My voice has dulled to a certainty.

'I wrote off the car.'

'It was an accident—'

'I fell asleep at the wheel.'

His expression is more confused. He tries to pick up the car keys to carry on with our old life. A new and darker light flares in his eyes. He looks back at the letter.

'Jesus.'

'I'm contaminated,' I repeat.

The implications tumble into place, one after another, like dominos.

'I've *been* contaminated these last seven years.'

'How could this happen?'

'You might be contaminated too.'

'No, I'm not.'

'How do you know?'

He doesn't want to answer. It will seal my fate.

'I haven't fallen asleep at the wheel.'

He folds up the letter.

'We need to get you to a doctor.'

He looks at his watch. It is almost seven o'clock.

'What time does the practice open in the morning?'

My hands fly to my mouth.

'Could the children be contaminated?'

'No, they'll be all right—'

'How do you know?'

'Well, it's blood-to-blood contact—'

'*Women bleed!*' I scream.

We stare at each other.

'*I bleed!*' I scream. '*Call the doctor!*'

'But the practice is closed—'

'*Call him!*'

He reaches the telephone first. By some miracle, the call is answered. I hear him explain. I cannot stop screaming. He holds me off with one hand.

'– absolutely demand that you tell the doctor not to leave his office until we get there. My wife has been notified *by letter* –' his voice begins to shake with disbelief and anger '– *by letter* –'

We race the stone steps, and the narrow pend, into the street for the car.

'*You make them see me!*'

'I will. Calm down!'

'*Make them see me! You make them—*'

'*I will!*'

At the medical centre, the car park is deserted save for a single car.

The glass entrance door has been locked behind double wooden ones. My husband leaps from our car. As he hammers on them, the double wooden doors open.

'Come in,' says a receptionist.

She is buttoned into a purple woollen coat. Her expression is disconcerting. She indicates the chairs in the waiting area.

'Just a minute.'

We wait. She turns behind her desk and presses a button on a telephone console. A glass screen divides her from us. Her lips move. I wipe my eyes with the heels of my hands.

The receptionist picks up two shopping bags and pauses as she reaches my husband.

'Room 5.'

She glances at me, her expression as disconcerting as before.

'Just go on up.'

She locks the double wooden door behind her. We go on up.

'She wasn't surprised,' I say.

'What?'

'She knows. She wasn't surprised.'

In Room 5, the doctor knows too.

'– an initial test will produce results within two days but can only prove there is no infection. If it is inconclusive, a further test will provide proof of infection within twenty days.'

'I want our children tested.'

The doctor raises his palms to acknowledge that twenty days is a long time to wait for a test result.

'I want our children tested.'

He lowers his palms in acknowledgement.

'Of course, of course. But there is an important consideration to bear in mind. Most patients who test positively for blood contact viruses have contracted them through the chaotic nature of their lifestyle. Drug addicts, primarily, using dirty needles. Or those who have unprotected sex with, for example, prostitutes.'

My husband looks as though he has been shot.

'As a consequence,' the doctor ploughs on, 'these diseases attract considerable prejudice. Current medical practice is to advise those who test positive for Hepatitis C not to make their condition known.'

There is a stunned silence.

'Of course, you will know how to talk to your own children,' the doctor continues, 'but the consequences of public anxiety about the virus are best avoided.'

The room starts to spin around my head. I reach the stairs on my husband's arm.

'Bring the children with you tomorrow,' the doctor tells him, unlocking the double wooden doors to the car park.

My husband drives to the school. A haar is piling thicker and thicker around the rooflines of the fisher houses on the cathedral headland. The air is tear-laden.

'What are we supposed to do now?' I weep. 'Lie to the children?'

'What?'

'Lie to them about tomorrow's blood test?'

'Well, is there any need to frighten them tonight?'

'And if they test positive? When will we tell them the truth that we are hiding?'

'They won't test positive—'

'Well then, when I test positive? How long should anyone conceal the truth from their own children?'

'At least leave it till after supper. Once you and I have had something to eat and a chance to discuss—'

I shake my head.

'This is the only chance. This is the only chance to say nothing was ever covered up. That whatever we tell them, or aren't telling them, they can trust.'

We drive to the school. The boarders are in the bootroom, auctioning stick insects. Our son has done a deal for two in a yoghurt carton for one pound fifty. He comes to the car window to tell me about it.

'Can I buy them?'

'Well, what do they eat?'

'Mulberry leaves. But his mum says they'll eat blackberry.'

'Listen, tomorrow we all have to go to the doctor.'

'Why?'

Our daughter's wide-eyed expression joins our son's at the window.

'For blood tests. The doctor thinks maybe a virus is making me tired. He wants to check I haven't given it to you.'

'I'm not tired,' says our son. 'I could go to school early and pick blackberry leaves on the way. What's a blood test?'

'Can I get one?' says our daughter.

'A stick insect?' asks our son.

She rolls her eyes at me.

'No, not a *stick insect. Yeuch.*'

On the way home we stop by the stream to gather blackberry leaves for the stick insects' supper. By the time we have set them up in a plastic box, our own is served on the kitchen table.

'I can't believe I just did that,' my husband is apologising. 'Liver and onions. *God.* I'm so sorry.'

I push aside my plate. The kitchen table starts to spin. I make it onto the stairs on my hands and knees.

'I'm so sorry,' my husband follows me to repeat.

I like the stairs. With difficulty, I persuade him I don't want to eat. He goes back down to the kitchen. Still on my hands and knees, I climb higher. By the time I reach it, the landing is spinning so fast I have to lie down on it. I close my eyes to wait until its window onto Argyle Street comes round slower and less often.

'She's not asleep,' our son is shouting back downstairs. 'But she's lying down. It's probably just the virus.'

'You know,' says my husband, once the window onto Argyle Street darkens and the buses which pass it are lit, 'we ought to get the children to bed.'

They are asleep on either side of me, our son in his grey shorts, our daughter in a pintucked summer frock. Without disturbing them, I unfasten their shoes.

'I don't want to put them to bed.'

My husband thinks about this. He goes downstairs and brings the cushions from the garden bench to tuck beneath their heads.

'Shouldn't *you* get to bed?'

'I don't want to.'

The landing has stopped spinning and we have not lied to the children. It is enough. Besides, the landing is a good place. It is warm, and I can keep watch along Argyle Street without being seen.

'Keep watch?'

'Because – we didn't see this coming, did we? We should have done.'

'Look, I can't let you sleep on the landing all night—'

'We should have seen it coming. But we weren't watching.'

'—and you're shivering already.'

'I'm scared.'

'Scared?' repeats my husband.

I hold out one hand at arm's length.

'It used to seem the future stretched to here.'

I pull back my hand in front of my face.

'Now it stops here.'

My eyes close against it.

They open to my husband's silhouette. He is sitting with his back against the bannister, facing Argyle Street, holding a cup of coffee in his hand. On either side the children sleep on a tumble of cushions.

I open my eyes again. The streetlamp has gone out and the sun is shining directly in the window. Beyond my husband's unconscious shoulder, Argyle Street continues uninvaded. The night is over. We have made it through.

'Well, the first thing I have to tell you,' smiles the doctor, getting to his feet in welcome, 'is that the children's results are absolutely clear. Neither has been or is infected with Hepatitis C.'

My husband hugs me and shakes the doctor's hand. I am speechless with relief. The children's future unrolls back into its proper distance.

'Though the only real risk was to your daughter,' continues the doctor, 'as the infection is transmitted by breastfeeding.'

My husband and I look at each other.

You're not sickening for something, are you? You're not coming down with something, are you?

'You had a fever—'

'I ran a temperature—'

'How old was she?'

'Nine, ten weeks?'

The doctor consults his computer. The incubation period for the Hepatitis C virus ends somewhere between six and twenty four weeks.

'And I am pleased to say,' the doctor turns to my husband, 'that you are also absolutely clear. Your test result was negative too.'

I catch the stricken glance my husband sends in my direction.

'What's the matter?'

'But I'm *sorry* to say,' continues the doctor. He looks down at the forms on his desk and back up again. 'I'm sorry to say that your own test result was inconclusive.'

I hear myself say *oh*.

'We hoped we were wrong,' says the doctor. 'But we were not.'

'It doesn't *have* to mean I'm ill,' I tell my husband.

The doctor gets up and wraps an inflatable tourniquet around my arm to take bloods for the definitive test.

'That's the spirit,' he says, in a fruitless attempt to keep up my husband's.

My husband is giving in to tears. When I get back from the school run he is at it again, this time behind his desk in the coal cellar.

'I thought we agreed that if we didn't worry about it, the children wouldn't worry about it?'

'She's nearly eight years old,' he shouts. 'Do you understand what that means? It means cancer or cirrhosis in another two.'

'I haven't any symptoms—'

'There aren't any symptoms, apart from *unreasonable fatigue*.'

My father arrives in a round trip of one hundred and forty miles. He sits on the brocade nursing chair, while my husband weeps, on the garden bench.

'It is only an inconclusive test result,' my father attempts to comfort him. 'We never know how life will turn out.'

'I know how this is turning out,' says my husband, wiping his eyes.

He gets up to make my father a cup of tea.

'Do you still go to church?' my father asks me.

'No,' I tell him. 'But then, neither do you.'

'You see?' says my father. 'We never know how life will turn out.'

I stop at the door of the coal cellar.

'For God's sake, could you stop crying long enough to do some work? I don't want to be ill *and* poor.'

'Where are you going?'

'I can't bear the waiting. I mean, not here. I'll wait in church.'

My husband stops crying.

'In *church?*'

'I know.'

'Which church?'

'Oh God. Who cares? Any church.'

'St James?'

'Only if the rest are locked. When the doctor rings will you—'

'I'll find you.'

In the university chapel a young man puts in an hour's organ practice. He tells me he is supposed to lock up after it. From another church I am moved on before my presence upsets mourners. At the end of the cliff top path to St James, its heavy iron gate is open. Inside, there are marble and mosaics.

'Can I help you?'

The priest is young, in a plain brown robe. I remember that they send the bright ones to St James, to ensure St Andrews' professors toe the doctrinal line.

'Probably not,' I tell him. 'I'm waiting for a test result after a contaminated blood transfusion.'

It is a relief to be savage. The young priest does not reply.

'I don't know why I'm here,' I add. 'I haven't been to Mass for years.'

He nods in silence. I can hear my own voice breaking.

'And – and now I turn up, without meaning anything, just because I am in trouble.'

'Oh,' says the young priest. 'That's fine.'

'What?'

'That's fine. It is fine to come just because you are in trouble.'

He doesn't wait for a response, but indicates the nearest pew.

'Please. Stay as long as you like. If you want to talk,' he points to the sacristy door, 'I'll be in there.'

I sit in the nearest pew. I do not go near the sacristy door. I do not thank the young priest, nor apologise. Hours pass. I slide onto my knees.

I will not pray to be well. It is anti-intellectual. It is fear-driven. But the alternative is taking me all day.

Dear God. You decide.

I get to my feet and walk back through the iron gate. The sky has lowered and darkened. Rain begins to fall. My husband meets me in the street. He is crying again.

'It's positive.'

With five minutes to spare, I have made my contamination necessary.

There is a state visit from the historian. It is preceded in the morning by a visit from her husband, to set things up. She will arrive at three o'clock, with cake.

'Instead of writing?'

'She's taking the afternoon off.'

'God. I must be ill.'

'Bad luck,' the historian's husband says to my husband.

'I know.'

'She's coming round this afternoon.'

'God,' says my husband, looking at me. 'You must be ill.'

We light the fire in her honour. It is the first time it has been lit. I walk to the ironmongers in South Street and buy a freestanding grate to light it.

'You've resigned?' asks the historian.

The freestanding grate is splendid. Huge flames leap from its coals and disappear into the black abyss of the chimney space above it. The draught is medieval. Leaves of ash, black as soot and big as pennies, float in the air, settling in our tea and cake.

'I had to. We will depend on his income. He can't spend half his day supporting me so that I can teach.'

'How very inconvenient for the headmistress,' observes the historian, not without pleasure. 'And why has it taken eight years to discover you are ill?'

My hand shakes so that my teacup rattles when I replace it in its saucer.

'Well, the official line is that a test has only just become available.'

'The Blood Transfusion Service didn't know its blood supplies were contaminated?'

I release the teacup at last.

'But then, they would say that, wouldn't they?'

She narrows her eyes.

'Are you telling me there won't be proper compensation?'

'God. I don't know. I haven't thought about it. I don't even know if there's proper *treatment*. I've got an appointment next week at the Royal Infirmary in Edinburgh. That's all I know.'

I blow out my cheeks and try to laugh. The historian is not amused.

'You need a lawyer.'

'I just need treatment, really—'

'Oh don't be silly,' she snaps. 'You have two young children. You *need* a lawyer. You've lost your job, for God's sake! Haven't you got a lawyer?'

'Not in St Andrews.'

'I'll talk to mine. It's—'

'I've heard of him. There's no way I could afford the consultation.'

'Let me talk to him. I can't see why you should have to pay for an initial consultation. We've had him to lunch often enough.'

'But—'

'And the children are clear? Thank God.'

'I know.'

The fire in my new grate rekindles in my happiness.

'And your husband too?'

'Yes. I know.'

It is some moments before I realise the historian's eyebrows are still raised in interrogation.

'Weren't you surprised?'

I have taken too large a bite of cake and am struggling to swallow it.

'Surprised?'

'Well correct me if I'm wrong,' drawls the historian, 'but isn't Hepatitis C generally contracted through sexual intercourse?'

My husband has taken her husband downstairs, to show off the printer he has installed, along with the geraniums.

'Yes,' I admit. 'Or dirty needles.'

'Somehow I don't see your husband as the druggy type.'

Downstairs, the voices fade and disappear into the coal cellar.

'Well,' I say. 'There has not been very much sexual intercourse.'

'You're unhappily married?'

I lean my chin on my hands, my elbows on my knees, and stare into the fire.

'No, I was Catholically married.'

'Gawd,' she interrupts.

I tell her a story of an old priest who advised me to *let the babies come*.

'But for how long? So you don't, of course. You try to play it by the rhythm method, which means having sex when the woman doesn't feel like it, and not having sex when she does. In the end, even the thought of sex is fraught with resentment.'

'And have you divested yourself of this medieval nonsense?'

'Too late,' I laugh.

The historian looks at her watch and brushes crumbs from her lap. The visit is over. She rises to her feet.

I open my eyes. The fire is low in the grate. Its embers, melded together in lumps big as apples, throw out an exhilarating heat. I am stretched out on a hearthrug.

'Where did this come from?'

'She sent him back with it.'

'What time is it?'

'Ten o'clock.'

I scramble to my knees.

'Why didn't you wake me? I've missed the children.'

'No you didn't. We made toast, remember?'

'So we did.'

He lies down on the rug beside me.

'How the hell did we get to here?'

'You mean, the transfusion?'

'No.'

There is a long silence.

'It's too late,' I tell him.

'I'll take the risk.'

'I won't let you.'

'I want to take it.'

'It's too late. I don't want to undergo some drug programme the NHS are about to talk me into, only for you to reinfect me.'

'You're only saying that to let me off the hook.'

'You are off the hook,' I say. 'I mean, if you leave now – well, what I mean is, a lot of men would leave now.'

He stares into the fire.

'Well, I'm not leaving. Ever,' he replies.

I have not forgotten our rows, nor his patriarchal attitudes, nor my unhappiness. I have not forgotten them, but I know there is something admirable in his staying now.

'Do sit down,' says the lawyer.

I am already awkward. The table to which he gestures is twenty feet long, and polished to a mirror. It is difficult to know which gilded chair to go for. I choose the nearest, and the nearest to the door.

'I know you are seeing me as a favour. It's very good of you.'

He brushes that aside with a careless, almost effete gesture.

'Oh for God's sake. If there isn't time to help someone in your highly unfortunate circumstances—'

'Are they?' I ask, desperate for official confirmation of *something*.

He raises an eyebrow.

'You've lost your salary, it is possible you will succumb to serious illness, possible that you will not see your young family grow up, that you will lose your pension rights, lose access to life insurances, private medical insurance, mortgage facilities—'

I am appalled.

'It is appalling,' agrees the lawyer. 'That is why these circumstances are outlined in a group action recently raised in Edinburgh against the East of Scotland Blood Transfusion Service. Unfortunately, under a Statue of Limitations the courts will disallow any negligence claim against the Government which is made more than three years after the date *of* the negligent action.'

'But they didn't tell me about it for nearly *eight* years.'

'I know.'

'Then – shouldn't the Statute of Limitations run from when the Government told me about it?'

He raises his palms off the table.

'You may well take that view. Whether it is a reasonable one would be a matter for a court to decide.'

The conversation has taken a surreal turn.

'You mean, I'd have to take the Government to court to see whether I had the right to take the Government to court?'

'Exactly.'

'Two court actions?'

'Yes.'

'When I doubt I can afford one?'

Outside the Royal Infirmary of Edinburgh a prison van pulls up on double yellow lines. There is a delay. The prisoner has travelled from Glasgow unshackled, and is not happy that he should attend his hospital appointment handcuffed on either side to two police officers.

'Fuck's *sake*,' he complains, as the back door of the prison van is opened, and the police officers step round the blue flashing light of their police vehicle to meet him.

They reach the lift at the same time I do.

'After you,' grins the shackled prisoner, and laughs when his captors struggle to extricate themselves from our muddle.

'Oh it's you lot,' says the young nurse at the reception desk. 'He been taking his medicine?'

'Yeah,' says the prisoner, 'and some.'

He winks at the young nurse, and grins at me. The sleeves of his cotton shirt are rolled up to the elbow, so that the tracklines of his heroin habit shine a livid white under reception's fluorescent light.

'Next?' asks the young nurse. 'Name?'

I give my name and date of birth.

'New patient, are you?' she asks. 'Must be, you're down to see the prof.'

We look up as another nurse bears down on me.

'There you go. The clinic nurse will look after you. Shut up, will you!' the young nurse leans over her desk to bellow in the direction of the waiting room, where the police officers are failing to curtail their prisoner's flow of obscenities.

I find an empty chair opposite them. The police officers, knowing the score, drift off to sleep. An hour passes. The prisoner spends it favouring the occupants of the waiting room, one after the other, with a malevolent glittering stare. I spend it on the edge of my seat.

The prof is genial and at the top of his game. He is attended by a court of lesser doctors – registrars and students – who are in awe of his erudition. A Swiss drugs company has recognised it to the tune of half a million pounds, funding his research laboratory in the hope that it will improve the recovery rate of Hepatitis C sufferers who are treated with Interferon.

'Interferon?'

'Is a synthetic drug which closely resembles the chemical compounds produced naturally in the body in response to a viral attack. You will inject yourself with Interferon three times a week for a year, boosting your own natural defences until the viral load we detect in your blood tests is reduced to zero.

'And then I'm cured?'

'Well not necessarily zero,' he allows. 'Our blood tests are not that sensitive. It is possible that we reduce the viral load, but do not completely eradicate it. In that situation, I am afraid a relapse is inevitable. I have to warn you that for this reason some patients do not respond to treatment.'

'How many?' I ask.

'How many do not respond?'

'Yes.'

'To take the more optimistic view, our positive response rate is currently thirty per cent.'

'*Thirty* per cent?'

The professor is offended.

'That's as good as most antibiotics. People don't realise that. Antibiotics are often used to treat infections which would have cleared up anyway.'

'Will Hepatitis C clear up anyway?'

He sighs.

'Spontaneous remission rates are negligible. So no, I'm afraid.'

In the corridor leading to the ladies' lavatory of the Edinburgh café, there is a payphone which lets you ring it back.

'A prisoner?' My husband is incredulous. 'In *shackles?*'

'Yes. And my nurse says—'

'Your nurse?'

'The clinic nurse. She's all right. She says we mustn't confuse our razors, or our toothbrushes.'

'Oh for God's sake—'

'And I said, what about my period? And she said no-one had ever mentioned that, but she supposed it was sufficient to wash the lavatory with bleach after I used it—'

'What?'

'– so I said sometimes I'm too exhausted –'

'All right. Stop now. This is nonsense.'

'No, it's not,' I sob.

I lean under the payphone's stippled metal hood so that no-one will hear me.

'These people are not joking. It's the only way to protect the children. They've given me a yellow infected sharps bin to keep in our bedroom—'

My sobs overcome this last anguish. I haven't even told him about the regime of Interferon injections.

'Listen. Stop crying. We'll sort this. You need to go and have a cup of coffee right now. Are you in the café? Go and buy a cup of coffee.'

'But do you think I ought to?' I sob. 'I mean, drink from their cup without telling them?'

'Thirty per cent?' repeats my husband.

Coffee and fifty miles of Fife's ancient kingdom at the speed limit have given me new hope.

'But thirty per cent takes into account all those chaotic lifestyles getting it wrong. I mean, if I do everything perfectly, maybe my chances will go up to forty per cent. Or even fifty per cent?'

Fifty per cent sounds like I might actually recover. It is the universal pass rate. Fifty per cent I can live with, even if I made it up.

'So will you come down from the landing?'

'I don't want to. I want to keep watch. They might try to deliver the fridge.'

The fridge arrives next morning. It is identical to the fridge in the kitchen we already own. We carry the new one past the kitchen, up to the landing and on into our bedroom. It fits perfectly between the wardrobe and the yellow infected sharps bin.

The first batch of Interferon arrives that afternoon. I collect it from the pharmacy and take it straight home to be stored at 4°C, in splendid isolation, on the middle shelf of its own fridge.

'Of its own *fridge?*' repeats my sister, on the telephone. 'Why didn't you just shove it in the fridge you've already got?'

I explain about the thirty per cent success rate, and the need to offset, statistically, the chaotic regimes of heroin addicts.

'Is this your own idea?' asks my sister.

'Yes, they just said to store the vials at 4°C. But how can you be sure, if everyone keeps opening the door for milk?'

Far to the north of the Mansard attic, my sister hangs up, walks out of her farmworker's cottage and calls her children.

'Come on, come on, get in the car.'

'Where are we going?'

She drives three miles to her local church.

'Right, out we go,' she orders the children via the rear view mirror. 'Follow me.'

They follow her through the churchyard into the church, and down the aisle. When my sister gets to the end of it, she puts her hands on her hips.

'Would You give her a bloody break?' she yells.

She turns round. Her children are open-mouthed.

'Right, come on, come on. Back in the car,' she tells them.

'Hello this is reception. I'm afraid it is seven-fifteen. Please forgive the delay in getting to your name on the list—'

'Hello this is reception. I'm afraid it is seven fifteen. Please forgive the delay in getting to your name on the list—'

'Hello, this is me. Call me back.'

'Hello, how can I help you?'

'So how late were you?'

'Fifteen minutes. I had to come in through the ballroom.'

'Where did you leave the bike?'

'In the ballroom. It's behind the chair stacks. I've left the door open. Will you collect it on the way back from the school run?'

'Yes, but this is crazy. We can't go on like this. It took me twenty minutes to waken you—'

'We have to. We need the money—'

'I'd rather have you well—'

'Well I'd rather have our children at that school—'

'But it's hardly giving your treatment the best chance, is it? Nor my income, if I've got to run around retrieving bikes from ballrooms—'

'I don't have time for this argument now. It's almost half past. I have to go.'

'Wait a minute—'

'I can't. I'm still not dressed.'

I flick back the silver levers on the switchboard, pull off my headphones and wriggle into a pair of black tights. Under my sweatshirt is a black uniform. In one pocket of the waistcoat is a wand of black mascara, in the other a lipstick.

I run round the reception desk to button up in a gilt mirror. In its reflection, lift doors open. An elderly man steps out. I turn to meet his frown.

'I would prefer you kept your shoes on.'

My fingers close around the wand of black mascara.

'Yes, sir. Sorry about that.'

'Have you the bar totals?'

I haven't a clue whether I have the bar totals. I know I am supposed to have them. I am supposed to total them before I finish a late shift, and leave them on the hotel reception desk in four neat elastic-banded rolls. I am not supposed to stuff a bankbag with loose bar receipts and rush home to punch an Interferon injection into my right thigh.

'The bar totals? Certainly.'

I march back behind the reception desk. Beneath the cover it affords, my bag opens to reveal four neatly elastic-banded rolls. My husband has not let me down.

'There you are. Can I order breakfast for you, sir?'

'I'll take breakfast in the dining room. Where's the porter?'

'I haven't seen him. I expect he's upstairs.'

The elderly hotel owner throws me a sharp glance, and proceeds out of the hall towards the dining room.

I open my eyes. I am sitting on my stool. The hand on which my chin has rested is suddenly reconnected with a blood flow, and starts to throb. The *thud thud* of the suitcase which woke me transforms itself into an irate guest stopped at the turn of the stairs.

'– particularly asked the waitress to send a porter to our room without delay –'

I get to my feet as the Interferon injection finally kicks in. Great flu-like shudders run down my spine and along my limbs.

'Can I check you out, sir?'

'No you can't. You can call a bloody porter to carry my case down this last flight—'

I glance around the hall to see whether the porter has turned up yet. As I move my eyeballs, sharp pains run round my skull. A second irate guest appears behind the first.

' – waiting in the breakfast room for forty minutes –'

To divide my apologies between them, I have to swivel my head so that my eyeballs remain stationary relative to my nose. The second guest condescends to check out. Unable to look down, I type an extra zero into the hotel's electronic check-in/check-out software.

'– tried to charge me three thousand pounds for two nights dinner, bed and breakfast –' the irate guest is complaining to the elderly hotel owner, when the porter steps through he hotel door.

He is unshaven, with his piped jacket over one shoulder and the wrong trousers. *Essay deadline,* he mouths over their heads. *Sorry.*

The hotel owner follows my eyes and turns on his heel.

'Where the hell have you been?' he roars, so that both guests nearly jump out of their skin.

The porter clicks his heels and pulls on his jacket. 'Snorting cocaine, I'm afraid. Won't happen again, sir,' he says.

The second guest laughs. The hotel owner doesn't. He comes round the reception desk, elbows me out of the way and overrides the check-in/check-out software to knock two thousand and seven hundred pounds from the guest's bill.

'Thank you,' I say. 'Won't happen again, sir.'

The hotel owner doesn't answer. From a distance he surveys with distaste the porter's attempts to manhandle suitcases down the hotel steps.

'If I thought for one minute that boy was one of those drug addicts, I'd turn him out on his ear.'

'Yes sir. I'm sure he's not.'

'We don't want that type here, nor the vile diseases they carry.'

He puts down my computer mouse and glances up.

'And what's the matter with you?' he demands.

'I – nothing, sir.'

'Sorry about the shrieks and the wails,' says the young nurse, rolling her eyes.

The din from the waiting room is ear-splitting.

'What's the matter?'

'New patient. Not very happy about the situation. Don't let her upset you.'

'Did I make a fuss like that?' I ask the clinic nurse, as she takes more blood.

'You were worse,' she grins. 'You and all your questions. Wait there. I've asked the prof to look in and see you.'

'Why?'

'In case you've got some more.'

'More about what?'

'About a liver biopsy,' explains the professor. 'It's the only way we can determined how far the disease has progressed, which it is essential if we are to treat you properly.'

'But can't you tell from the blood tests?'

'We can tell a great deal from the blood tests.'

The professor addresses his remarks to his court of registrars and junior doctors, who listen and smile enigmatically whenever I catch their eye.

'We can tell that there is dysfunction, which suggests the inflammation of the liver. This is typical of Hepatitis C infection. Over the longer term continuous inflammation will lead to structural change, indicative of secondary disease, such as cancer. A biopsy will tell us the degree of inflammation, and whether pre-cancerous change is evident.'

The court of registrars and junior doctors gaze back at me. The most junior, a slim blonde girl, breaks ranks with a grimace of sympathy. The professor turns back to face me across his desk.

'The biopsy itself is carried out through keyhole surgery,' he beams, 'so you've nothing to worry about.'

The slim blonde doctor and I exchange enigmatic glances.

I flick the latch to open the gate. My husband emerges from the coal cellar and hands me a parking voucher.

'The lawyer called. You're to go round to his office.'

'What now?'

'He just called. He wants to see you as soon after five as possible. I told him you were driving back from Edinburgh and it would depend on the queues at the road bridge.'

He is hustling me back through the gate. I have forgotten to wind my watch.

'What time is it now?'

'Half past. Take the car and use the voucher. How did you get on at the hospital?'

He slams the driver's door without waiting for an answer, but the window is open.

'They want to do a liver biopsy.'

I am indicating and turning into the traffic lane.

'Tell the lawyer!' he shouts after me.

I waken with a start. The car is parked outside the lawyer's office. It is five minutes to six. I scramble from the driver's seat.

The parking voucher is an outsize scratchcard designed for year-round use. Car key poised to scratch, I stare helplessly at its matrix of silver squares. Month, day, nearest quarter of an hour.

In reverse order, I scratch out a guilty six o'clock. It is a guilty five past before I give up trying to remember the date of the hospital appointment from which I have just returned. I take a look at the tree next to my parking space, consider that it is not yet budded and guess *March? April?* But I can't remember any birthday presents so I scratch *March*, shove the voucher on the dashboard and arrive in the lawyer's office an hour late.

The lawyer agrees that the queues at the road bridge are a nightmare. He is fielding a call from his wife. We proceed to the polished table. I explain my liver may already be damaged. I forget to mention the biopsy. We are sitting at the polished table before I wonder why I am there.

'Well –' the lawyer opens a file and lays it on the table.

The file makes me nervous. I am aware that the files of even the most junior lawyers rack up legal fees faster than our precarious income will keep up.

'– well, you must be wondering what all the urgency is about. Our initial investigations had suggested that you would not be entitled to make a claim for compensation, owing to the Statute of Limitations. However, a way has been found around this difficulty. I mentioned to you that a group action is being raised, in Edinburgh, by lawyers representing some of the other people who find themselves in your situation.'

'Yes.'

'They have decided to raise an action against the Blood Transfusion Service itself under the laws governing Product Liability. They will argue that the transfusions, as products, were not fit for purpose. In other words, they will sue the Blood Transfusion Service as the supplier.

And the reason they will raise this action, rather than make a negligence claim,' continued the lawyer, 'is that the Statue of Limitations for Product Liability is not three years, but eight.'

'God. I don't know. I'll have to think about it.'

He is looking at me as though I have missed the point.

'Hence the urgency.'

'I'm sorry?'

'Well, you received the transfusion in 1988. As I said, the Statute of Limitations for Product Liability claims is eight years—'

'*Oh.*'

'Exactly.'

'Oh God. It How long have I got left to decide?'

'Thirteen days.'

'This is my husband,' I tell the surgeon who is drawing blue crosses on my stomach.

'Sssh,' says my husband. 'He knows.'

'This is the surgeon,' I whisper. 'He gave me valium.'

My husband looks at the surgeon and laughs.

'You'd love it,' I whisper further.

'I'd love valium?'

'Yeah. valium. I love it. Do you love me?'

My husband blushes with pleasure.

'You know I do.'

'I love you too,' I tell him.

The surgeon explains that there may be some little pain, but the incision is very small and he will be sewing me up again within ten minutes.

'Are you happy that I carry on?'

'I love you,' I reply.

I am happier than I have known it was possible to be. The surgeon sews me up again. I am ecstatic with happiness.

'But what was I raving on about?' I ask my husband over and over, as we drive home from Edinburgh next morning. 'What did I say?'

'You said you loved me.'

'Did I?'

He blushes with pleasure all over again.

'Yeah. You also said you loved the surgeon, but I'm ignoring that.'

'I'm going to light the fire,' says my husband.

Huddled beside me on the garden bench, my daughter sits up. She watches as my husband rolls pages of an old newspaper into a makeshift kindling.

'I'm celebrating,' says my husband, taking another sheet. 'I said all along the hotel job was a stupid idea.'

My daughter slides off the garden bench and races upstairs.

'He's going to light the fire!'

The sticks of newspaper ignite in a merry blaze. My husband is already lit by a grin.

'So two Wall Street bankers book in for a night—'

'Yes.'

'—and ask you to enter their names in the golf ballot?'

Our children race down the attic stairs and slide onto their knees on the hearth-rug at our feet.

'Yes. To play the Old Course. They telephoned from New York at seven o'clock yesterday evening.'

'And then what? They must have driven straight to JFK and got on a plane?'

'Yeah, they did. They showered at Heathrow, then caught the afternoon flight to Edinburgh and took a taxi to arrive in time for the result of the ballot.'

'Only you'd forgotten to enter them,' grins my husband. 'Were you sacked on the spot?'

'We came to a mutual understanding. He said he'd pay me to the end of the week if I would go straight home and never come back.'

Our eyes meet. My husband's are dancing with suppressed laughter.

'He said, apart from the bar totals, I was a walking disaster,' I complain. Tears prick the back of my eyes.

'He said if it weren't for the bar totals he'd wonder what I was on?'

'Welcome to our play,' recites a pupil trusted to behave front of house.

He hands me a photocopied programme which someone has coloured in. Beyond the school door, a boy with a greenish expression is slumped on a stuffed chair. There is a large basin on his knees.

'He's been sick twice,' Front-of-House informs us, with relish.

Alice in Wonderland could not hope for a more bizarre introduction. While we wait for the play to begin, there is a glass of Chablis. Thereafter, the audience roar approval. Fathers, not easily confined on plastic chairs, play up.

'Go again, go again!' they applaud the scenes they fail to capture on the camera film they aren't supposed to be using.

On stage, our son clenches his fists and waits for his cue. A heckling father to my left introduces himself as the aristocrat's husband.

'I've heard so much about you,' I tell him, shaking hands.

'Christ. I hope not,' he grins, leaning past me to shake hands with my husband. 'And I notice my wife isn't here yet, despite issuing me with a three line whip. Which is yours?' he goes on, settling himself back into his plastic chair. 'The long-tailed mouse? Where are you sending him next year?'

'He'll go to the local school,' I reply.

The aristocratic husband winces.

'Good school and all that, but far too bloody big. Can't see your mouse making his mark there. Why don't you apply for a bursary to a boarding school?'

I am embarrassed.

'Too proud, eh?' he nods with another grin. 'Well, I'm not. I've no bloody option, not with four to get through. Two of them aren't even mine. Excuse me.'

He pulls a telephone, which is buzzing, from his jacket and attempts a sotto voce conversation with its electronic irritation.

'Yes I sacked her. Look darling, I can't discuss it now. I'm at the play remember? Why didn't you come?'

There is electronic explosion. The aristocratic husband rolls his eyes towards my husband and puts the telephone away.

'Sacked my secretary. Now she's gone blubbing to my wife. Gawd.'

His misery redoubles a minute later, when the telephone buzzes again.

'Look, I told you I'm at the *play* – oh, hello, mummy. How are you? Yes, I did sack her. Yes, I know who puts up the money—'

This time the electronic outrage will not be fobbed off.

'Well, maybe I'll reconsider. I'll reconsider if she apologises. *What?* Apologise to *her?*'

In the interval, the telephone is still ringing.

'*For God's sake.* Would you get me a top up?' he asks my husband, passing his glass over the row in front.

We find him ten minutes later. The greenish boy has vacated the stuffed armchair. The aristocrat's husband is slumped upon it instead.

'– do ask you to accept my most sincere apologies –' he is pleading.

The White Rabbit is counting down the seconds. We return to our plastic chairs.

'Should we send our son to boarding school,' I worry. 'Depending on the result of the biopsy?'

My husband laughs.

'We can't afford boarding school fees.'

'We can if we win an action based on Product Liability.'

Our eyes meet. My husband tries to find a way out.

'He wouldn't go.'

The cast are reassembling. In the wings, the long-tailed mouse has set his jaw to follow them back on stage.

'He would go,' I start to cry. 'If we asked him, he would go.'

'I've decided to join the group action,' I tell the lawyer. 'I want the money to send our son to boarding school if this all goes wrong.'

The lawyer shakes his head, flipping pages of my file.

'If your case were to go forward, the last thing I would do is mention boarding school. We would want to emphasise your suffering, not a privileged lifestyle—'

'*Privileged* lifestyle?'

'Well, the common perception of boarding school is—'

Someone's fist has just banged on the table.

'Do you think it will be easy to send our son away?' I shout. 'I'll tell you how easy it will be. About as easy as dying and leaving him behind. No, that's easier, because if I want to give him a shot at life without me, I'll probably have to send him away *now*, for what could be the last couple of years I've got—'

The lawyer sighs.

'Then, at the very least, I suggest we commission, on your behalf, a barrister's opinion. He will advise us whether such a claim has any chance of succeeding in court.'

I am embarrassed to be on my feet. It does not occur to me to ask what barristers charge for their opinion.

'I just need school fees.'

'Yes,' interrupts the lawyer. 'I think we have established that.'

'This is another of your mother's daft ideas,' I hear my husband tell our son as he passes the open door of the coal cellar, '*designed* to keep me away from my desk.'

Our son loads the tent into the boot of the car and runs back up the pend for the sleeping bags.

'She'll only wear herself out,' my husband's voice predicts. 'Make sure you collect my sleeping bag from the garden bench, will you?'

'Dad says make sure—'

'Tell him we're packed. I'm going upstairs to inject so he's got ten minutes.'

Our daughter arrives on the landing.

'Dad says make sure—'

'Are you ready? Is everybody ready? Right. Tell Dad I'm going upstairs *now*.'

They clatter downstairs as I climb up. In our bedroom I forget which thigh I last injected and lose a couple of minutes trying to decide which looks the more bruised, but I'm dressed again on schedule.

'Just coming,' says my husband, still at his desk.

'But I've taken it now.'

'I'm just coming—'

'It's a three hour drive. You won't get the tent up before the side effects kick in.'

'I will. I'm just *coming*. Did you make sure—'

'Well come *now*. We're supposed to be giving the children a normal family holiday. I don't want to have to lie down in the bloody *field*.'

We drive three hours north to Rannoch.

'Stay in the car,' orders my husband, leaping out to help our son light the stove.

Our daughter has the tent unfolded on the grass, and is sorting poles. The urge to lie down grows too great. I open my eyes as they lift me off the gear lever and help me to my feet. In the tent, my sleeping bag is unrolled. A hot water bottle waits inside it.

At dawn, I open my eyes. The children are asleep in their own sleeping bags at the bell end of the tent. By its zipped up door lies my husband, wrapped in *The Times*.

'You're still shivering.'

'I know. I've spilled my coffee.'

The spill runs through the ironwork of our table, to water a bed of hollyhocks. Below the hollyhocks, the slope to the lawns is steep and alive with the laughter of our children, who are rolling down it. From the terrace of the restaurant, I gaze out over the tops of a pinewood, to the loch and the mountains of Rannoch beyond it.

The laughter of our children is rhythmic, waxing during the roll downhill and waning in the exertion of the scramble back up. Pitstops at the ironwork table on the terrace are silent save for hurried sucking on straws.

'Just a minute,' I say, grabbing each in turn. 'Tick inspection.'

Despite the rolling, the children's limbs are free. My son inspects my husband and reports two.

'That's what comes of sleeping in *The Times*,' grumbles my husband.

Two knobs of butter are applied to his left ankle, to encourage the sheep-ticks to release it. In a spirit of vengeance, he insists on inspecting me.

'I only just got up since Friday.'

'Yeah, but if one of the little bloodsuckers has found you, then he's got what's coming to him.'

My husband lifts my arm to peer beneath it.

'And speaking of bloodsuckers, the barrister's opinion came through.'

'Which is?'

'He says you have a case, but the government will fight it through the courts. He reckons that could take ten years. Which means ten years of legal fees.'

'Which means we can't afford it.'

He flashes a wry glance.

'Not without your salary. It's a Catch 22.'

I put my apple-cake back on its plate.

'But if we can't afford legal fees we'll never win *school* fees.'

'Let's face it, if we had ten year's legal fees we wouldn't *need* to win school fees.'

'You're not on top of this,' I begin to panic. 'It's not funny. It's bloody unfair. And don't say anything,' I stop him, with one raised hand, 'I'm the *last* person who needs telling that life's not fair.'

'I wasn't going to—'

'How much did the barrister's opinion cost, in the end?'

'Fifteen hundred and eight pounds.'

'*Fifteen hundred—*'

'Calm down. Your lawyer friend says that's par for the course.'

'*Fifteen hundred and eight pounds.*' I put my hand to my forehead. 'He might at least have knocked off the eight.'

My husband picks up the bill the waitress has left beneath his saucer.

'No, the barrister only charged fifteen hundred. You asked what it cost *in the end.* It just cost eight pounds for enough apple cake to tell you about it.'

I tear off a handful of blackberry leaves from a bush growing by the stream.

'No, not like that,' says our son. 'They don't like them chewed up. Tear them one by one.'

His own careful selection takes several minutes to harvest. Our daughter disappears behind a holly tree to re-emerge ecstatic.

'I've found an island!'

We exchange glances. At its widest point, the stream is not quite a metre across.

'No you haven't—'

We follow her round the holly tree and down the bank. At its foot is a slope of grey rock, a narrow channel of rushing water and, midstream, a solitary tussock of grass.

'You see?' says our daughter, hopping onto it.

'That's not an island,' begins our son.

'We could have a picnic,' she cries. 'Mum could bring lollies and we could eat them on the island.'

'That's true,' says our son. He takes a flying leap to join her. 'Lollies, or choc ices?'

'Come down mum!' she shouts from a distance of eighteen inches, once she has regained her balance. 'It's really deep on the other side.'

'I think it's a two man island.'

'No it's not,' argues our son. 'There's loads of room. It's a brilliant island. You could definitely bring choc ices tomorrow.'

Our daughter basks in his admiration.

'And you can bring your stick insects if you like,' she offers, 'so long as you don't let them out of the box.'

'They'd be too scared to get out,' I reassure her. 'It would take all day to explore this island, if you were a stick insect.'

The telephone rings.

'For you!' yells my husband from the coal cellar, so that I will pick up the extension in the kitchen.

'Have you surfaced?' asks the historian. 'The new housekeeper must have made her mark. We are invited to lunch.'

I begin my excuses.

'I'm still pretty spaced out—'

'You may think that,' she interrupts them, 'but wait till you see the castle.'

The castle stands on the bank of a river, six miles outside town.

'Hi,' calls the millionaire's wife, from a battlement.

She waves a hand over a sizeable tract of Fife.

'Park wherever you like.'

In the Great Hall around two dozen women, at least half in mohair, chatter around a thirty foot table. The historian is buttonholed at once.

'There you are!' bellows a familiar voice. 'What've you been up to? We've had a dreadful report from the girls' school.'

'Hello,' I grin.

'God, you look worse than ever,' says the aristocrat. She kisses both my cheeks. 'Come and sit next to me. I can drive you back to school. The boys are playing in a match at half past three.' She breaks off to assist in another conversation. 'You must have seen him on telly? His mother lives underneath you,' she turns back to startle me.

'Underneath?'

'In the pantiled cottage? You must know whom I mean. She's ninety-two. Haven't you been in to say hello?'

At quarter past three we reach the playing field. The opposition's mothers are already on the touchline.

'Hello!' cries the aristocrat. 'Thought I might see you all here.'

Our son appears with the team, his face contorted around a gumshield. He looks me up and down.

'Your skirt is too short,' he says.

'Remember to cheer when I score,' the historian's son is telling her. 'Don't just stand there gabbling.'

The match gets underway.

'Where's your lovely daughter?' asks the aristocrat.

'On expedition with her class,' I say. 'She had a note to bring a change of socks.'

'Her teacher told me all about it,' says the historian. 'It is an expedition to an island. Your daughter offered to lead it.'

'Island? What island?'

'The one you said would take all day to explore?' says the historian, with a straight face.

'Come in,' says the historian's husband, who has stationed himself by the door with a very short script. 'Have a drink.'

His eyes are unseeing, his posture uncertain. Inside the house, the historian's son is crying. At his side stands the aristocrat's son, as she has ordered him, in a cousin's suit, miserable, with nothing to say.

The historian is dead.

The lawyer has delivered her eulogy. His words have resounded from car to silent car in a cavalcade of grief along the farm roads of the Pitscottie valley, from the crematorium in Cupar back to her house in St Andrews.

At her husband's behest, men drink uncomfortably. Women whisk about, temporarily making up for her loss.

'For God's sake,' one attempts to joke, kneeling on the kitchen floor in a black silk coat to load the washing machine from an overstuffed laundry basket.

The door to the historian's study stands open, as it always stands open, because piles of books are stacked against it. Her desk still faces the window and overlooks the garden. Hollyhocks jam its flowerbeds.

I have to turn away. On the opposite wall is propped a lifesize heat-sealed portrait photograph. It is the one used by publishers to promote the historian's novels in America. The photograph is a good likeness. It has caught the vivacity, not to say ferocity, of her eyes. As that fire faded a doctor prescribed an asthma inhaler. When the mistake was discovered, there was pandemonium.

'I'm coming this afternoon,' I tell her husband, in a panic. 'Tell her I will come at three o'clock, with cake.'

'No, don't do that. She told me when you are to come. You are to come at six, with gin.'

'And it's definitely not asthma?' asks my husband.

'Bowel cancer.'

'Christ, are they sure?'

'She's going into hospital tomorrow to have the tumour removed.'

By six o'clock the news is worse.

'I wouldn't let him tell you,' the historian announces. She has taken up camp in a leather chair by the fire. 'They suspect the tumour has done for my liver.'

I am horrified.

'Bizarre, isn't it?' she acknowledges the irony. 'Hopefully not, of course. But the test results aren't great.'

A week later she is released from hospital. There is no hope left. Chemotherapy fails. All her hair falls out. She takes to wearing a cap of embroidered silk. I find it now, where she has taken it off after a final sentence, got up to leave the room and dropped it on her chair.

In the hall awkward friends have begun to make awkward withdrawals. Ring anytime, they tell her husband. He has stationed himself back by the door again. Drink has temporarily steadied his posture. His script is even shorter.

'Thanks for coming to see her off.'

Across these agonised leave-takings, my rush of tears meets the lawyer's urbane self-control. She asked him to help me when none of us knew it was she who stood in danger. He meets my eyes. We both know there is no reason for him to help me now. He turns away.

'Lundi, mardi, mercredi—' I start out, once we reach the stream.

'Lundi, mundi—' begins our son.

'No mardi. *Mardi*.'

'Uh. Yeah. Lardi mardi—'

By *vendredi* we are on course and past the holly tree. By *dimanche* triumphant and home. On the kitchen table lies a letter from the Royal Infirmary of Edinburgh.

'Wait,' says my husband, covering it with his hand. 'Before we panic, we've already agreed that the statistics apply to junkies, not to us, right?'

I know what he's trying to do. It is an inept attempt. The fact is that the greater the progression of Hepatitis C infection, the less likely a patient to respond to Interferon.

'I'm all right,' I say, 'I know there's likely to be some inflammation.'

'Well there's *bound* to be,' my husband goes on, his hand still over the envelope, 'after eight years. I mean, there will be at least mild inflammation. That's what the hospital said, wasn't it?'

'Yes.'

'They said you have to expect mild inflammation?'

'At the very least.'

'What?'

I put out my hand for the envelope.

'They said at the *very least*. Just let me open it, will you?'

'I just want us to stay calm and—'

'Well stop winding me up then. I am calm. And I'm not stupid. It's been eight years. There will be mild inflammation. Give it here!'

He hands me the envelope.

'The other thing to remember,' he continues, 'is that you *are* being treated now. That's the difference. Now that you're being treated, you're actually in a much safer position.'

I tear the envelope across. A letter falls out. I see the test result before there is time to read its message.

'Fuck.'

'What is it?'

'Moderate.'

'What?'

'Moderate. Moderate inflammation.'

I scan through the letter's contents and refold it.

'Let me read it.'

'No.'

'Why not?'

'I told you. Moderate.'

'But what else does it say?'

'Oh for God's sake! It says moderate!' I shout, unfolding the letter and flattening it onto the table. 'Moderate inflammation and some striation at cellular level around the portal lobes. *All right?*'

'What the hell does that mean?'

'I haven't a bloody clue,' I am still shouting. 'But it doesn't sound very good, does it?'

'Please,' he is saying, 'sit down. We need to sit down and talk—'

He follows me to the landing, remonstrates, goes back down to the kitchen to read the letter, comes back up to plead.

'Just come down. Come down and sit in the kitchen, where we can talk this through.'

I cannot answer. I look into his eyes but no words come.

I watch him go back downstairs, listen as he scrambles eggs, calls the children to supper, carries my plate back up. I don't refuse it. I can't. I stare into his eyes, immobile, until he gives up and takes the plate away.

On the landing the light begins to fail. My world is shutting down with it. Assumptions, expectations, hopes eventually – one by one they break and fall away. Without them, the future flat-lines. It is a deadening experience.

'Do you want to talk now?'

Aeons pass. He tries again.

'We can talk here. That's fine. Do you want coffee? No?'

The light fails further, with the last of my courage. Their eyes wide and anxious, the children climb the stairs. They sink to the floor beside me.

'Lundi mundi—'

My husband stands in the shadows. When our son falters, he nods encouragement.

Our son turns back towards me.

'Lundi mundi—' he starts again.

My eyes meet his.

'Lundi mundi—' he repeats. 'Lundi mundi—'

'*Mardi,*' I whisper.

'Lardi mardi—'

I am driving along the slope of a long low hill. Beneath me, pasture curves into meadowland. Beyond is the sea. It is hidden by woodland and distance, but I know it is there.

The safe place is within the woodland and overhung by its lowest branches. They form a circlet of foliage around the few sun-warmed paces of its diameter. I am on its edge, beneath the leaf-laden boughs, or possibly beneath the ground. The difference is immaterial.

I open my eyes, and am not surprised to discover my husband with his back to the bannister. On the other side of the landing, framed in the window onto Argyle Street, hangs the moon, full and the colour of butter.

'Feeling better?'

'Much.'

I lean on one elbow to take off the children's shoes. He gets to his feet and picks up his cup.

'I'll put the kettle on. Back in a minute.'

'For coffee? I'll put the children to bed while you make it.'

He stops on the top step, surprised.

'You don't want it up here?'

'No, I'll come down.'

'We're not spending the night on the landing?'

I glance with him, over my shoulder, towards the window. Shafts of moonlight strike and splinter against it, illuminating the landing to the street below.

'I know a safer place.'

My husband stares, mutters what might be *Oh, God* and carries on downstairs to put the kettle on.

'Come with me,' I whisper to the children.

They scramble from their blankets, still asleep, and into bed. Downstairs, a cafetière of coffee waits on the kitchen table.

'I've been thinking,' says my husband, 'that we should ask for a second opinion. They keep these things on a microscope slide, don't they?'

I shake my head.

'It doesn't matter whether I recover or not. It *can't* matter. Or whatever life there is left will become unbearable.'

He falls silent. Excitement overtakes me.

'I had a dream.'

'I knew you were going to say that.'

He takes a forlorn draught of his coffee.

'It was a green place.' I tell him. 'Surrounded by trees.'

I'm screwing up my eyes, struggling to remember the details.

'There was a circular edge. Like a circle of overhanging boughs. And it was safe. I mean, really safe. No matter what happens.'

He puts his cup down on the table.

'But it was just a dream?'

'I know.'

'I mean, even if we wanted to, we'd never find it?'

'I've no idea where it is,' I agree.

'Just a lovely dream then.'

'Yes. Really lovely.'

He lifts the cafetière and gets up to refill it.

'It made me think—' I say.

'What?'

'If I *am* going to die, we ought to look for a cottage. Somewhere you and the children would be happy. In the countryside, I mean. If I am going to die, we ought to send them to boarding school and find a cottage for when they come home for the holidays.'

My husband puts down the cafetière with a thump.

'I *knew* you were going to say that.'

At the gates of the boarding school in Edinburgh, we almost lose courage. They stand as tall as a man might stand on another man's shoulders. Their great ironwork arch is almost tall enough to frame the distant steeple of the school's clocktower. Beyond the gates, a Pipe Band of schoolboy warriors is marching away, down an avenue of trees.

'Well, we've come this far,' I say.

My husband engages gear and drives on through. I glance towards the backseat. My son is wearing his kilt and his set jaw. It gets him into a panelled hall, facing the sweep of a staircase carved with lion and unicorn. His kilt ascends between them, its swing the only motion in an exchange of frozen expressions.

Three chairs have been arranged on the intimidating side of the Headmaster's desk. My husband and I explain about the moderate inflammation and the lack of compensation for my salary.

The Headmaster sits back and puts his fingertips together. He watches our son through narrowed eyes while he considers. Then he sits forward.

'We do have funds available with which we can support families in difficult circumstances,' he begins. And then, turning suddenly to our son. 'What do *you* think? Would you like to come here and board with us?'

I know that entrance examinations, school reports and statements of income can only be triggered by our son's reply. If he says no, the interview is over. If he says yes, my heart will break. I suddenly understand the arrangement of the chairs. My son is looking at the Headmaster and cannot see my distress.

His answer rings out sooner than I expect it.

'I'd like to come.'

'You won't miss home too much?'

'Well I will, but I want to play in the Pipe Band.'

'Ah. You're a piper, are you?'

'No.'

'A drummer, then?'

'No.'

The Headmaster bows his head for a moment. It is unaccountable, because when he raises it his expression is still serious.

'Well, we like young men of ambition here.'

The interview is over. Everyone shakes hands. We will send all the paperwork. In two weeks, the Headmaster will inform us of his decision. He reserves his brief smile for our son.

We arrive back to St Andrews in time to collect our daughter. As we turn out of town again the backseat grows animated.

'Aren't we going home?'

'Where are we going?'

They recognise the Anstruther road. There is a fish and chip shop at Anstruther. It is the Shangri-La of fish and chip shops, more often wished than visited, owing to the eight miles of fields which divide it from the Mansard attic.

'Are we going to Anstruther?'

Their voices are incredulous. My husband's is loaded with sarcasm.

'Well, your mother's plan is that we drive until we find a cottage which some farmer has decided to sell off cheap. Though if we get as far as Anstruther without spotting one, I'll buy the chips.'

On the way back, we share a bag between four. At the mid point, where the road climbs highest and the sea is on three sides equidistant, the shout goes up.

'Stop!'

A broken bough of honeysuckle obscures the For Sale sign from the St Andrews direction. The cottage is poorly constructed, has a pantile loose on the roof, and a derelict garden.

'It isn't derelict,' points out my husband. 'It's full of stones. It's never been a garden.'

The children report two apple trees and a Victoria plum. Their harvest lies unwanted and shrivelled in long grass.

'It won't have any heating,' warns my husband.

'It's got a chimney,' I say, to his scorn.

He turns to walk back round to the front of the cottage, and shakes his head at the bare woods behind.

'It's a desolate spot—'

'It's the time of year—'

'Look at the window renovation,' complains my husband. 'They've taken out the stone mullions. Horrible.'

But the ugly modern windows are already succumbing to two climbing roses, planted to grow around the door. I can't stop talking about it all the way back into town.

'It's as if, despite all its drawbacks, you just can't keep that cottage down,' I say.

In the third estate agent's window we locate its photograph. *Estate cottage, Dunino.*

'Even cheaper than our attic!' I shout, to call my husband from the car.

He saunters round the bonnet to take a look. I point to the guide price.

'I wonder why it's so low?'

'Because Dunino is four miles out of town?' he drawls.

'We could buy that cottage now!'

He holds open the passenger door with heavy courtesy.

'Get in. No we could not. We'd have to find a buyer for the attic first. And you are too ill to have viewers in and out for months.'

'Couldn't we arrange a private sale?'

'If we had a buyer,' he agrees. 'But I don't see Argyle Street queued out with private developers desperate to get their hands on a Mansard attic.'

When we reach it, he shepherds us up the pend and stops by the coal cellar to check his answering machine. The children and I climb the steps to the kitchen with four Victoria plums salvaged from the long grass in the cottage garden.

'Leave the kitchen door open,' I tell them. 'Dad's coming up in a minute.'

So we hear the latch of the gate when it rattles again behind us.

'Hello?' says my husband's voice.

'Have I come to the right place?' replies an unfamiliar one.

There is an exchange of architectural drawings and introductions.

'Most of the time I buy flats with a view to student lets,' explains the unfamiliar voice.

I hold my breath.

'You wouldn't like to buy this one, would you?' asks my husband.

'I'll take a look at it.'

In the kitchen, I leap to my feet and for the stairs. Whether I live or die doesn't matter. What does matter is that I reach the bedroom first, to ram the yellow infected sharps bin into the bottom of my wardrobe, lest its offensive presence tempts this miraculous twist of fate.

I am standing in the shower. Through the window, I hear the door of the coal cellar bounce back on its hinges.

'He's in!' yells my husband.

From the kitchen, my son shouts *yes!*

I sink to my knees. The shower splashes on and, fast as I weep, washes the tears away.

'Coffee?' I ask, hearing my husband climb the stone steps.

He doesn't answer, until he has reached the kitchen and closed its door behind him. I look round in surprise. The kitchen door is never closed.

'The old lady downstairs?' he mouths.

I nod.

'She wants you to visit her.'

'Now?'

'In half an hour.'

I decide that we are whispering for no reason, and raise my voice.

'Well, I'd be glad to visit her.'

'For Christmas?' asks my husband, with a straight face.

'Do come in,' says the old lady, who is waiting my arrival in her porch. 'Merry Christmas.'

We shake hands.

'Merry Christmas,' I say, 'though we're five months early, I think, aren't we?'

She ushers me into a narrow passage.

'Oh, I never celebrate Christmas early. I always make sure that last year's decorations are put away in good time for Advent. That's why I thought I'd send you an invitation, otherwise you would have missed them.'

We have reached a tiny sitting-room. Its crooked windows and ancient fireplace are dwarfed by an artificial Christmas tree swathed in silver lights. Merry strings of Christmas cards hang between doorpost and bookshelves. In the corner, an ivory Nativity is serenaded by a plastic music box tinkling *Away In A Manger*.

'Tea?' beams the old lady, already presiding over her hearth, on which a plate of mince pies has been laid to warm.

'It's quite unusual, isn't it?' I say. 'To celebrate Christmas right through till August?'

'There's no doctrinal impediment in church liturgy,' she explains. 'I asked my son to check that for me specially.'

She mentions the name of an eminent professor of philosophy. My mouth falls open.

'He bought the mince pies,' she adds. 'I rang him at the university when your husband told me you would come.'

'Crumbs, I mean, he shouldn't have bothered—'

The old lady leans forward to confide.

'I meant to ask you long before this, but –' she indicates the empty room around her with a merry shake of her head '– you know how it is at Christmas. And you're not at all well?'

'Uh—?'

'Oh I pick up bits and pieces,' she nods.

Above our heads, I hear our son run into our kitchen and then out again.

'Where's mum?' he asks, quite clearly.

The old lady beams like an angel, and offers another mince pie.

It is the end of the summer, and the month of the harvest moon. Field after field slides past my windscreen, at seventy miles an hour. In every one the headlights of farm vehicles trace out lines of furrows. Like me, they have a long night ahead of them.

'Do you have to drive like a maniac?' asks my husband.

It isn't Sunday. I have fiddled my injection schedule to leave me drug-free on a Tuesday.

'I want to get home to check the answering machine.'

'But we left him an hour and a half ago,' objects my husband. 'He's *fine*. He ate three meringues.'

In Argyle Street, I leave my husband to park the car, racing the pend and the stone steps to the bluebell urn. There are no messages. In the sitting room the answering machine's little red light glows with steady reassurance.

'Told you,' says my husband, coming in behind me.

'This is awful. Now I don't know *what's* happening.'

'Nothing's happening!'

'But how do we *know*? I think you ought to ring.'

'I ought not. We *saw* him two hours ago.'

'Well, I'll ring then.'

'You'll sound like an idiot.'

'Sorry to sound like an idiot,' I apologise to our son's housemaster, 'but would you mind checking that he's fine?'

Our son is fine. He ate bangers and mash, ran around the High Field till dusk and has been asleep since nine thirty.

'Oh God,' I say to the housemaster, 'and now I've got you out of bed.'

He laughs. Apparently there is no going to bed on the night of new boarders' arrival.

'You mean, other mothers—?'

'You did quite well, holding out till midnight. And you only called once.'

I find my husband in the kitchen.

'I didn't sound like an idiot,' I tell him. 'I held out till midnight and I only called once.'

'In the two days it has taken us to empty the coal cellar and relocate my office,' frets my husband in a wooden shed attached to the gable of our new cottage, 'Dunino's field mice have developed a taste for engineering drawings.'

He lowers another cardboard box of lever arch files onto his desk.

'I'm supposed to archive these for seven years,' he worries further. 'I suppose I could stack them in date order and hope mice chew at a steady rate?'

At midnight, he is reduced to feeling his way along the climbing rose to locate the front door.

'And there's no lock,' he comes into the kitchen to report. 'Someone's removed the barrel.'

The kitchen overlooks desolate woodland at the back of the cottage. The butter-coloured moon has returned to hang above it, like a familiar friend.

'It was locked when we came to look round.'

'With a padlock. The estate agent must have taken it off. I'll have to find something to jam it shut while we sleep tonight. When are you taking your injection?'

We have been moving since Friday's injection, to take advantage of the extra day's grace before Monday's.

'I just took it.'

'How do you feel?'

'Rubbish. Even my teeth hurt. I think I'll take a bath.'

In the middle of the night, I open my eyes, step out of the bath, and walk into a tree.

'Careful,' shouts my husband, who is in the kitchen, cleaning a saw in the sink.

I know at once that it is a tree. There are bits of bark in my hair. He has sawn a trunk from the woodland outside, and jammed it diagonally across the cottage's tiny passage.

'It's free,' he points out. 'Not bad eh?'

'But I can't get into my bedroom.'

He rolls his eyes, and holds the saw up to the light, to check its teeth aren't clogged.

'Yes you can. Just step over it. We're not living in town now, you know.'

The dentist's wife sits in a white coat at the dentist's reception desk. She sets her knitting aside to answer her telephone, and pushes a form across the desk towards me.

'I'm a new patient,' I smile.

She taps the form with a manicured fingernail, and doesn't.

'Sorry,' I mouth, reading *Medical History (New Patients)* on the form.

'—not prepared to make you appointments unless you are prepared to keep them,' the dentist's wife remonstrates into the telephone receiver.

My eyes slide round the waiting room. A young mother smiles back.

'Come here,' she adds in a low tone, as her child strays too near the reception desk.

I take out a pen and fill in the form. *No, no, no, no* its columns of empty squares are ticked until I reach *Current Medication?* Yes, *Prescription Drugs?* Yes (*Please detail*) Interferon *For?* Hepatitis C.

At the end of the form there are ten centimetres for *Any Other Relevant Information.* I spend half a dozen outlining the circumstances of the contaminated blood transfusion. The dentist's wife is still remonstrating. I leave the completed form on her desk and check my watch. The young mother exchanges another smile, then a grimace for the whoever is on the other end of the telephone. We pick up magazines, to hide our laughter.

The dentist's wife says she will send an invoice for the missed appointment and replaces her telephone receiver. She picks up my form, reads it and leaves the room, closing the door behind her. Low voices in the passage engage in urgent conversation.

The young mother frowns and checks her watch. She asks me what time is my appointment.

'Ten thirty.'

'Ah,' she smiles, relieved. 'You're after me.'

But she has time to check her watch and frown again. The dentist's wife returns. She opens the door and holds it wide, apologising to the young mother.

'I'll take you through now.'

'Will you keep an eye?' the young mother asks me, pointing to her child.

'No, bring him with you,' interrupts the dentist's wife.

The door closes behind them and reopens almost at once, to reveal the dentist. Without preamble, he says my name.

'Hello,' I say, offering my hand.

He doesn't offer his.

'Although we have the greatest of sympathy for your situation—' he begins.

I stare at him. It seems to put him off.

'—ah – the greatest of sympathy—' he repeats.

I suddenly realise that we are alone in the room by design.

'You won't treat me?'

'I *can't* treat you. The fact of the matter is I *can't* treat you.'

Now that he has declared himself, his manner gains conviction.

'We have nothing but sympathy for your situation, but I have my other patients to consider. If I were to treat you, I would have to disinfect all my instruments, before it was safe to treat anyone else. And clearly, there would always remain some risk of cross-infection.'

He holds open the door to indicate that I should leave. I get to my feet.

'But – but I have a toothache—'

He shakes his head.

'The best advice I can give you is to try the dental hospital. I believe there are special clinics there for people who – people in your sort of situation.'

'The – the dental hospital?'

I am on the pavement without knowing how I got there.

'The dental hospital?' I am still asking.

He nods, doesn't smile, and closes the door. There has not even been time to get angry. There is only, as I fumble for my car-keys, confusion. And then, in the privacy of the driver's seat, the first tears of humiliation.

'His sterilisation procedures are supposed to assume that patients have infections,' rages the clinic nurse when I ring her. 'Some patients may not *know* that they have. You should tell him that he has no reason to refuse to treat you. No. Give me his telephone number and I'll tell him myself.'

She rings back half an hour later. The dentist is putting up considerable resistance.

'It won't cut any ice with the BDA,' she snorts. 'He's ringing them to check his professional obligations.'

'Maybe they'll support him?'

'No they won't!' scoffs the clinic nurse. 'There's not the slightest medical justification for the stance he's taking.'

She adds that it is common for hepatitis sufferers to lose teeth and hair as the disease runs them down, and that I am therefore entitled to a wig. I decline the wig and am starting to think better of the dentist when the clinic nurse rings back. The BDA are of our opinion. The dentist has apologised and rescheduled my appointment for seven o'clock.

'Seven o'clock?'

'I suppose,' says the clinic nurse, 'his appointments must be running late?'

From the bath in the cottage I can see two windows. One faces the direction of the distant sea, and is permanently closed against an onshore wind. The other is permanently open and permanently green because a wisteria has grown so thick that the catch cannot be closed. Leaves and petals fall into the wash hand basin, which have to be removed. As soon as the tap is run, daddy-long-legs dance out of the water's path, and scramble through the open window.

'Are you all right?' calls my husband through the wisteria.

'No.'

'What's the matter?'

I am trying to keep my voice steady so that he will not realise I am crying. It is not easy with a jaw full of novocaine.

'They clingfilmed the surgery.'

'*What?*'

'Everything. The chair, the arm that the drill hooks on – they even clingfilmed the doors of the cabinets where they keep the amalgam.'

'*Cling-filmed?*'

'As though I were unclean.'

'Didn't he treat you?'

'He said he was only prepared to do a quick extraction and I was too humiliated to argue. So when I got home I had to bleach the steering-wheel and the gearstick, and wash all my clothes, and I'm still bleeding –' my sobs finally filter through the leaves of the wisteria, '– I can't cope with this. I'd rather not see anyone than this.'

The wisteria is silent for a few moments.

'Avoid our friends, you mean?'

'Well, this is horrible, wondering who else isn't comfortable with it—'

'Nobody else isn't comfortable with it.'

I am not sure any more. I lie in the bath and decide on retreat. When my gum stops bleeding. I get out of the bath, empty it and clean it with bleach. Then I take a shower, to get rid of the smell of the bleach. Two hours after I leave the dentist's surgery, I reach our children.

'Telephone,' says our daughter, with her ear to the receiver. She holds it out to me. 'Are you remembering the reels party on Saturday?'

I close my eyes and take the receiver.

'Hello, I am remembering,' I say, 'but do you mind if we pass?'

'I do actually,' says the aristocrat. 'I've already said I'll take a table for twenty. What's the matter with you?'

I explain about the dentist.

'I don't want to make people uncomfortable. And there's a lot of physical contact at a reels party.'

'What?'

'Well, some people might not want to take my hand?'

'Not want to take *your* hand?' she repeats. 'It would make more sense if you didn't want to take *their* hand, considering half of them have probably had the clap.'

I stare at the telephone in amazement.

'Have they?'

'I'd be amazed if some of them don't have it now,' scoffs the aristocrat.

'*Yeuch*,' I say, before I can stop myself.

Winter tightens its grip. I regret the boarded-up wall of our sitting-room. An outline of old cement on wooden floorboards demonstrates the width of the hearth which someone has removed. Above the boarding, indentations in the wallpaper reveal that there had once been a fire surround too. I tap around its perimeter.

'Actually,' I say to my husband, 'should that ring hollow?'

He raps his knuckles against it.

'That's the chimney space you're hearing. Someone's just nailed a piece of plywood over the gap. No wonder this room's so bloody cold. The wind's coming off the North Sea and straight down the chimney.'

I stare at him.

'Is it usual for someone to go to all the trouble of removing a fireplace just to nail a piece of plywood over the gap?'

'Well, they must have done, because it's ringing hollow. Unless they just—'

My husband stops, and looks again at the boarded-up wall. I am already feeling my way along the bottom of the boarding for a loosened corner of wallpaper.

'No, wait,' says my husband. 'We can't afford to replace that. You'd have to repaper the entire wall. Wait. Wait!'

The first strip of wallpaper comes off in one long roll.

'Wait!' shouts my husband, coming in from the passage with his toolbox. 'For God's sake, wait a minute! Don't hammer at it like that. You'll crack the plaster.'

Together we wedge screwdrivers under either side of the boarding, and lever it off the wall. There is a loud splintering noise. The adjacent strip of wallpaper rips unevenly up to the ceiling in long jagged tears.

'For God's *sake*,' my husband groans.

The boarding suddenly comes away, toppling onto the carpet between us. Behind it, beneath a heap of soot and dead leaves, stands a Victorian grate. It has vertical panels of ironwork to hold back the coals, and a hob for a kettle.

I am ecstatic. *Nothing* can keep this cottage down.

'We'll have to have the chimney swept,' warns my husband, on his knees and peering up it. 'That won't necessarily be cheap. And God knows what we'll do about this.'

He waves his hand at the desecrated wallpaper.

I am dancing around the room. We will have a fire for Christmas. We will sing carols around it. Our son will come home to sing them.

'You can't light a fire without a hearth,' my husband shakes his head. 'It's a big job, building a hearth. We can't afford it.'

He puts his toolbox away and goes back out to his office in the wooden shed to answer the telephone.

'Yes?' he asks, hanging up half an hour later.

'I found a hearth.'

'What?'

'A hearth.'

'Where?'

'Here,' I say, pointing towards the ground.

He gets up to look. At the door of the wooden shed are laid two large stone slabs, to act as doorsteps.

'They're my doorsteps.'

'You don't need two.'

'You can't cement a doorstep in the middle of your sitting room—'

'It'll be great.'

'You'd have to cut the carpet—'
'Did you phone the sweep?'
'Who?'
'The sweep? The *chimney* sweep?'

I miss the historian. I finish the new fireplace in time for Christmas, and remember how she sat at the old one, in Argyle Street, picking soot out of lemon cake.

'Love the fireplace,' says the aristocrat. 'Perfect setting for a book club. Where'd you get the wallpaper?'

I explain it is left over from our financial heyday, when we built a house and wallpapered four lavatories.

'And the mantelshelf?'

The mantelshelf was emptied of cans of oil in the wooden shed outside, unscrewed and brought indoors to be painted to match the wallpaper's *fleur de lys*. The plain wooden frame of the mirror hung above it is painted too.

'We're going to light the fire at Christmas,' I explain. 'We've cut deadwood from the den, and stacked it over the seven year archive.'

She nods.

'So first book club in January. But you ought to issue invitations, to give people time to read your recommendation.'

'I wish I could,' I apologise, 'but I can't stay awake long enough to read a book right now.'

The injections are taking me longer and longer to get over. The next time I get over one, my husband tells me the millionaire's wife is on her way.

'Here?'

I am fussing around the tiny sitting-room, when it is pitched into darkness. A large and expensive car has pulled off the road in front of the window.

'I have to take you round the back,' our daughter is explaining, 'because that door's jammed shut with a tree.'

'Wallpaper is very good,' the millionaire's wife nods and smiles, and clambers over the tree trunk. 'They told me you have built a fire to start a bookclub. Thank you. I would like to come.'

I explain that it is not possible for me to read a book. The millionaire's wife nods and smiles in complete understanding.

'Yes. I cannot read a book in English either. I am coming for the coffee.'

We are interrupted by a voice calling from the garden. It is the wife of the farm. She has heard about the tree trunk from the postman and knows to come round the back. She gives me a blue and white striped cream jug, in welcome.

'It's beautiful! Thank you very much.'

'Oh, and someone mentioned a bookclub,' the wife of the farm turns back to say on her way out. 'Can you let me know a title asap? I'll read it before Christmas, in case there isn't a chance after.'

There is not even time to argue, if I am to catch the post before collecting our daughter from school.

'This is my mum,' she is pointing through the car window to tell one of our son's old classmates.

'Hello,' says the classmate. He is shy but determined. 'My mum says thank you very much. She'd like to come.'

I close my eyes.

'Would this be to my bookclub?'

'Yeah,' says the shy boy. 'Mum's always reading. When you tell us what the book is, me and Dad are going to buy it for her Christmas.'

I drive our son from Edinburgh into Dunino. The cottage is invisible in the shadow of its surrounding firs, but there is no mistaking the smell of wood smoke. It is the first time he has entered his new home. At school, he tells us, boys ask him where he lives, to prompt the reply 'Dunny-know.'

In his new bedroom, which he shares with our daughter, we dunny-know where to put his trunk, let alone its contents. In the end we put it in the sitting-room, between the fireplace and garden bench, and on top we put plates of cheese on toast, with a slice of tomato grilled between. Our son reads out his report. Its marks are excellent in every subject except mine.

He pulls a practice pad and drumsticks from the trunk and plays a March, Strathspey and Reel. It is the new pattern of his life. We thrill to its beat.

Later, when we are alone, my husband confides that while I was away the clinic nurse rang to say my latest set of blood tests are still HepC positive. I am failing to respond to the Interferon treatment.

'And don't say it doesn't matter.'

My husband's voice breaks as he speaks. He has had to bear the news alone all day.

'It doesn't matter,' I insist. 'Not compared to a March, Strathspey and Reel.'

But at dawn, we waken on the hearthrug. We have run out of money, and now we are running out of strength.

Dunino Church sits on hallowed ground above Dunino Burn.

Its churchyard is marked out by a wall which rises on the higher side to iron railings, and a gate, but on the lower side is reduced to a few crumbling stones hidden in bracken. The church is never locked, because there is nothing in it and because no-one knows it is there.

It is never heated either. On Christmas Eve, over the hour of its carol service, centuries of damp seep into my veins, freezing blood and Interferon together.

'We couldn't waken you,' says my daughter. 'We thought you'd miss Christmas.'

'What's that noise?'

She peers between curtains drawn to conserve heat. It is already snowing outside.

'They're chopping logs for kindling.'

When the fire is lit, more logs are piled higher than the ironwork guard. The heat is tremendous. I waken again, this time on the hearth-rug, to find the curtains open. A slow drift of snow across the window leaves the fields and barns of Dunino sparkling. It is magical.

'How long should we leave potatoes in the fire?' asks my husband.

'Ten minutes?'

He seizes the coal-tongs and searches the flames for blackened silver foil.

'They might be a bit well done. How long should we leave the drumsticks?'

'Two minutes?'

'Hmmm,' says my husband, searching faster. 'This is not good news.'

'How long have they been in?'

He glances at the clock, lifts a blackened drumstick onto the hearth and peels back its foil. Inside, there are cinders.

'Three quarters of an hour?'

To make up for the loss of their Christmas dinner, I promise the children a bedroom each.

'It's not really practical for them to share,' I tell my husband.

'Yeah,' says our son. 'My bed is bounded on three sides by wall. I can't reach it unless I walk over hers. And I've got to keep all my stuff in your new coffee table.'

Our daughter realises that if our son is moved out, the millionaire's daughter can move in for sleepovers.

'But where's the other bedroom?' she stops celebrating to ask.

'An interesting question,' says my husband. 'Where *is* the other bedroom, dear?'

'Give me a minute,' I tell him. 'I found a cottage, didn't I? I can find another bedroom. Make coffee.'

My husband hesitates.

'Well go *on*,' says our daughter.

I have a bedroom in mind. At the back of the sitting room a door leads into a curious cupboard-like space which for some reason has a window onto the garden. It is filled with packing cases.

'Most of that could go into the loft—' I begin.

My son's expression falters. There is not enough space in the cupboard for his bed, never mind the couple of mates he too has in mind to ship in.

'Well it must have been a bedroom at some point,' I argue, looking round the door to try to work out how it could have been.

My husband says that it was more likely the pantry. The cottage's kitchen, which is adjacent, is a more modern extension.

'I can't sleep here,' says our son, lying down in demonstration. 'You wouldn't be able to open and close the door.'

'All right. Give me a minute.'

I meet my husband's eyes. I am thinking that if he chopped logs for a fire every night he and I could sleep on the hearth-rug. The trouble is that there is not much space on a hearthrug for a fridge and a yellow infected sharps bin.

'No he can't have our room,' my husband interrupts. 'Don't be stupid. You need to get well in it.'

'All right. Just give me a minute—'

My husband sighs.

'Let's cut this short. The only possible space is in the loft. But even if there were a window, which there isn't, I doubt he would able to stand up in it.'

'The loft,' repeats our son.

His eyes are shining.

'No, not the loft,' I say, looking up, above the jammed tree trunk to the trapdoor in the roof of the passage. 'He might fall out.'

'No I wouldn't.'

'He wouldn't,' says my husband. 'It's not that high and we'd get a ladder. But it's a pitched roof. He wouldn't be able to stand up.'

To prove the point my husband gets a chair and pushes the trapdoor aside with his fingertips. There is a lot of heaving and kicking the air to get his elbow through the hatch and wedged inside.

'What can you see?' our son asks his legs.

The legs kick the air again and disappear.

'No!' I order, as our son's legs follow.

'What can you see?' I am forced to negotiate.

There is some scuffling, and an argument.

'I can stand up!' yells our son.

'No you can't,' says my husband. 'That doesn't count. Ten centimetres left or right and you'll smack your head off a rafter.'

'I can walk this way though, backwards and forwards.'

'Don't be daft—'

'It's not daft. The bed can go here, in the low bit, because I'll be lying down anyway. And we can get rid of this whatever-it-is—'

'—no we can't. It's the water tank.'

My son's head appears in the open hatch.

'You'll have to come up and talk to him.'

'I can't get up there—'

'Yes you can,' says our daughter, grim-faced with determination. 'Hold up your hands and Dad'll pull you up.'

Fifteen minutes later we are all four in the loft space. The thought of getting back down is making me feel faint. Our son is walking up and down the roofline, to demonstrate that one end is located above the hatch. I look round as my eyes grow accustomed to the lack of light.

'We'd have to partition off the water tank.'

'The space that's left would be far too small,' my husband is insisting. 'You'd never get planning permission for a bedroom.'

'We could say it was a storeroom. It would really only mean the cost of putting in a window.'

'Why would anyone put a window in a storeroom?' asks my husband.

'But I'm still not happy that he won't fall out,' I argue in the opposite direction.

'Oh don't be *daft*,' my husband immediately contradicts himself.

'That's it, then,' says the joiner, sticking his head into the kitchen at midnight. 'Window's made a big difference. And I've donated my ladder to the cause.'

I am overwhelmed.

'Now, now,' says the joiner. 'Fourth rung's missing. Only fit for scrap. But your husband can saw it down to size.'

I show him out the back door, and follow my son into the passage to secure the ladder. He jams it widthways, between the hatch and the wall, missing the jammed tree trunk by millimetres.

'I'm not sure about this—' I am already complaining, as I follow him up.

The loft is half its former size. A huge velux window slants from floor to roofline, high enough to look down on the woodland in the den below. Against a starlit navy sky, crowns of firs stand in silhouette.

'Get Dad,' I say, sinking to my knees in awe. 'Tell him it's happened again. You just can't keep this cottage down.'

My husband explains that the Velux window had been marked for scrap, until the joiner rescued it and put it in our loft. It has therefore cost almost nothing. Nor does my husband charge for advising the joiner what size of lintel he would require, were he ever to build the conservatory of his wife's dreams.

'So this is the breakfast room,' explains the joiner, showing us round it, 'and through here is her potting shed.'

There is considerable banter. My husband remarks that it will be a great shame if the joiner has to pull the conservatory down, given that he didn't apply for planning permission to put it up. The joiner is shocked by this slur on his reputation.

'I certainly *did* apply for planning permission.'

My husband apologises in surprise.

'Fair enough, planning permission was refused,' the joiner allows. 'But I did *apply* for it. And how's your new storeroom? Now, would you be storing the lad's bed up there, by any chance?'

Driving back up the Anstruther road, my husband says he has applied to Fife County Council Planning Department for a *Letter of Comfort*. A *Letter of Comfort* will reassure me that although our loft conversion is news to them, Fife County Council will not be instigating court proceedings to dismantle it.

Back home, in the tiny sitting room, the answering machine's little red light is berserking. There is a message from the clinic nurse. In the final fortnight of a year of Interferon injections, I have tested HepC negative.

The answering machine message pauses. My husband and I scream, and punch the air.

'*You did it!*' he yells.

No you didn't, the answering machine is quick to contradict. After a year of injections, a negative blood test is almost inevitable. In fact, mine is late. The real test is whether there is a subsequent relapse. I am to show up at fortnightly intervals, so that the clinic nurse can check for one.

'*You probably did it!*' yells my husband.

There is no restraining our jubilation. After a year of HepC positive blood tests, of fortnightly disappointment, the dream has come true. *I am well!* I sing in the den behind the cottage. *I am well!* I exult to the crowns of firs silhouetted in the Velux window.

I am *so nearly* well. All I need are a few more negative blood tests and there will be a *Letter of Comfort* from the Royal Infirmary of Edinburgh. It will tell me that with each succeeding negative blood test, a relapse becomes increasingly unlikely.

There is an outbreak of foot and mouth disease. Straw is laid across the end of the farm track. A bucket of bleach stands beside the straw. There is a mop in the long grass of the hedgerow, for our shoes, and a stiff broom for our car tyres. We sweep and clean and pray for a clean bill of health.

One day, the wife of the farm is waiting at the end of the track. The straw is brushed away, and the bucket of bleach emptied into a field drain. The farm's agony is over.

'I wanted to catch you. What book are we to read?'

There is no hope that I will recall the last book I read, but when I get home I check my bookshelves and discover a volume out of place. I ring the farm.

'*The Beginnings of Humankind.*'

'What's it about?'

'Palaeontology.'

'You're a strange one,' she observes, writing it down.

The book club likes the new fireplace, but *The Beginnings of Humankind* nearly finishes it off. The wife of the farm is particularly scathing.

'Am I right,' she opens her copy at the fossil photographs, 'that this book attempts to prove a three million year old fossil is more human than not?'

'Yes, the previously oldest fossil of a hominid—'

'From a couple of teeth?'

'No, that's why this fossil is such a fantastic find. In fact, besides the teeth, there is a jaw, a shinbone and several vertebrae from a young female and an adult male—'

The shy boy's mother is a weaver. She weaves seaweed and fibre optics at a prestigious art school and hasn't had time to read the book.

'Is it a romance?' she laughs.

'It is a biography?' suggests the millionaire's wife, trying to be helpful.

'No, it can't be –' says the wife of the farm, struggling to convey some sense of how ridiculous is palaeontology as a bookclub choice. '– it can't be, because this woman is three million years old—'

'Does she have a child?'

'No, of course not—' the wife of the farm grows frustrated. 'Well, yes, there is a child but it's a fossil too. They are all dead in a heap in a dried up riverbed.'

The millionaire's wife is shocked into silence.

'A tragedy, then?' asks the weaver, with a straight face.

My husband sticks his head round the door.

'I've a contractor on the phone. He's offering us topsoil for the price of its delivery. Do we want some?'

I hesitate. I am too tired to think about it.

'Yes!' says the weaver. 'Yes, the garden desperately needs it. How much is he offering?'

'Well,' says my husband, 'he says he's going to deliver it on a sixteen ton loader—'

'Very good!' she nods. 'You'll need that, once you've built the terrace.'

'Terrace?' asks my husband.

'I think it's your only option,' she shrugs, 'otherwise you won't have anywhere to put your garden furniture.'

'We haven't *got* any garden furniture,' says my husband.

The millionaire's wife sits straighter on the beech-slatted sofa and smiles her inscrutable almond-eyed smile. We appoint the wife of the farm *Bookclub Secretary*.

'Shall we go for a *novel* for next month?' she asks.

'What about *The Leopard?*' suggests the weaver.

'Very good,' says the millionaire's wife. 'I like very much not to read *The Leopard.* Thank you. I will come.'

In the auction house in St Andrews, there is a sofa small enough to fit before the cottage's hearth, and a table minute enough to stand in the pantry. The reserve prices are all we can afford. My husband is fretting.

'I know you. You'll get caught up in bidding and put an extra tenner on. We don't even need a sofa,' he goes on, 'at least, not until the grass grows.'

'I'm sure I saw a green mist from the kitchen window—'

'No you didn't. It takes a fortnight with a decent rainfall, and we haven't had rain for a month. If your heart is set on the sofa and the table, I'll ring in and offer the reserve prices. That way, if you're meant to get them, then you will.'

I have no faith in this arrangement.

'You might as well not bother,' I complain. 'Someone will put in a higher bid.'

'Anyway, you're busy tomorrow afternoon,' my husband remembers. 'The old lady downstairs in Argyle Street rang. She wants you to take her to church.'

I show up at her pantiled cottage in a temper.

'You are not taking me to church,' explains the old lady, buttoning herself into a long black coat. 'I am taking *you*. I discussed your wretched circumstance with the priest at St James, and he has offered to anoint you with the Sacrament of Extreme Unction.'

'But that's one down from Last Rites, isn't it?'

'There's a special Mass at three o'clock,' she nods over her shoulder, turning away to switch off the lights of her Christmas tree, 'and he's put your name on his list.'

'No, wait,' I say, following her into the pend. 'Wait a minute. I really don't think I should accept Extreme Unction. I'm not *that* wretched—'

'Take it, take it!' she urges. 'I always do. Every winter. Extreme Unction and a flu jab.'

I am still protesting on the path along the cliff top. A passkeeper hurries to meet us.

'Just come for Mass?' he enquires. 'Or are you down for Extra Munction?'

'Oh yes,' beams the old lady. 'Two please.'

On the way home, we stop at the auction house. It is deserted. By the door, labelled with my name, are the sofa and the minute table.

'The topsoil came?' asks the weaver at a drinks party.

'Sixteen tons. It was only just enough. We gathered all the stones and built a terrace in a curve, so that it would reach the apple tree. Then we sowed it all with grass seed, but it hasn't grown yet.'

'You must be exhausted!'

'I am,' I laugh.

'I am quite tired,' I repeat to my husband, as we drive home.

'God, that's not surprising,' he says, so that I know that he has noticed. 'These drinks parties are exhausting. Did you talk to the millionaire?'

'He asked me what I was reading. But I was so tired I couldn't remember.'

There is a silence. Fifteen miles pass unnoticed. I open my eyes on the Anstruther Road.

'*The Leopard*,' says my husband.

'What?'

'You're reading *The Leopard*.'

There is no reason to worry. Long term medication with Interferon often results in memory loss. Nor does unreasonable fatigue have to mean I have relapsed.

I drive to Edinburgh with our last ten pound note, to buy my husband boxer shorts and keep my hospital appointment. The clinic nurse is not there.

'On holiday,' confirms the receptionist. 'But she's back on Monday, so I'm sure she'll be in touch. And you're down to see the professor, but he's not here either.'

I am not alarmed. There is no reason to be alarmed. The clinic nurse is on holiday, that's all. And besides, I am too tired to be alarmed. I am so tired after driving to Edinburgh that the receptionist has to waken me to tell me that I will be seen by one of the registrars.

'Ah,' says the registrar, indicating a chair with a courteous hand.

He looks a little harassed. His shirt sleeves are pushed up to his elbows. There is no warning.

'I'm afraid there has been a relapse.'

'What?'

'You have relapsed, I am sorry to tell you.'

I am aware of a silence.

'What?'

The registrar nods and grimaces, to show his sympathy.

'The professor did discuss this eventuality and so I know that you will have been to some extent prepared for it. But it is a disappointment. I am sorry.'

'But – but I thought that after a whole year—'

He nods again in sympathy.

'We gave it our best shot.'

I leave the hospital. Rush hour traffic is log-jamming the Mound. It is raining. On Princes Street, in the window of Marks and Spencers, tailor's dummies model a new collection of lycra miniskirts. Their ticket price is nine pounds ninety nine.

'I didn't get the boxer shorts.'

My husband reacts with despair.

'He said it was a *disappointment?*'

'Yes.'

'What did you say?'

'Nothing. I went to buy the boxer shorts, and saw this miniskirt –' I wiggle my hips to model it for him, '– and spent the ten pound note on it instead because,' I shout at last, 'I will probably never sleep with you again!'

'You need a lycra miniskirt to tell me that?' my husband shouts back.

We explain my relapse to the bank. It withdraws our overdraft facility.

A hammering on the cottage door wakens me out of an Interferon fever. I am in bed, in a derelict cottage surrounded by empty fields, and someone is hammering at its door. I pull open the bedroom curtain. Two men stand outside, wearing black suits and unfriendly expressions.

'It's locked,' I say through the window, 'and I am not dressed.'

The unfriendly expressions grow derisive. I have no idea of the time. I guess from the position of the sun that it is about eleven o'clock.

'Sheriff's Officers,' says the nearest, flashing a wallet.

He asks me to confirm my address. I have no clear idea what a Sheriff's Officer is. I offer my husband's telephone number.

'You're pretty isolated here,' says the second. 'You must have a car?'

'Yes, we have a car,' I say. 'My husband has gone to town in it.'

I offer his telephone number again.

'What make of car?' asks the first Sheriff's Officer.

'I'm sorry?'

He leans closer to the window.

'What make is the car?' he enunciates.

I start to shake. It is a physical reaction. I do not yet understand that these men mean to seize our car. I shake without understanding and point to the road.

'Please go away. I am not dressed.'

They step closer to the window. They argue. There is a reference to the Inland Revenue. They walk to the side of the cottage, inspect the wooden shed and saunter back to the road, where their own car is parked on the grass verge. For several minutes after they get inside, it remains there. I stand at the window until it moves away.

Without my salary I have no access to the judicial system. Yet if I am not awarded compensation, I will be presumed undeserving of it. I will be hounded for tax and legal fees and bank charges. I collapse onto the hearthrug and beat my fists upon it.

The telephone rings. It is the clinic nurse, returned from holiday and returning my several calls.

'Are you all right?'

'No,' I point out. 'I relapsed.'

She knows. She has checked my medical file before she rang. She is very sorry.

'But why is nothing happening?' I wail.

'Well, it's up to the professor, really. He gets back before your next appointment. I expect he'll have a word then. And I will take your bloods, obviously, to monitor how you're doing—'

'Yes but never mind monitoring. We *know* how I'm doing. I've relapsed. Surely it's worse to delay the next course of Interferon? I mean, surely it's better to get back on it while the viral load is relatively low?'

There is an embarrassed pause.

'Well, like I said, that's a decision for the professor,' repeats the clinic nurse.

I realise what she is saying.

'A *decision* for the professor? What decision? He won't decide to stop the treatment?'

'I'm really sorry,' she repeats, over and over. 'I'm so sorry.'

'But why?'

'Because,' she explains, 'all the evidence we have is now against your recovery. The response rate to Interferon drops through the floor where a patient has failed to respond to it already. In order to save money, it's currently NHS policy not to treat non-responders. It all comes down to money, in the end.'

She hears my intake of breath.

'I'm so, so sorry,' she says.

I drive into St Andrews to collect our daughter from a hill-walking expedition. Beneath the trees, a line of headlit cars await the arrival of the school minibus.

'Took them longer to get down than we estimated,' the headmaster comes out of his study to explain at my rolled-down window. 'I'm afraid the minibus won't be back until nearer half past.'

I lock the car and walk through the blackberry bushes to the stream. It is smaller than it lives on in my memory. I walk to the island and on almost as far as Argyle Street. When I turn back, and put the lights of town behind me, the path has grown too dark to follow.

I walk on regardless. In Dunino we have grown used to darkness. In any case I have walked this path so often. The school cannot be more than a quarter of a mile away.

Though I have forgotten the intersection with another path from a different part of town, which comes in over a footbridge. On the footbridge might be shadows.

I tell myself to get a grip. The shadows mutter and laugh. I quicken my pace. They quicken theirs behind me. For a moment I am afraid, and cannot believe I have been so stupid.

Though it is an unlikely spot for murderers and even if they are, it looks like I'll die anyway, in the fairly near future. I can't be robbed for much, since we haven't even got the tax. And if they are rapists, then I will infect *them* with a life-threatening virus.

I start to laugh. First silently, then loud enough to hear, then great shouts of laughter I can't control. I have to stop on the path.

Two hooded figures sidle past my hysterics.

'I'm not going to worry about this,' the weaver says. 'Place has huge significance. That is why, in the end, you will recover in Dunino.'

Her husband has made an apple crumble and is holding it over the table, between oven-gloves.

'It's too much of a coincidence,' he agrees.

'What coincidence?' asks my husband.

'Oh God!' the weaver puts her hands to her temples. 'I don't believe it. They have bought the cottage at Dunino and they don't know why they are there.'

'She rang last night,' says the wife of the farm, who won't come in but has pulled over onto the grass verge on her way into town, 'and asked me to give you this.'

It is a few typed and photocopied pages bound between two sheets of blue card.

A History of Dunino Den.

I take the booklet into my husband's wooden shed.

'Listen to this,' I say.

'In 208 AD on the orders of the Roman emperor Septimus Severus two legions were diverted to the Stone Circle of Dunino to subdue local tribesmen. The Roman camp was fourteen hectares in area, suggesting a force of ten thousand men.'

'*Ten thousand* men?' says my husband.

I drum my fingers on his desk.

'So it's not just this cottage. It's Dunino. They couldn't keep Dunino down.'

We are standing in Dunino Den around a man-made pool carved into rock by an ancient people.

The pool is just over a metre wide. Its depth cannot be measured by the branch our son sticks in its leaf-laden waters.

Above the pool, in four equal quadrants, smaller post-holes have been cut. According to the *History of Dunino Den*, the post-holes allowed the erection of a canopy to dignify religious and political ritual.

'– similar pools have been found carved into rocks in Ireland and France –' I read.

'Wild,' says our son, enacting throat-cutting ceremonies to distress our daughter.

In the interests of serious research, I am trying to downplay the human sacrifice angle.

'It is likely the pool was used for ceremonies of cleansing and renewal—' I read.

Our daughter is not convinced. She looks up at the fields and cottage chimneys which loom high above our heads.

'I'm never coming here again,' she vows. 'And I'm never going into the garden again, unless you or Dad come with me.'

'The Celts were a civilised people,' I say. 'They valued art and learning. Only primitive societies go in for human sacrifice—'

'Like ours, you mean,' says out son. 'Which is sacrificing you.'

My husband grins.

'It was your idea to educate him,' he justifies himself.

'And anyway,' says our son, 'you said that communion was a left-over re-enactment of primitive human sacrifice—'

'Which just goes to show,' I comfort our daughter, 'that nowadays nobody gets eaten.'

She casts a wary eye towards our son, to see whether he agrees.

'Well, not in Dunino Church,' he allows.

'There's absolutely no difference between this ancient place of worship and Dunino Church,' I interrupt. 'Or any other church. They're all the same, and anyone who thinks otherwise is just being daft.'

The professor turns from me to his registrars for their opinion. They purse their lips. One or two shake their heads.

'We hear what you are saying,' agrees the professor, turning back to me. 'And if the typical graph for viral load reduction continued in a straight line to complete eradication then another month of Interferon might make the difference. The trouble is that Interferon isn't very good at virus eradication.'

My heart begins to hammer.

'But the fact remains I tested HepC negative for a whole fortnight,' I plead.

'Patients often test HepC negative on Interferon, only to relapse as soon as treatment is withdrawn,' continues the professor. 'It works well at reducing heavy viral loads, but isn't so effective mopping up at reduced levels. It is not therefore our policy to offer Interferon therapy to non-responders—'

'But I *did* respond—'

'—partly because it's a very expensive treatment,' the professor explains. 'And partly because there is no point subjecting patients to the side effects of Interferon unnecessarily.'

'But it might not be unnecessarily!' I cry. 'The fact remains, I tested negative—'

'Moving on,' the professor puts his hands together, 'to the next phase of our research programme, we are about to trial a new drug.'

'I did respond,' I am appealing to the slim young Asian doctor, 'only not for very long. But I did *respond.*'

The slim young Asian doctor slides her eyes towards the professor, with a significance I do not understand.

'Ribavirin,' the professor is declaiming, 'may be the virus *eradicator* we have lacked. It has the ability to slow the rate of replication of viral cells, thus rendering Interferon more effective at reduced viral load. Used in a combination therapy, Ribavirin may well improve our response rate out of all recognition.'

'—tested negative for a fortnight,' I am battling on, in a general appeal to anyone who will listen, 'which hardly counts as non-responding—'

The slim young Asian doctor gives up throwing significant glances, and rolls her eyes at me instead.

'What?' I say.

The professor puts his hands flat on his blotter to repeat himself.

'In order to establish an improvement in response rate, we will trial Ribavirin in a control group of patients who have previously failed to respond to conventional Interferon therapy. For the purposes of our research, failure to respond will be defined as a failure to maintain a HepC negative status beyond the period of treatment. In other words –' the professor raises his voice to finish.

'Oh!' I say.

'—in other words, patients who have suffered a *relapse.*'

'Meaning me?' I say.

The professor opens my medical file.

'Because I was only pointing out a technicality,' I tell the registrars and junior doctors. 'The fact remains, I *have* relapsed.'

'However,' the professor is confessing, 'there is a catch. You cannot take part in this, or indeed any other drugs trial, without signing away your medical rights—'

'That's fine,' I interrupt him. 'That's absolutely fine.'

'You will of course need time to consider our offer,' the professor concludes.

He closes up my medical file, having noted the offer within it.

'No, that's fine,' I am light-headed with relief. 'That's absolutely fine. Don't worry about the medical rights. I accept. Thank you very much.'

I walk through the garden. There is no sign of Septimus Severus' two legions, but when I open the door to the wooden shed, my husband is fighting a rearguard action on the telephone.

He has seen off the helpline tax advisor and got himself put through to a tax inspector, who has access to our file. But not, the tax inspector claims, with any authority to call off Sheriff's Officers.

'Then can you put me through to somebody who has?' my husband is repeating. 'I am not disputing my tax bill. I want to pay. I need you to give me time to pay, because my wife is ill and we have lost her salary—'

The tax inspector has not the authority. My husband takes a deep breath.

'Then can you let me speak to someone who *has* the authority—' he repeats and points to the clock to indicate to me that he has been on the telephone an hour.

But the tax inspector is tiring. He tells my husband he will speak to his manager. He says it won't make any difference.

'Thank you,' says my husband and slumps over his desk.

'You're too nice to them,' I whisper.

'They've a fair point—' he shrugs, putting his hand over the receiver. '*Fair?!*'

The Inland Revenue manager comes on the line. The tax inspector was right. It has made no difference.

'Six months,' my husband is pleading. 'I can settle in six months. My wife has lost her salary. She is too ill to work. She has signed away her medical rights—'

The Inland Revenue manager raises her voice, so that I can hear what she is saying.

'I am not interested in your wife's medical condition,' she is saying.

Adrenalin pumps through my veins so fast I hear my ears sing. As though in action replay, I watch myself spin from the wooden shed's door and spring towards my husband's desk. I wrench the telephone receiver from his hand.

'AND I AM NOT INTERESTED' I bellow at the Inland Revenue manager 'IN ONE GOVERNMENT BUREAUCRAT TELLING ME SHE IS NOT INTERESTED THAT ANOTHER GOVERNMENT BUREAUCRAT HAS *CONTAMINATED MY BLOOD!*'

I thrust the receiver back into my husband's hand. There is a shocked silence.

'Three months to pay,' sniffs the Inland Revenue manager. '*Three* months.'

The line clicks as she hangs up. My husband stares at me. The battle-fever still has me in its grip.

It is as infectious as hepatitis. My husband leaps to his feet. Screaming and circling, we war-dance around his desk and out into the garden.

My husband strips a branch of birch to make a curtain pole. I stand on the minute table and lay the curtain pole across two cup-hooks screwed into the frame of the pantry window. My handsewn gingham curtains refuse to draw against the birch but don't have to, since not even Septimus Severus could fight his way through Dunino Den to look in.

'It's raining again,' I say.

My husband stops refilling his toolbox and looks at my reflection in the window. Water is running down it.

'God,' he moans, 'I hope none of the pantiles are loose. I hope it doesn't flood my wooden shed, now you've nicked one of my doorsteps. I hope—'

'I hope the grass grows,' I interrupt him.

'I hope that rain doesn't wash all the seed into the den,' my husband countermands me.

Next morning, the rain has stopped. I stop too, en route to the bath, to check out my new birch curtain pole in daylight. Its gingham curtains, necessarily open, frame a miracle. The grass has grown.

Greenness floods from the pantry window in a level ripple, curls around the apple tree and waterfalls over the terrace to meet, not desolate ranks of tree trunks, but boughs swept low with the weight of newly budded leaves. Bough after bough glows darkly green in the shadows deep in the den. Where the wood meets the edge of our garden the boughs sweep low, continuing the curve of the terrace to form a perfect circle of green grass.

It is exactly as I dreamt it.

'Well, here we go again,' I say.

We are signalling to turn onto the Anstruther Road. The car is packed with our son's belongings. Behind us, in the cottage bedroom, my fridge is newly stocked with Interferon.

Our son flicks open the car's music player and inserts a cassette.

'This is one for you, mum.'

It is Chumbawamba singing *Tubthumping*.

I get knocked down

But I get up again

You're never going to keep me down.

Our eyes meet in the rearview mirror. We both know that in his absence I will play it every day.

The tree jamming the cottage door has dried out, slipped and jammed the letterbox. The postman throws our letters through the bedroom window. One bears our son's handwriting. I scramble for it over the duvet.

'He's written a letter.'

My husband opens his eyes.

'Not of his own volition, I bet.'

The notepaper bears the school chaplain's address.

'Told you,' says my husband, closing his eyes.

Please accept this invitation to our Ceremony of Confirmation on the final Sunday of term—

'Oh yeah,' says our son, when I ring him, 'I forgot to tell you about that. We're all getting confirmed.'

'But hang on,' I say. 'Have we stopped to think about this? I mean, which church are you being confirmed into?'

'I don't know. Episcopalian? Possibly Episcopalian and they've invited an Anglican bishop for the English boys. So, half and half?'

'But these are Protestant churches,' I protest. 'This is not a Catholic confirmation.'

'I know *that*,' argues our son, 'but you said anyone who thinks there is a difference is just being daft?'

There is a moment of silence.

'Oh yeah,' I say.

Our son is right. The atmosphere in the school chapel at the Ceremony of Confirmation is exactly the atmosphere in Dunino Den.

Sunlight filters, not through green boughs, but with an equal iridescence through tall arched stained glass windows. Between them wooden columns branch into wooden rafters. Through the arches of the windows, upper classrooms and the topmost tower of a girls' boarding house loom over our heads.

Beyond the lectern sits the Headmaster.

'He would have to be crazy to let our daughter sit his scholarship examination,' is my husband's gloomy assessment, as we climb the stair between the lion and the unicorn after the ceremony. 'We're an even worse bet, financially, now that you've relapsed. We'll be out of his study within five minutes.'

The Headmaster makes his decision faster than that. He presses his finger-tips together and looks at me through narrowed eyes.

'You need to go and get well,' he decides. 'Send your daughter to sit our scholarship examination. But I am telling you now, regardless of its result, that we will take her.'

I punch a hypodermic needle of Interferon into my thigh, and before its side-effects kick in, walk round Dunino Church and down its path. In the silence of Dunino Den, I close my eyes. The Headmaster says,

'*But I am telling you now, regardless of its result, that we will take her.*' I open my eyes. Sunlight is filtering through stained glass windows and the trunks of the trees are branching into a canopy of rafters. Shivers are already running up my spine, but Dunino Burn is flowing down the aisle of the school chapel, where our son is marching, in kilt and tweed jacket, to confirm that there is a God.

The weather is warming. Soon I will be able to eat at the table under the apple tree. Our son and daughter already are. I watch them from the shelter of the pantry and regret in mime-play that its window does not open.

'What?' they ask, coming through the kitchen for more toast.

'It's a pity the window doesn't open. Though what we really need here is a patio door.'

Our son inspects the pantry window as he munches.

'You could replace it with a window which opens,' he tells me, 'but not with a patio door. The window is sitting on a metre of solid stone.'

The idea of a patio door makes me regret the metre of solid stone in louder tones.

'You're stuck with it, mum,' laughs our son. 'Unless we take a sledgehammer to it. Come and sit in the loft if you want fresh air.'

They take their toast to its ladder. I follow with my coffee. The joiner's ladder holds no fears for us now. We scramble up and down its rungs, using the missing fourth to tell us when to twist and brace ourselves against the wall, to lift whatever we are carrying through the hatch. When the first thunderous blow is struck, I don't even spill my coffee.

'What was *that?*' asks our daughter.

She is standing wide-eyed next to our son's bed. Our daughter has free run of the loft, because she is not yet tall enough to bang her head against a rafter. She uses the advantage to dive past us in the rush to the Velux window.

'It's Dad,' she confirms, leaning in again to let our son lean out.

He leans out, then leaps out, onto the kitchen roof.

WHAM!

'Dad!' he yells.

WHAM!

'He's knocking it out,' reports our son.

'What? What's he knocking out?'

'The metre of solid stone. He's knocking it out.'

WHAM!

This time the thunderous blow is quickly followed by a thunderous shattering of glass. *Stop! Stop!* I am yelling, as I scramble back down the ladder and out the kitchen door.

'*Stop!* What are you *doing?*'

It is too late. The pantry window lies in shards on a tumble of broken stone. Beyond, the gingham curtains have begun to flutter in synchrony with the wisteria against the bathroom wall.

My husband drops his sledgehammer and wipes his forearm along his brow. I am practically speechless.

'Wh—what have you done? Don't we need planning permission for that? What if it's not safe?'

'They ask me what's safe.'

'But – but – surely we should have waited, for a *Letter of Comfort* at least?'

He picks up the sledgehammer again.

'A *Letter of Comfort?*' he howls. 'You've just signed away your *medical rights!* What's *comfortable* about that?'

WHAM!

'You haven't *time* to wait for a Letter of Comfort!' he howls again. 'You might only have this summer!'

WHAM!

'Stop!' I yell above the din. 'Stop!'

WHAM!

'All right! Stop! You can stop now –' I am almost as breathless as he is.

'– stop, stop. It's – it'll be great. It's just that – we haven't got a door.'

He leans on the sledgehammer for a minute, then lets it topple onto the grass.

'Well, I'll find one. I'll ring the joiner's yard on Monday. They're bound to have an old door—'

The children appear in the pantry, and stick their heads round the hole in the wall.

'Good effort,' grins our son.

My husband surveys the hole with pride.

'But what about this evening?' I say.

'What about this evening?'

'The farm are expecting us for supper.'

There is a pause. The children hold their breath.

'Ah,' says my husband.

Their laughter explodes around him.

The internet discovers Dunino in the nick of time. My husband provides structural analysis for a timber-frame manufacturer seventy miles away without moving from his wooden shed. We start to pay off the tax bill.

He shows me an email open on his screen. It is from the lawyer. The advent of email has facilitated their invoicing too.

'What do they want?'

'Four and a half thousand pounds.'

I am shocked.

The school fees are still two terms behind and I am swallowing cocktails of unlicensed drugs. It is not a strong financial position to be left in. It doesn't feel like four and a half thousand pounds worth.

'Tell him to stop representing us.'

'Then if the group action succeeds, you won't get any compensation.'

'Well then, tell him to take his fee from the compensation, when it comes.'

My husband clicks to open another email. The lawyer has forseen and precluded this argument. He has represented us – fair enough, unsuccessfully to date – and he is not a charity. His fee is due.

I dictate an emailed reply.

'—willing to sign a mandate that when the penury to which we have been reduced finally drives us from our home, you can take your fee from the proceeds of its sale.'

'Click send,' I tell my husband.

'You'll annoy him.'

'Click send.'

'He can arrest our bank account.'

'Much good that'll do him. Anyway, he won't. He knows I'd never shut up about it. He'd make himself *persona non grata* at every drinks party from here to Edinburgh.'

The wall at the front of the cottage has no gate.

There is not much need for a gate when a tree is jamming your front door. Our son decides to construct one all the same. The weaver's son is called in to help.

They saw and split logs in the den. They hammer them together with six inch nails. When the gate is levered into place, it is massive and splendid.

'Very good job,' approves my brother. 'If you're attacked from the west, this will buy you half an hour.'

It is a stockade of a gate. It holds out even in the face of viral replication. I test HepC negative again.

Above the theatre in St Andrews, there is a gallery which is a little like a landing. I see the weaver before she sees me. A moment later, her head appears at the top of the gallery's stairs.

'What are you doing up here?'

I explain I have reapplied to study for my post-graduate degree and that I am testing HepC negative again. The weaver raises her hands to clap them.

'No don't,' I stop her. 'It doesn't mean anything. It won't mean anything for months. Last time it didn't mean anything at all.'

She stares in silence for a moment.

'Is that why you're up here?'

'Well, you know. It's a gallery. It's neither one place nor another.'

'Ah,' says the weaver.

'I can see what's coming,' I say before I can stop myself, 'like I saw you.'

'Ah,' she nods.

She nods again, towards my A4 pad and pencil.

'What's this?'

'I'm putting together a portfolio of poems to support my application.'

'May I read this one?'

'It's a trilogy,' I keep interrupting. '*Into Dunino.* Because you said place was significant.'

She holds up the final poem of the trilogy.

'It's not finished?'

'No,' I agree.

The weaver smoothes the unfinished poem back into place behind the others, back *Into Dunino.*

'Can I keep these?' she looks up to ask.

Her eyes are full of tears.

I ring the clinic nurse's mobile number.

'What's up?'

'Listen, I just rang your reception desk, to check the time of my appointment at next week's clinic?'

'Yeah?'

'And they told me it's been cancelled. Either I've cancelled it in error, or my husband has, or somewhere down the line we've got our wires crossed, or whatever, so I'm very sorry and can you put me in again for Friday—'

'I cancelled it,' says the clinic nurse.

'—or anytime to suit you,' I say. 'What?'

It is the first time I have heard her laugh. It is a lovely deep friendly laugh.

'Well, you can come if you want,' she says, 'but only to take me out for a drink.'

'What?'

'You're through,' she says. 'Cured. Recovered. Off my caseload. Go away.'

'What?'

'Oh all right,' she laughs again. 'If you insist. Friday at four o'clock. I'll meet you in the pub around the corner.'

'Mum's driving,' says our daughter, once we have collected our son from his boarding house, 'because Dad got drunk with the nurse.'

I tell our son I am recovered at last.

'And Dad's not drunk,' I make his excuses. 'He's just worn out with the excitement. I'm sure he'll want to celebrate as soon as we get home.'

There is a whispered exchange in the back of the car.

'Does the celebration have to be at home?' asks our son.

I turn out of the gates of the boarding house. Instead of joining the dual carriageway north to the road bridge, we pull over into a parking space.

'No, I don't suppose it does. Where do you want to celebrate?'

'Paris,' says our son.

'*Paris?*'

I twist round in the driving seat. Our daughter is nodding.

'*Paris?*' I repeat.

I glance at my husband, who is still asleep in the passenger seat.

'We'll never get another chance like this one,' points out our son.

Our daughter starts clapping her hands.

'Paris here we come!'

'No. Wait a minute,' I say. 'This is mad. I mean, we can't just drive to Paris. For a start, we haven't got any luggage—'

'I just put my trunk in the boot,' points out our son. 'I've got *loads* of luggage. You can all have some of mine.'

Our daughter is asleep in the backseat, wrapped in our son's dressing-gown. He and I are listening to Chumbawamba's *Tubthumping* at seventy miles an hour on a dark deserted bypass. A roadsign looms in the headlights. My husband opens his eyes.

'Birmingham 8,' he reads.

We hold our breath.

'Interesting,' says my husband, and closes his eyes again.

' *– you're never going to keep me down –*'

'Let me introduce you,' says the professor at the launch of his new collection.

I look into the lawyer's eyes.

'We are old friends,' I laugh.

'Wasn't he embarrassed?' asks my husband's profile, driving home.

I wince as I pull off an unaccustomed ear-ring.

'Lawyers don't get embarrassed.'

'What did you say?'

'I congratulated him on his retirement, he congratulated the prof on his new collection and then they both congratulated me on my recovery.'

I pull off the other earring.

'Why don't you wear pierced ones now you're not infectious?'

'The holes in my ears have closed up.'

My husband frowns as he examines the nearest.

'Look at the road,' I admonish him.

'And did he say anything else?'

'He had the grace to apologise that he had not kept up with the case. So I told him the bookclub saw a BBC news report about it.'

'And what did he say?'

'He said he hadn't seen it.'

My husband is silent. He changes gear for the Stravithie corner. At the end of a long avenue of beech tress, Dunino is asleep beneath its butter-coloured moon.

'But did you ask him if he thought it could be true that the government is waiting for blood victims' deaths?'

'I did.'

'And what did he say?'

'He said it was his great pleasure to learn that the government is no longer waiting for mine.'

My husband signals for the cottage and turns under the sycamore.

'Bloody lawyerspeak,' he complains. 'Come on. There's enough light to follow the path.'

We follow the path to the door and on round the corner of the cottage. In the light of the full moon, daisies gleam at the edges of our glances. Above them, Dunino Law blacks out so many stars its outline is traced over them.

'Where are you?' says my husband's voice.

He laughs as he follows my laugh, down to the silver thread of the stream, up to the churchyard's Celtic altar, on matted straw along a field of furrows, to leap a ditch, cross the road and turn at the beechwood.

The cottage is watching for our return, the butter-coloured moon reflected in each window. In its light, dog roses are opening around the door. The leaf buds on the apple trees are wakening from a longer, deeper sleep.

'Bloody lawyerspeak,' my husband repeats.

He shuts the stockade gate behind us.

'One year of Interferon was bad enough,' he says, 'but there was never a chance we could afford a second. I wouldn't change a thing, but the fact is we'll have to sell.'

Dear Headmaster,

Enclosed is a copy of a mandate which my lawyer has just obliged me to sign, ensuring that most of the funds we released from the sale of our home are now diverted to him.

I cannot put into words my frustration that the little he has achieved, in raising an unsuccessful court action, should count more than the kindness you and the school governors showed our children.

Since Edinburgh Royal Infirmary have confirmed that I am in remission, and it is not their expectation I will subsequently test Hepatitis C positive, I will find employment to ensure their education continues now that I am well. Please let me know if you have any teaching post for which you think me suitable.

'Hmmm,' said the professor in his book-lined study in St Andrews University. 'Would the teaching job in Edinburgh you failed to mention in your application be a full time occupation?'

'Please,' I say. 'I'll have everything in on time.'

'And your tutorial time with me?'

'They're giving me Tuesday and Thursday afternoons off. I was hoping you might see me then?'

Once he has closed his diary, the professor pushes back his chair.

'When do you leave for Edinburgh?' he asks, in a conversational way.

'In time for the start of term,' I say. 'Why don't you come to lunch this Sunday, in Dunino? My husband would like that.'

My husband and the professor hit it off at once. They share a Scottish respect for the technical aspects of one another's trade and a rueful disdain for the lack of reward of their own. We eat haddock, which my husband has baked in milk.

'It's just as well you can cook,' the professor tells him, 'since your wife wants to spend her time writing bloody poetry.'

He tells us that the award was for a collection he wrote on the death of his first wife, twenty years before. By then we are at the cottage fire, in a twilight of Gaelic coffees.

'Damn woodsmoke,' he and my husband agree, as it gets into their eyes.

'Did we get to keep the gate?'

In the garden, the flowers have died back. Wisteria and apple blossom are blown away together. Cow parsley and bluebells are trodden underfoot. In his wooden shed, my husband's tone is equally autumnal.

'No, we didn't. It's a fixture.'

'Didn't you offer to replace it?'

He nods and shrugs.

'They wouldn't budge. All fixtures as seen.'

My eyes widen.

'Including the *tree?*'

But my husband has bought a barrel for the cottage lock at last. He has hauled the log which used to jam the door across the grass, and let it roll into the den.

'We'd never have got the tree in the car anyway,' he consoles me.

I push the door of the wooden shed wider.

'We'd have got it in the hired van,' I wail. 'We could have taken the gate *and* the tree.'

My husband narrows his eyes to gauge the van's capacity.

'We could pack the seven-year archive in that. And the children's trunks are already in Edinburgh. If we're lucky, we'll only need a couple of trips.'

But apart from the tree and the stockade gate, I want to take the view from the velux window, the synchronised fluttering of wisteria and gingham curtains, the shadow of the apple tree over the garden bench –

'We can take the garden bench, can't we? It isn't fixed to anything—'

My husband shakes his head and reads from the missive the lawyer has sent him.

'– garden as seen, including all plants, exterior lamps, patio and garden furniture –'

I am in a panic.

'Is the bluebell urn garden furniture?'

'Well—'

'No it isn't,' I argue, 'and it's not fixed to anything either.'

My husband consults his contract again.

'Though it does say, garden including *all plants*. So technically, I suppose, the vine is—'

'—not planted in the garden, and bloody well coming to Edinburgh.'

Once the van is packed, we fall asleep on the hearthrug for the last time. At dawn its fire has crumbled to cold grey ash.

'Damn woodsmoke,' we curse all the same, switching on the windscreen wipers, as though that will make a difference.

'Hello. I'm the secretary.'

The school secretary has a clear gaze and a friendly smile. She reaches under her desk and brings out a plastic bucket of Maltesers.

'So what do you teach?' she beams, holding it out.

'Poetry and Latin.'

'Ouch,' she grins.

'And I'm to supervise the boys' boarding house. The Headmaster has given us a flat in it.'

'Ah,' says the secretary. 'Then come and meet your Gaps.'

I swallow my Malteser.

'Gaps?'

She laughs.

'Gap year students. From Australia. You need them to staff your weekend expeditions.'

'What you must do now,' my husband tells me, 'is submit an expenses claim for last weekend's expedition.'

'I can't do that,' I explain. 'I already told you I can't. I asked Accounts for a budget and they said there wasn't one.'

'Yes,' argues my husband. 'I know they said that. But only because there wasn't time to get the Headmaster's approval before the expedition. Now that you're back, it is perfectly in order for you to claim expenses.'

'But—'

'You have to take a professional attitude to expenses,' my husband points out. 'For example, you wouldn't expect to pay for the fish and chips you stopped to buy the boys on the way back to school?'

'Oh God,' he continues, almost at once. 'You did expect to pay for the fish and chips. Are you crazy? Forty-five fish suppers?'

'It was a *treat*,' I say. 'I didn't have a budget for fish and chips either.'

'Oh *God*,' groans my husband. 'Then you shouldn't have stopped for them. This is completely unprofessional. No wonder Accounts are annoyed with you. You need to agree budgets and then you need to claim expenses.'

'No I needn't,' I say.

'What?'

'No I needn't. Just like the Headmaster needn't have given a place to our son when the biopsy said moderate. Just like he needn't have given a place to our daughter, when my treatment failed.'

'But that's got nothing to do with this—'

'It's got everything to do with this!' I shout. 'I don't care about the money. He's given us a home! He's given our children a future! He's given me a salary to pay for it! And you want me to ask him for *forty-five fish suppers?*'

My husband hears about the Rome expenses row because Accounts relays it to the secretary, verbatim.

'Um – I've just been in the office,' he says, rushing back to our flat and trying to look calm, 'and apparently Accounts are refusing to give you a budget for the Rome trip?'

I look up from my desk.

'Well, not refusing,' I have to say in Accounts' defence. 'They can't create a budget for that amount without the Headmaster's approval. And obviously I don't want to ask him for the money.'

In order to process this information without betraying anguish, my husband is nodding.

'You don't want to ask the Headmaster for the money,' he nods, 'because—'

'*Because* he's already given our children a future, and me a salary and—'

'Yes, yes,' he nods. 'Yes. I understand where you are coming from on this. I just wondered whether you've gone ahead and already booked – maybe – the flights or—?'

'Yeah I had to, otherwise I couldn't put the trip in the school calendar. I've booked the flights—'

'Right,' nods my husband, swallowing hard.

'—and the hotel.'

'*And* the hotel? Right. Flights and hotel accommodation.'

'Yes.'

'For forty-five boys.'

'Of course.'

'Of course!' he echoes, an octave higher than his usual one. 'Forty-five return flights to Rome plus hotel accommodation. So how much – I mean, we must be talking – five, six—?'

'Seven thousand pounds.'

The unaccustomed octave is lost in his awe.

'*Seven thousand pounds.*'

'Hello,' I say as I pass the open office door.

The secretary is typing and doesn't turn round. In the common room, in my pigeon-hole, is a solitary white envelope. There is no-one else in the common room. I put a cup into the coffee machine, press the espresso button and rip open the white envelope.

Private and Confidential its letter warns, too late to prevent my gasp.

– *Governors and Headmaster are pleased to award a discretionary salary increase of seven thousand pounds per annum* –

I turn at once. The secretary is still typing, still with her back to me.

Private and Confidential repeats the letter.

'Did you type this?' I demand, holding it up.

'Don't ask me anything you're not supposed to,' she replies.

She stops typing long enough to pass me the bucket of Maltesers, before realigning her keyboard on her desk and carrying on.

'Right, listen you,' says the secretary. 'I've just had a call from the Director of Studies. You're ruining his life.'

'Ah yes,' I get to my feet to apologise. 'I meant to mention that.'

The common room looks up.

'You're forgetting to check the cover list again,' accuses the secretary.

'No, no, I *always* check it. But by the time the lesson comes around, I forget I'm down to cover it.'

'I'm not making your excuses for you next time,' she warns. 'He is not a happy man.'

I blow out my cheeks.

'But everybody knows I forget stuff like that. Why doesn't he give the cover to someone else, if he's so unhappy about it?'

'Well, he knows you're available,' the secretary argues. 'All those injections you gave yourself must have left you virus-proof. When was the last time you even had a cold?'

'Am I likely to remember?' I complain.

'I've nowhere to put the seven year archive,' complains my husband. 'You must empty some bookshelves. They're only filled with books you've already read.'

'I've read them, but I can't *remember* them.'

'Then make a list of those you do. I'll help you. *Lord of the Flies?*'

'This is what I'm telling you. I know I've read it but I can't remember any of it.'

'What about *The Letters of Pliny?* Can you remember those?'

'Not a word.'

'*The Beginnings of Humankind?*'

'Not really, and I reread that in Dunino—'

'Do you know,' my husband raises his eyes from an Excel spreadsheet to tell me, 'you've even forgotten the books you read before Interferon?'

'I know. That's why I need to keep them here, on the shelves.'

'Where's the point? You haven't time to read them now.'

'The point is,' I am insisting, 'if I don't keep them here, then everything I ever knew is *gone*.'

'So what's this column here?' asks our son.

Delete, clicks my husband's mouse.

'No, don't delete it. That's your column, isn't it?' says our son. 'That's how many of mum's books you've read.'

'No it isn't.'

'Yes, it is. You've kept a total for yourself.'

'Only an approximation—'

'*Eleven?* Is that *all?*'

'*Approximately* eleven. And anyway I bet you haven't read as many.'

'I bet I have.'

Lord of the Flies, Pliny, The Beginnings of Humankind, our son starts clicking into an Excel column of his own.

'If you find him an acceptable archive,' suggests my husband, 'I could pack the ones he's read?'

'This is seriously weird,' I tell the secretary at the fire doors. 'This is happening more and more. I just forgot the *school.*'

'How could you find your way back to it, if you'd forgotten it?'

'Well, I *knew* about it, I just couldn't *remember* it. So I followed the roadsigns, then I followed parents from the car park. Then I pushed open the firedoors and recognised this corridor.'

'Weird,' says the secretary.

'And then at other times,' I say, 'these really vivid memories come out of nowhere. One of them is an invitation to a school play, as vivid as though I had just received it. But I can't remember which play it is.'

'Is one of your children in it?'

'I can't remember,' I frown. 'There's so much of their childhood I can't remember now. What ones have they been in?'

'*The Insect Play,*' starts the secretary, as though at the top of a list. '*Grimm's Fairy Tales, Les Miserables, Fear and Misery of the Third Reich*—'

'*Were* they?'

'*– Midsummer Night's Dream, Paradise Lost* –'

'Was our daughter Gabriel in that?'

'No,' says the secretary. 'I take it you're remembering *No Time for Fig Leaves?*'

'No recollection whatsoever.'

'That's because it starts in ten minutes,' she says.

I stop on the threshold of the office. Inside, a girl is crying. The secretary pushes past my shoulder, carrying a cup of coffee.

'Here you are, love. You drink that up. It's not the end of the world though, is it?' she comforts the sobbing girl.

'Can I help—?'

The secretary glances round and straightens to face me.

'What's the matter?' I am mouthing.

'Nothing's the matter,' she says. 'I think someone was looking for you in the common room.'

Then she is mouthing too. The expletive is unmistakeable. I recoil from it into the corridor. The secretary steps forward and closes her office door on my surprise.

'Don't you look at me like that,' she follows me into the common room to say. 'Poor girl's heart is breaking –'

I look at her like that.

'– for your son,' she grins.

Unlike the secretary, the Headmaster's Lawn does not live in sunshine. It lives in mist and rain. It is the perfect setting for a pipe band, whose music is the howl of tempest, through which a thunder rolls. I reach my husband's side at the turn of a March.

First our daughter, then our son, spin to face us.

Our daughter's sticks are dyed scarlet, to spin around her wrists. Behind the patterns she spins, the last smile of her childhood plays upon her lips.

Our son wears colours for *outstanding contribution*. His drumsticks move so fast that younger boys who try to match them miss their beat.

We reach the clearing in the forest at Rannoch, and find the weaver's car.

'You're here!' I call, winding down a rear window.

'Yes!' she calls back through hers, holding up her hands like a conjurer.

The weaver's son is slamming his passenger door. Our son leaps out as the handbrake is pulled. Hands in the pockets of their shorts, they exchange insults, shoulder one another off the path and set off for the river.

'What a wonderful *place!*' cries the weaver. 'What a wonderful place for the boys to recall, in their colleges in London.'

My husband spins for trout off the footbridge over the ravine. The weaver's husband grills the trout over a Primus stove. Our sons dive into its deepest pool from an overhanging rock.

'Hey!' waves my husband from the riverbank. 'Lunch!'

For dessert we feast on blueberries at the ravine's edge. Our lips are stained as purple as our sons' limbs are frozen. The weaver gathers as many blueberries as her hat will hold, and carries them back to the camp to dye the sheeps' wool she is teaching our daughter to spin.

'Place is so significant,' she tells her, 'places hold memories in the same way this sheepswool will hold dye. But first let me help your mother with that tent.'

My husband is calling our son.

'Did we dry out the tent last time we were here? Remember there was the thunderstorm, and by the time we got back mum should have taken her injection?'

Our son is shaking his head.

'We didn't dry it out.'

The weaver has helped me strip the tent from its bag. We grasp its corners, bend to shake loose its folds and stretch to roll its length along the grass.

'Hang on a minute!' my husband shouts.

The plastic groundsheet springs apart. Inside, the tent is mildewed and rotten into holes.

The secretary and I are in her office. Beyond its window, on a sun-baked pitch, a lacrosse practice has broken off for orange quarters.

'I don't know why,' I tremble, 'but I'm exhausted. I mean, exhausted like when I used to inject myself with Interferon. Which is odd, because Tuesdays and Thursdays I don't have to drive to tutorials any more. I'm only coaching *lacrosse*.'

'You do look ill,' she says. 'What happened to your sunhat?'

'I left it in the minibus. It's gone on a Duke of Edinburgh expedition.'

In the sunhat's absence, I am wearing my old Laura Ashley hat. Back on the pitch and looking up through its brim at the sun, every warp and weft of its weave frames a shining pinprick of light.

After the match, it is all I can do to make my way back along the stream to the school. The Headmaster is standing on its overgrown bridge, hands in his pockets, talking to the secretary.

'I thought I recognised that hat,' he says.

I take the Laura Ashley hat off. He is teasing, but his glance holds an interrogation.

'Are you overworked?' he asks, kindly. 'Are we working you too hard?'

With the Gaps and the secretary to help me, dozens and dozens of daffodils are secured in milk cartons to the top of high windows. Swathes of ivy fall twelve feet from their trumpets to the ground. There are more daffodils in milk cartons fastened in a dado rail around the walls, and ice buckets of them on every linen-frocked table.

'I don't see why I should help with bloody Guest Night,' complains my husband. 'That's your job. I've got projects which are *weeks* behind.'

'You have to help me,' I argue, 'I'm exhausted. And there are still the lanterns to wire up.'

'For Christ's *sake*,' swears my husband.

He follows me to bed at three o'clock in the morning, after the eighth. The following evening, after a full day's work, he wires up the remaining four. Ten minutes before the first guests arrive, the lanterns are lit.

'This,' he snaps at me, returning to the office dinner-jacketed and in a foul temper, 'is the *last* time I'm giving up a weekend to help you. Do you understand? *No more.*'

'Go away,' says the secretary, who is struggling to zip me into black velvet, 'before the boys see her cry.'

'But you don't know how tired I am—' begins my husband.

'I know how tired she is,' the secretary replies.

I throw my husband a reproachful glance.

'And you can shut up,' snaps the secretary. 'You and your bloody daffodils.'

'The Headmaster thinks you're working too hard,' says the school bursar. 'The secretary has told him you give out your mobile number and take calls from parents on the treadmill in the gymnasium. He asked me to have a word.'

He pours me a cup of coffee and pulls his calculator across his desk. I am uneasy.

'Not hard,' I protest. '*Fast.* I'm working fast. I'm short of time.'

'When you say you're short of time,' says the bursar, 'do you mean, time to recoup the income you lost following the infected transfusion?'

'Well, obviously. I need to work to make up for the years I missed.

We've debts to pay, and a new mortgage to save up for, and now our son has gone to London, there are tuition fees and his accommodation costs. I need to get to where we would have been financially—'

'You can't,' the bursar interrupts.

'—and I need to go to the gymnasium to get strong again,' I say. 'I've been feeling really tired in the afternoons.'

'You can't,' he repeats. 'At least, you might manage to turn back the clock in the gymnasium, but not financially, you can't. Do you know how much the infected blood has cost you?'

'Well, I haven't worked it out to the penny but—'

'How old is your daughter?'

'Sixteen. But—'

He is scribbling numbers.

'You were teaching before she was born?'

'Yes, but—'

'And paying into a pension? What sort of pension?'

'Oh the basic scheme set up for teaching staff—'

He draws a double horizontal line beneath his calculations, looks up and smiles.

'You can't catch up,' he repeats. 'No matter how hard you work. On the back of the proverbial envelope you have lost, to date, more than three hundred thousand pounds in salary, pension investment, and secondary benefits in kind, such as the school fee reduction to which your teaching post is entitling you now. Let's imagine you are still unwell. How old are you?'

'Forty-five,' I choke.

'Easy sum.' He holds up his hand to preclude my interruption. 'Yes, I know the virus has been eradicated. But we also know a good deal of damage was done. As the Headmaster said, we're in uncharted territory here. If you become unable to work, until retiral, you will double that loss. At a conservative estimate, you will have lost three quarters of a million pounds.'

I am shocked.

'They're offering me ten thousand pounds, with no admission of liability.'

He shrugs.

'They're hoping to bribe you. They want you to sign away your legal rights, the way you signed away your medical ones.'

He hands me his scribbled calculations.

'So all I can advise is that you refuse the bribe and listen to the Headmaster. Try to work out where you can take some time off. And stop giving parents your bloody mobile number.'

'So this father said where are you going for half term,' I report to my husband, 'and I said nowhere, because you have projects which are weeks behind. Then he said, if we had no plans, we must spend half term in his five-star hotel.'

'*Five*-star hotel?'

'I think the Head put him up to it. It's crazy, isn't it? They're trying to make me take time off.'

'No,' says my husband. 'No, it isn't crazy. The crazy bit is you said *no?*'

'I thought you said you couldn't do weekends?'

'So I can't make a five-star exception?' complains my husband.

'In my country,' explains the rear-view mirror of the Rolls Royce sent to collect us, 'we say that these are your golden years.'

'Oh really?' I try not to reflect disbelief. 'Why do you say that?'

'Because your children are grown and you are young enough to enjoy the freedom that affords you. You won't need a dinner jacket this evening,' the mirror goes blank to tell my husband. 'You'll eat in the private dining room.'

In the private dining room there is a private waiter and the crystal glasses he leans forward to refill have taken centuries to collect.

'Antique,' he tells us, 'but only the liqueur goblets are Jacobean.'

Dish after dish is served, and goblet after goblet poured to match them, until the Jacobean is reached at last. It is impossible to gauge the degree of intoxication this represents, because the preceding five glasses have never run dry. It is just as well we have our own waiter, to relocate the door once the dinner is over.

He shows us to our room. In it, the conversation of the dinner table is conjured into life. The Mozart symphony I mentioned is playing in the background. The whisky to which my husband referred is waiting on a silver tray. My bath is run, and scented with a scattering of apple blossom to remind me of Dunino.

My husband holds a whisky goblet up to the chandelier to check that it is Jacobean then pours us another measure. Yet we waken to a perfect recollection.

'Oh *God*,' I shout. 'How long have we slept?'

He is already out of bed and in a panic.

'What shall I do? Shall I call a doctor?'

I kick the duvet aside to panic with him.

'Is it too late? What time did we go to bed?'

'What time did the unprotected intercourse take place?' repeats the village pharmacist, once we have tracked down his pharmacy.

I am scarlet with embarrassment.

'About – about ten hours ago?'

'And when did you last have intercourse before that?'

I glance at my husband for confirmation.

'About – about ten years ago?'

We argue all the way back to Edinburgh.

'What do you want me to say?' I ask him. 'If I had infected you, our children would have been at twice the risk. What happened, happened. It couldn't be changed. *We* changed to deal with it.'

Tears are running down his face.

'How can we turn back the clock?' I ask him. 'I love you the way soldiers love one another, who fought together, and slept in their clothes together, and ate mouldy food together. What *golden years*,' I sneer, 'can recompense for what that cost? But take them if you want them. Whatever you do with them, it can't affect what we've become.'

'Are you talking about a separation?'

'Of course.'

'That's a big step—'

I am exhausted.

'God, after all we've been through? No it isn't. It's nothing. What we've become, even a separation can't destroy.'

Later, when we are calm, he asks if he should separate our bank accounts.

I stare at him.

'Have you been listening to me *at all*? I mean the school will pay my salary into your account as usual, and you will use my money to support our children as usual. If I need money, I'll ask you for it.'

'You're still comfortable with that?'

A sadness grips me.

'I wouldn't say that to you,' I reproach him.

There is a little silence.

'I'm sorry,' says my husband.

I remember that once our daughter had spun her wool, and dyed it, our son fashioned two sticks into knitting needles for her.

I remember this because a parcel arrives. It contains a square of uneven purple knitting, mounted over a photograph of our son diving into the ravine. Its frame is labelled *Spinning at Rannoch*.

It is the world I have lost.

'What about this one?' I ask, pointing to the third and last schedule in the estate agent's folder.

My husband shakes his head.

'It's in the old market so there won't be any parking. I only picked it up because it was in my price range.'

'You might as well take a look,' I say.

We arrive in the old market through a high forbidding Victorian arch, still bearing the inscription *Meat, Poultry, Fruit, Flowers*. There is an iron side gate, then a set of worn steps down to a flagstoned floor, where a double row of stalls has given way to a double row of trees.

'Oh!' I say.

My husband is unlocking the door to the ground floor flat in the corner of the courtyard. Inside a short passage leads to a boxroom and, at the end of the passage, a Victorian sitting-room. It had a tall window with wooden shutters. I open the shutters, and a trickle of light spills through the trees.

'You can't have this,' I say.

'No,' my husband is agreeing, 'I told you. There's nowhere to put the car—'

'Because I want it,' I say.

'What?'

'I want it. You can't have it.'

He starts to laugh.

'When would you ever come here? You're on duty every evening and on expedition each weekend.'

'I'll come here at night. I'll come to sleep.'

'Then who'll sleep at the school?'

'You,' I say. 'You can sleep at the school and I will sleep here. The headmaster said I should work out how to take time off.'

'To *sleep?*'

'To sleep, and to start writing poetry again.'

I fold back the shutters and push up the window behind them.

'It makes sense, doesn't it? You need a flat but you've got one at the school. And I need,' I turn from the window to declare, 'a literary salon.'

'*A literary salon?*' asks the secretary.

'Yes. I wish I could show it to you. But I can only go at midnight. It's all agreed with the Headmaster. Between midnight and seven my husband will sleep at the school, and I will spend the night in my literary salon, writing a verse-biography of the empress Josephine.'

'But,' argues the secretary, 'surely the Headmaster has given permission for all this in order to let *you* sleep?'

'Well, technically, yes,' I have to admit. 'But actually I never *feel* tired at night. Only in the afternoons. Though obviously I'll sleep as well,' I add to reassure her.

There is a short pause.

'Does your husband know about the empress Josephine?' she asks.

The question surprises me.

'I don't know. He came in late last night. He's bought a second hand dinghy, to race off Berwick.'

'While you write verse-biographies in your literary salon?'

'Well from now on, as soon as he gets back, I can go and write them.'

There is another pause.

'Apart from your children,' says the secretary, 'do you two actually have *anything* in common?'

'Not any more,' I say. 'We used to, but then I recovered. So no, not any more.'

'Did you notice the music?' asks the manager of the charity shop. '1812 Overture. I put it on for you specially. How's the empress Josephine?'

Several metres of linen cloth in eighteenth century military stripes is rumpled across his counter in a careless display.

'Left over from a refurb in Danube Street,' he tells me.

Our eyes meet. We are impressed. Danube Street is seriously wealthy.

'You see,' I am explaining, once the linen curtains have been cut to length and a washed-out pair of *broderie anglaise* sheets folded on top of them, 'one would think the worst part is waiting for the tumbril driver to carry you off from prison to the guillotine. But it isn't. The worst part is when they tell you that it's over. Your life is saved. You're released. And Josephine is standing there, in the rue des Chantereines –'

The charity shop's manager's expression is growing concerned.

'– and – and they have taken *everything*,' I tremble. 'Her children are grown. Her marriage is guillotined. She doesn't even know how many of those imprisoned with her are still *alive*.'

There is a hand on my arm. I stare at it until my voice steadies.

'It was the Terror,' I explain. 'There was no-one to whom she could appeal save the authorities who had unleashed it.'

His arms are full of chinoiserie and lace. We stop at the vintage rail so that I can pull out a full length navy velvet opera coat.

'How did Josephine survive the Terror?' asks the charity shop manager.

I take a deep breath.

'She found a house in the rue des Chantereines. More of a folly than a house. She persuaded a friend to put up the money for it. And then, in a great rush, before she was too old, she started holding salon parties.'

I lay the opera coat on top of the chinoiserie. The charity shop manager looks at it and raises one eyebrow.

'To keep out draughts,' I explain, 'while I'm writing her verse-biography.'

'You aren't on the phone so much these days?' we ask our son.

'Well, I'm spending most of them in the lab,' our son's voice replies. 'It's a bit of a conversation-stopper, theoretical physics.'

'Don't you have any lectures?' persists my husband.

'Yeah, I had a lecture this morning.'

'Well, what was that about?'

'Infinity.'

'Infinity! Most interesting. Tell me something about infinity.'

'Well, there's a theory that there isn't just one universe, but an infinite number of *universes*.'

'What? An infinite number of universes?' cries my husband. 'How can that be right?'

'It must be,' sighs our son, 'because in the urinals under that lecture theatre there are mirrors on opposite walls. So I could actually see my infinite number of other selves, all wishing they were doing something else.'

'It isn't finished,' I explain, opening the cardboard folder around empress Josephine's verse-biography.

I make coffee. The professor lights a another cigarette, draws, picks up *Thermidor*, exhales, reads *Fructidor*, draws, *Wendemiaire*, exhales, *Brumaire*, draws.

'Jesus,' I say. 'You're making me nervous.'

Frimaire, Nivoise, Pluvoise, Ventoise—

'Well?' I say.

'Well,' he stubs out his cigarette, 'it isn't finished.'

'After the Revolution,' I explain to the charity shop manager, 'the new Chamber of Deputies divided the year into ten months, instead of twelve, and renamed them. So I've borrowed those names as titles, for ten sonnets, and addressed them to the ten most influential of Josephine's lovers.'

'Only the ten?' asks the charity shop manager, po faced.

'Oh, these were desperate times,' I tell him, leading the way into his shop. 'Everyone who survived the Terror was damaged by it. Women like Josephine set the most outrageous fashions.'

I pick up an empty perfume bottle with a rubber bulb.

'They draped themselves in the finest muslin, sprayed with water, to keep it damp and clinging. It's not difficult to attract ten influential lovers when you wear damp muslin to your own salon parties. It's difficult *not* to.'

We arrive back at the counter. The charity shop manager unloads an armful of tulle and muslin curtains with an anxious expression.

'Surely the verse-biography must be written by now?'

'Not quite. I showed it to my supervisor. Though I don't know what he made of it.'

'I've a fair idea,' says the charity shop manager.

'If you're not enjoying physics anymore,' I telephone our son to say, 'you ought to give it up'.

'No,' says our son.

'A degree in physics from Imperial must be one of the toughest in the world. It's not worth the effort, if you're not enjoying it,' I argue on.

'No, wait a minute,' my husband tries to reason with me. 'A degree from Imperial is worth having. All right, so he doesn't enjoy it any more. Everyone feels like that at some point when they're taking their degree. It doesn't mean he *hates* it.'

'Yeah I do,' says our son. 'I hate it.'

'Then give i*t up!*' I tell him.

'No,' says our son.

'Guess what?' I say, arriving in the secretary's office with two cups of coffee.

'What now?' says the secretary.

'Estates just invited me to their Christmas party.'

'Estates?'

'Yeah, I stopped at their office on my way in this morning and they said did I have a party dress? And would I like to come? It's an honour. They haven't invited any other teaching staff—'

'Dear God,' says the secretary. 'This literary salon malarkey will be the death of me.'

She pushes her telephone across the desk.

'Ring them up at once and tell them you can't come.'

'But I can,' I explain. 'I said I was never free until midnight and they said midnight was when the fun started—'

The secretary pulls the telephone back again.

'I'll tell them myself,' she snaps, and does, in no uncertain terms.

'*Estates Christmas Party!*' she chides me, hanging up. 'Do you realise the wrong message all this Josephine business is sending? In and out of the school gates on CCTV like a –' she presses her lips together, tries to stop herself then continues anyway, '– and your husband tells me that you're off to Rome at the end of term?'

'I've been invited to Rome,' I protest, 'I haven't decided if I'll go yet—'

'He said you might go to Athens?'

'I might—'

'With whoever has invited you to Rome?'

'No, with someone else entirely—'

'Jesus,' breathes the secretary.

'Look,' I have to defend myself, 'I know what you're thinking—'

She swivels on her office chair to face me.

'No you don't.'

The swivel startles me.

'But I'll tell you what I think,' offers the secretary. 'I think that this is not what you're about.'

'Now listen,' I say. 'You're doing this for us. We both know you're doing this for us. You won't admit it, but we both know that and now it is making you ill.'

The telephone line is silent.

'*Will you just give up?*' I yell.

'No,' says our son.

I throw myself back in my chair.

The Tiber snakes around the ramparts of the Castel Sant' Angelo. From the *ristorante* on its battlements, I watch the sun reach and illuminate the ancient contour of the Palatine Hill. The view affords a moment of perfect clarity.

'I just gave up,' I say.

The verdict hangs, silent and terrible, in the air beyond the battlement. I get to my feet and pick up the Laura Ashley hat. An uneaten breakfast watches from a linen cloth as I back away.

'I'm sorry about this—' I am apologising.

Stone steps clatter into the courtyard below. I am walking fast. Sword raised, Raphael's iron-clad angel looms and is left behind. On the bridge over the Tiber I look back once.

Back at the hotel an Art Deco lift opens onto the concierge's desk.

'Chiave, signora?'

He lifts it from its hook.

'Do you speak English?' I ask him.

The concierge smiles and holds out the key.

'Inglese?'

'No signora.'

I start to panic.

'I need a telephone number for the airport—'

He stares at my panic in silence.

'Aeroporto?' I guess.

'Si si. Aeroporto,' he nods.

In the hotel room I throw open the shutters and copy the scribbled number into my mobile telephone. By the time it rings out my case is open on the bed.

'Benvenuto all' aeroporto di Ciampino. Si—'

I press button 1 for informazione, button 2 for dettagli del volo, button 5 for operatore telefonico.

'Ciao! Benvenuto all' aeroporto di Ciampino —'

'Inglese?' I beg.

'No signora.'

I run back downstairs to find the concierge. He is talking to the hotel manager. The hotel manager takes in my tears and comes around the desk. He offers me a chair. I offer the mobile telephone.

'Please – it's an automated service —'

The hotel manager snaps an order to the concierge, who disappears downstairs. I offer the mobile telephone again.

'Please – if you press button 5—'

The concierge reappears with a tray bearing two cups of espresso. The hotel manager puts my mobile telephone on the desk to take it from him.

'Please – it's eleven o'clock and I still have to get to the airport—'

'Prego,' he insists, leaning round my chair to pull one up for himself.

I take one of the cups of espresso. The hotel manager takes the other, drains it and retrieves my telephone. He dials the number for the aeroporto and is at once embroiled in a furious argument.

'Scozia?' he breaks off to ask.

'Si, Scozia—'

I sit back in my chair in relief. The espresso kicks in to dry my tears. The hotel manager wins his argument and rings off in grand style.

'Grazia, grazia—' I applaud him.

He nods in acknowledgment and returns the telephone.

'No possibile,' he confirms.

'No – no possibile?'

'No possibile,' he nods again. 'No possibile vigilia di Capodanno, signora.'

My panic returns before his reason is translated.

'Vi - gil - ia -' I watch his mouth as we separate the syllables together, 'di - New Year's Eve? Then tomorrow?' I panic further. 'Can I fly tomorrow? Capodanno?'

'Si signora. No possible Capodanno,' he confirms.

Back in the hotel room, leaning against the door, its slam is still resounding when my husband answers his telephone.

'Are you all right?' he shouts. 'What is it? What's happened? '

He cannot translate my sobbing.

'—just gave up –' I am sobbing, '– after all those years! I just gave up—'

'No more than I gave up,' my husband comforts me. 'Stop crying and get yourself to the airport.'

'I can't,' I sob. 'It's too late. It's too late anyway, for our failed marriage—'

'We haven't *got* a failed marriage,' scoffs my husband. 'We've got a failed separation. Stop crying and get to the airport.'

The navy velvet opera coat follows the Laura Ashley hat into the waiting case. The taxi follows the aquadotta Claudia to Ciampino airport. My husband rings back as I drag my case across its concourse.

'All right, there aren't any flights to Scotland. I've booked you on one to East Midlands. Once you land, you've got thirty minutes to catch the last train north on the East Coast mainline.'

'Oh God!' I whimper, dragging my suitcase faster. 'I dread to think how much a same-day flight has cost—'

'Seven hundred and thirty pounds,' says my husband.

'*Seven hundred and thirty—!* ' I choke, tripping over the suitcase and only realising I have stopped when he does.

'For God's *sake!*' howls my husband. 'Don't bloody *miss* it!'

The East Coast Mainline guard is making his way through the train, repeating his tannoy announcement.

'Owing to the storm, passengers may prefer to leave the train at York. After York and to ensure stability in exposed areas, this service will travel on to Edinburgh at high speed.'

After York, my mobile telephone rings.

'– might have to wait for me –' my husband is yelling.

A gust of wind tears something along the carriage windows in a high-pitched scream.

I press the telephone to my ear to make out what he is saying. The guard is moving back through the carriage, directing passengers to pull their luggage from overhead racks onto empty seats. The thud of heavy cases is lost in the defeaning rattle of the speeding train.

'– closed the road bridge,' my husband is shouting, 'so I'm going round by Kincardine—'

'Is it worth another fifty miles?' I shout.

'What?' he shouts back.

Another gust hits the carriage in a thunder of hailstones. The train accelerates through it. The gust of hailstones builds to a frenzy and breaks. My husband's voice cuts out with it.

'They've closed the bridges,' I tell the guard.

'Yes,' he nods. 'They're closing Waverley too, as soon as we get in. If we get in,' he adds, peering through the juddering window.

In the tunnel to Waverley Station, passengers cheer. The train's brake pads squeal. Platform eleven flashes into the carriage windows. My husband is racing along it.

'Leave the platform,' the station tannoy is shouting. 'All passengers, leave the platform. All passengers—'

The carriage door opens. I throw out my case. My husband pulls me after it. A huge black waste disposal bin rolls along the track, bounces over the end of the platform and bowls towards us.

'Leave the platform! All passengers—'

There is a flash of lightning. We leap for the steps to the bridge over the track. The waste disposal bin slams into them below our feet. High above our heads, the bells of St Giles Cathedral ring out into the storm.

'*Happy New Year,*' we shout to one another.

The Director of Studies sits on the Headmaster's right. He is frowning. The Deputy Headmaster sits on the Headmaster's left. She is concerned. I sit facing the window behind them. My complexion is red and agitated.

'But I am not agitated,' I tell the interview panel. 'This is some sort of reaction. There's something the matter with my skin.'

Yet in the sunlight streaming through the window, my complexion is agitated. Those considered capable of a senior post are never agitated.

'I wouldn't promote me in a state like this,' I admit to my husband.

'Don't be upset,' he comforts me.

'I'm not upset. There's something the matter with my *skin*.'

He shows me a letter.

'It's from the lawyer. The Department of Health is offering a charitable donation of twenty thousand pounds.'

'*Charitable?*'

'He says here that it's nothing to do with the court case. It's a one-off charitable donation.'

I take the letter and read it.

'Why?' I look up to frown.

'I don't know. They've fought us in court for a decade. Maybe they're getting embarrassed?'

'Or maybe the bursar's right,' I say. 'Maybe there is something going on we still don't understand.'

I fold up the letter and hand it back to him.

'Please accept it,' says my husband.

'Their *charity?* We ought to give it to the school. I don't need charity. I've got a job.'

'I meant our situation. God knows, twenty thousand isn't much of a deposit, but if we wait any longer, we'll be too old to get another mortgage.'

The moment my husband sees the For Sale sign on the coach-house on the corner of the cobbled mews, he turns on his heel.

'It's not even big enough for a *coach!*'

I follow the selling agent inside. My husband is left to complain about the doorstep.

'Well, for a start, look at this! Three steps up from the cobbles, and inside, three steps down! How mad is that? The front door's in mid-air.'

I frown over my shoulder.

'– compact culinary arrangements –' the selling agent is explaining.

'You'd have to raise the floor level,' says my husband, following us into the carriage room and going to the window, to shake his head at the gradient of the lane outside. 'You couldn't leave it as it is. That far corner will be lucky if it isn't below the water-table.'

'– compact stair to attic accommodation on an upper level –' the selling agent continues.

'Where's the kitchen?' my husband is demanding.

Upstairs I realise he is right. The larger bedroom extends over almost all the floor space of the carriage room below. It is just about conceivable that I will be able to persuade our son and daughter to share it. But the smaller bedroom is, in consequence, miniscule.

'It didn't used to be a bedroom at all,' says my husband. He examines its dormer window. 'The big bedroom was for the carriage driver, and this was the hayloft. Before this partition was put in,' he rattles the miniscule bedroom's doorpost, 'this was where they kept the hay for the horse. That little window, above the stairs, was for pitchforking it out onto the cobbles.'

I ask the selling agent if there is space to fit two beds into the miniscule bedroom.

'Of course you wouldn't get two beds in it,' scoffs my husband, before he can reply.

'There is actually just enough space for a double,' the selling agent tells me. 'But only just. You'd have to keep your wardrobe on the landing—'

'Now that's a more sensible idea,' interrupts my husband. 'That's a possibility. Let me go back outside and take another look at those floor levels.'

In her topmost tower in the school, our daughter has been painting my portrait for her portfolio.

'Oh,' I say, closing the door and leaning on it to get my breath back.

It is not the portrait I expected.

It is really a portrait of the sun, which has cast me into a blood-red shadow. Broken phrases of a line from one of the portfolio of sonnets – *there is a shame which sinners deserve but share with the sick* – are inscribed in gold paint.

'Wow. It's – uh – it's big, isn't it?' I say.

'I like big paintings,' decides our daughter. 'Once we've moved into the new house, I'm going to buy a bigger easel—'

'A *bigger* easel—?'

'—or two,' she enthuses.

'Yes, I'll be home for Easter Sunday,' says our son. 'How far is the new house from the station?'

'How far from that station? I don't know exactly—'

'Within walking distance? Because the kayak won't fit in a taxi. I'll have to carry it.'

'You're bringing your *kayak*?'

'Of course. I'm taking it back down to London for the summer term.'

'But where are you going to keep it while you're here?'

'Well, if there's nowhere else,' says our son, 'I'll keep it in my bedroom—'

'Mind the ice at the end of the track,' says my mother, 'and we'll see you in the summer.'

I wave until she is out of sight.

'I wouldn't put money on that,' warns my husband. 'Your face has swollen up again. You look quite ill.'

The hired car skids and slides down the mountainside. I watch snow drift across the windscreen.

'When I *was* ill,' I remember, 'we used to put money on the Celtic altarstone in Dunino. I've got a good mind to drive down there and put some on it now.'

'I hope you're joking?'

'No I'm not. For one thing, *place* is so significant—'

'Oh God!' wails my husband. 'For one thing, no *place* isn't, and for another, it would put a hundred miles on our journey!'

'A hundred miles doesn't matter.'

Large snowflakes are obliterating the windscreen. The wipers falter with my resolution.

'Though I suppose the hired car's due back in Edinburgh tonight?'

There is a silence.

'Yes, but in fact that doesn't mean anything,' admits my husband, 'because the hire office is closed until seven o'clock tomorrow morning.'

I open my eyes. Everywhere is just as we left it, frozen in time and a deep frost. Mile after enchanted mile opens to our windscreen and rushes past either side in a never-ending frieze of hill and forest, field and farm.

'You fell asleep before the crash corner,' says my husband.

'Yes,' I admit. 'So I did.'

There is no moon, Dunino churchyard is pitch black. We stumble around its frozen turf. My soaked gloves freeze onto my fingers.

'Found it,' says my husband.

The coin offerings on top of the Celtic altar stone clink as we add our loose change. It is too cold to stay a moment longer. We drive back down the farm track to the Edinburgh road.

I am bent double over my frozen hands. The crowns of the firs, silhouetted against a navy sky, are left behind again.

The exam hall seats itself in alphabetical order. I give out papers all the way back to the tall arched windows at the back. The pupils leave them face down, and watch me make my way to the invigilator's desk. I look up into their anxious faces, and into a spring sun.

'Turn over your papers. This examination has begun.'

I cannot look down at the desk, for fear a boy in the back row will start cheating. I stare at him, and at the sun, and he stares at me. After five minutes, with a resigned expression, he picks up his pen and begins to write.

I stare on. My nose is swelling. My forehead swells so much the hairs of my eyebrows stand upright. The boy in the back row looks up and looks back down again.

I touch my fingertips to my swollen cheeks. The skin is thickening and hardening. My eyes feel as though they have been punched. I clench my fists.

'Are you all right, miss?' wonders the boy in the back row.

'No talking, please,' I snap.

The skin over the bridge of my nose splits. I slide off my chair and make a pretext of inspecting desks back to the arched windows. The boy in the back row slides a covert glance as I pass. His back hunches when I stop behind him.

There are windowblinds. I pull down the first and turn to scan the rows of chairbacks. No-one moves. I pull down the second blind and cross the aisle to pull down the third.

'I can't see, miss.'

The boy in the back row is still hunched against me. But further up the hall, shoulders are twisting in concern.

'We can't see the paper, miss,' their voices multiply.

I release the window blinds. The entire examination hall is staring at my face.

'My apologies.'

They are still staring. I surf their derision all the way back to my desk.

'Mine said I wasn't to wear a hat,' says the other mother. 'Apparently no one does these days. I like your velvet coat.'

We stop at the gates of Holyrood House to give our daughter's names.

'This way,' smiles a courtier, directing us, not to the palace door as I expect, but towards another gate. 'Since the weather is fine, the Duke will join you in the gardens.'

'You needn't look so surprised,' the other mother is greeting her daughter. 'I told you I brush up well.'

Our daughter appears at my elbow.

'We're in the gardens. And you didn't bring your hat.'

My husband appears at my other elbow.

'It's in the gardens,' he tells our daughter. 'Where's your mother? Oh there you are. Did you bring your hat?'

'No, I didn't want to – I mean, it's so old now – and no-one does, these days.'

'I told you to bring it,' chides my husband. 'You'll have to walk behind my shoulder until we find you a tree.'

Through the gate, the blind spot in Edinburgh's map is suddenly filled in, with rolling lawns and gracious avenues. I blink in surprise.

'Keep behind my *shoulder*,' my husband's still directing me.

'But where are you going? She's over *there*.'

'I'm going to find you a tree.'

'I won't be able to see her from that tree. There isn't any point in coming if I have to stand under that tree—'

'There isn't any point in coming if I have to carry you home on a stretcher—'

'This way, sir, madam,' insists another courtier, directing us back into the glare.

'We thought you'd taken her home,' the other mother greets my husband. 'I know she hasn't brought her hat. I wonder if I have something in my bag?'

A lady-in-waiting is making her way through the crowd. Beyond her, our daughters wave tanned arms to alert us to the Duke.

'It's a beautiful day,' smiles the lady-in-waiting.

'Here it is!' cries the other mother. 'I knew I'd have one somewhere.'

She hands me a black collapsible umbrella.

'Beautiful,' I agree with the lady-in-waiting, as I put it up.

'You should always be properly equipped,' our son reproves me.

I am holding open the bathroom door. He heaves a kitbag into the bath and shakes it upside down. The bath explodes in a tumble of muddy rope.

'Phew,' says our son, slinging the empty bag on top.

I roll up my sleeves.

'I'll rinse the helmet,' he goes on. 'You wash out the ropes.'

I know how to wash out ropes because our son has taught me. I know to squeeze every inch of rope in cold water until the grains of silt caught in its fibres are released. I freeze and squeeze, freeze and squeeze, methodically, for seventy-five feet, then empty the bath, refill it, and start again in the opposite direction.

'Why haven't you collected your award?' I use the hour to complain.

'I'd lose my discount to buy new kit,' says our son.

He rinses his spray-deck in the shower and shows me a jagged tear.

'How did that happen?'

'Wee out-of-boat experience,' he grins, 'on the Ubaye.'

I steady myself against the bath.

'Throwing yourself over waterfalls! It's far too dangerous a sport.'

Our son lifts the wet rope out of the bath and starts to coil it round his arm.

'It isn't dangerous if you understand how rivers work. Like you need to understand how light works.'

'What is there to understand? I can see how sunny it is —'

'No you can't,' says our son. 'That's the point. The human eye works on a logarithmic scale. No-one can *see* how sunny it is.'

At the bridge over the school stream, the line of oaks which follow it are in full leaf. Beyond their canopy lies one hundred and forty metres of rugby pitch. I squint into a cloudy sky and walk on.

By the try line, my head is spinning. It is the spinning of a concussion, a numbing dislocation of neural pathways, an endless loop of electronic dysfunction. The emollient I have smeared over my face melts in the heat of its inflammation. I wipe it from my jaw and smear it back.

Shivers run up and down my spine like pistons, pumping exhaustion. On the other side of the rugby pitch, in the mirror on the hayloft landing, feverish eyes stare back aghast, at my disfigurement. I soothe them with more emollient, wiping a finger along each lid, and watch them leak faux-tears of suppuration.

'Well, it isn't an infection,' says my doctor. 'Those were powerful antibiotics, and you've been taking them for a fortnight. All we know is that the swelling is exacerbated by sunlight, and you think by the light from your computer screen?'

'But the IT department say that isn't the problem,' I wail. 'They've replaced my desk top twice but only because the Headmaster told them to. They claim there's nothing wrong with the old ones, and I'm just stressing out. They say the swelling *proves* I'm stressing out.'

The doctor is typing up his notes on the failure of the antibiotics test. *Undiagnosed photosensitive reaction*, he types. *No bacterial cause. Previous Hepatitis C.*

I consider my options.

'Though I suppose it could be stress,' I allow. 'I have been getting really tired in the afternoons.'

The doctor clicks to *save* and turns round.

'You mean you want it to be stress. You want it to be something you can fix. First you wanted it to be an infection, and now you want it to be stress. It isn't stress.'

'But I feel stressed!' I cry.

The doctor nods.

'It is the other way round,' he explains. 'The measures to which you must resort to cope with photosensitivity are fairly onerous. They create their own stress. Stress is certainly a consequence of photosensitivity, but it is not the cause.'

'Well *something* must be the cause!' I shout. 'It's getting worse and worse!'

The pharmacist looks my prescription up and down.

'I cannot dispense steroid ointments,' he insists, 'if you intend to apply them to your face.'

'But they are prescribed for my face.'

'There must be some mistake. These steroid ointments are hundreds of times more powerful than those we dispense without prescription. If you apply them to your face, then over time—'

'There *is* no time!' I cry. 'I just walked five hundred yards in the sun to collect this ointment!'

'—steroid ointment is *not* suitable for application to the face,' the pharmacist is repeating. 'Do you intend to apply it to your face?'

We lock glances. On my face waits the inflammation that will disfigure me. On my lips waits the lie that could deliver me.

'Because no-one is telling the truth!' I tell my husband. 'Why is the doctor still writing *previous Hepatitis C* all over my medical notes?'

'Did you or did you not lie to the pharmacist?' shouts my husband.

'Do I look like I lied?' I shout back.

'Your parasol has arrived,' says my husband.

He has ordered it from a shop in London which made parasols for the British colonies. It costs seventy pounds. Our daughter and I take it for a trial run.

'I don't like it.'

'What's wrong with it? It's pretty thick canvas.'

'What's wrong with it is all the people who told us it wasn't raining.'

My husband laughs.

'They're just being friendly.'

'They were all staring,' objects our daughter.

I am not aware of people staring. Unless I keep the parasol tilted over my face, there isn't any point in carrying it.

'Look at him, for example,' mutters our daughter. 'What are *you* staring at? Fuck *off.*'

I lift the parasol to remonstrate. Her forearm reaches the pinnacle of an exaggerated sweep.

'Will you both calm down?' my husband intervenes. 'There's no point getting worked up about it.'

By way of example, he ignores the next passer-by who tells me it isn't raining.

'All right, it's irritating,' he concedes, after the third.

I don't hear the fourth. But I lift the parasol in time to grab his arm as he strides across the path towards a grinning youth.

'Who's getting worked up now?' I cry.

'Ooooh!' mocks the grinning youth, to add to my husband's wrath.

Several friends suggest a burka.

'Have they actually thought about what they are saying?' I rage.

'Email for you,' says my husband. He prints and holds it out to me. 'This one says he can get his hands on a decontamination suit, if that's any use to you?'

The door to our daughter's bedroom opens as I rattle it.

'He's got a new girlfriend!' I tell our daughter.

She looks at the mobile telephone in my hand.

'And he wants us to meet her!'

Her eyes widen.

'Are you sure?'

'He just said so. Next time we're in London. Only we never are in London. I'll have to ask him to bring her to Oxford when we take you down.'

'I wouldn't ask him yet,' protests our daughter. 'I've only just applied.'

'Or should I ask him to invite her to Edinburgh for the summer?' I wonder.

'Where would you put her if he did?'

I haven't begun to think about it.

'Where am I supposed to sleep if you invite her for the summer?' persists our daughter.

'A new girlfriend!' I am telling my husband.

'Because I'm not sleeping in the kitchen,' she warns.

'What? No, of course not,' I reassure her. 'You can have the hayloft landing.'

Her eyes light up.

'Don't you need it?'

I am already clearing its tiny desk.

'You can have it. I want you to have it. A new girlfriend!'

Our daughter sits at its tiny stool.

'But what about your wardrobe?'

'I'll donate it all back to the charity shop.'

'You can't donate the navy velvet opera coat,' she argues. 'It's beautiful and practically antique.'

I help her to try it on.

'Very pretty,' I am insisting. 'You'd better have it too.'

Log in, I type, *Marks Database,* and when its window opens *English Literature.*

In the computer screen my reflection is watching itself, at first warily and then with increasing dread.

– combines industry with a flair for the cadences of language – I begin to type.

My reflection stops typing. I watch its eyes watch mine, aghast. Fever is flooding into them.

He is predicted to score highly at examination – I try to type on.

Blood pulses to fill each eye socket. My cheeks throb in synchrony. The skin over the bridge of my nose thickens, hardens and splits.

'This can't go on,' I wail. 'I can't keep asking you to type for me. They've already given my lacrosse team to someone else. If the Head reduces my timetable any further, I'll have to pay *him.*'

'Well, what did the doctor say?' asks the secretary.

'He said there's no bacterial cause, and it isn't stress.'

'Am I done?' she goes on, handing me back a sheaf of papers.

'No, not nearly,' I fret, handing her the next.

A dreadful thought disables me.

'You don't think it's divine retribution, do you?'

'Don't be daft,' says the secretary. 'If it's divine retribution, what did I do to deserve you?'

'If it's a photosensitive reaction,' says the specialist in the private medical centre, 'then for some reason light is triggering your immune system to attack you.'

My fingers are pressed to my disfigured face.

'Most obviously your skin,' nods the specialist, 'but possibly your heart muscle. We will have to conduct an array of laboratory tests. Do you have medical insurance?'

'I can't get medical insurance because—'

My voice breaks. The private medical centre is wrapped in clingfilm. I close my eyes and open them to unwrap it all again.

'—because I once had Hepatitis C,' I force myself to say.

The specialist raises his eyebrows.

'Then you can't afford to pay for this. You're in this for the long haul, I'm afraid. I will transfer you to my NHS caseload and see you in six months.'

I am speechless with despair. A nurse wraps an inflatable tourniquet around my arm. The specialist fills in a request for the first laboratory test, scribbles *previous Hepatitis C* in the form's top left hand corner and wraps it around my blood sample.

'Until we meet again,' he adds, 'I must advise you to avoid those light conditions which provoke a reaction.'

'Avoid light?'

'That is my advice.'

'But how can I?' I protest. 'I'd have to *resign* to avoid light!'

The specialist does not meet my eyes.

'You're telling me to resign?' I cry. 'Without a diagnosis? The school would think I had gone mad!'

I drive to St Andrews in fourth gear, late at night, through fifty miles of Fife. There is no moon. The first floor room in the bed and breakfast overlooks the courtyard of the lawyer's office.

'I would like you to request my medical file. I think that's possible? I need to know what's happening to my face.'

The lawyer who has inherited my case is of an ancient Scottish lineage, but he himself is very young. He has not learned the advantages of lawyerspeak.

'There's no point. Your file would be filleted before we got it.'

We are seated at the same polished boardroom table over which I faced his predecessor. In the silence that follows this remark, its mirrored surface rocks back and forth.

'You can't be serious?'

He reaches for the coffee-pot.

'I have given you a shock. Apparently other people given contaminated transfusions have requested their medical files. And that has been their experience.'

My mind is reeling. I put an elbow on his polished table and lean my head into my hand.

'*Your file would be filleted before we got it?*' repeats my husband, when I relay the conversation to him that evening.

My elbow rests on the kitchen table. I lift my head out of my hand.

'Other people have requested their medical files and when they got them the relevant sections were deleted.'

We stare at one another.

'So what am I to *do?*' I wail. 'I've spent four hundred pounds in a week, and I don't know what to *do.*'

'Ah,' says the secretary. 'Have you got a minute?'

'What is it?'

'Sit down.'

I sit down. We are in the common room. She sits down too, which alarms me. The secretary never sits down in the common room. She has no need. She has her own office, where there are Maltesers.

'What is it?' I repeat.

'I'm leaving.'

Since I have no recollection, it is impossible to tell how long I stare into her eyes, stricken.

'*Leaving?*'

A tide of panic is already sweeping us apart. She puts her hand on my arm.

'Of course I don't want to leave,' she comforts me. 'My husband has a new post.'

The sun sets below the mews houses further up the hill. I step outside.

'I can't cope any more,' I am trying to say.

My husband sets a cafetiere on the doorstep. Our daughter waves from the hayloft window and runs downstairs. In expectation of the new girlfriend's arrival, the vine is blossoming in the bluebell urn.

We take our coffee onto the cobbles.

'I can't cope,' I am repeating.

'We need more information,' my husband agrees. 'I mean, these streetlamps, for example? Are they capable of triggering a photosensitive reaction?'

'What?' frowns our daughter.

They walk back across the cobbles to examine the nearest one.

'I cannot cope,' I try to warn them. 'Not any more.'

'I suppose I could board up our bedroom window?' suggests my husband.

Below the bedroom window, our son and the new girlfriend appear around the corner.

'*Hello!*' cries our daughter.

'What's wrong?' our son asks me.

'I CANNOT COPE!' I scream. 'I CANNOT COPE ANY MORE!'

'It's *lovely* to meet you,' continues our daughter, shaking hands, 'and this is our mum—'

I burst into tears. The new girlfriend gives me a hug.

'You're nocturnal, that's all,' she tries to comfort me. 'You come out at night.'

Our son puts his arm around my shoulders.

'One step down from a vampire,' he tries to cheer me up.

The shutter over the hayloft window is closed, yet the hayloft landing shimmers with emotion. The Headmaster is waiting. I am not dressed, but he is waiting.

'I can't see a doctor for six months,' I rehearse, 'and the lawyer says my medical file would be filleted before I got it.'

The hayloft stairs are lost in a tunnel of darkness. So is the miniscule bedroom, and the cobbles beyond the shutter. Only the hayloft landing flickers and gleams like a candleflame.

'All they'll tell me is I'm in this for the long haul.' I try to explain. 'And I can't let you pay me for the long haul. Not after all you've done for us already.'

The hayloft landing is burning with a fiercer and fiercer light.

'So – I – resign,' I force myself to say.

I glance up to see whether the Headmaster will think I have gone mad. He isn't there. The hayloft landing begins to spin. My husband calls upstairs to warn me it is eight o'clock. The echo of his call attempts the stairs and falls back unanswered, over and over again.

It's eight o'clock. It's eight o'clock. It's eight o'clock.

Each echo whips the landing to a faster spin. There is a thump. On the stairs beneath my head, feet scramble. My husband helps me up and throws open the shutter for air. The landing is suddenly illuminated.

There is a shame, glitters my portrait, *which sinners deserve, but share with the sick.*

'Here,' says our daughter, ripping half a dozen pages out of her printer. 'Your resignation speech. All typed up. Take it, and take these –' she hands me a packet of tissues '– and get going.'

My husband climbs three steps up to open the door onto the cobbles.

'You're not going to cry, are you?' frowns our son, looking at the tissues.

'No,' I gulp.

'Because it wouldn't be right to cry,' he says. 'Not in front of everybody.'

The common room is waiting for me with its blinds pulled down.

'When no-one would help us,' I say, 'not the government, nor the civil service, nor the lawyers, not the banks, you gave our children their future.'

I have to stop, and breathe hard, before I can raise my voice again.

'Our son says it would not be right to cry. Not in front of everybody. But after this speech, when none of you are looking, I'm going to cry my eyes out.'

The blinds go up. I turn to the Headmaster. He is smiling and I am smiling and I walk very quickly past the Deputy Headmaster, who has tears running down her face, and the Headmaster's Wife, who is sobbing, and through the common room, who are wiping their eyes.

I walk quickly past them all until I reach the door, pass through it, and hear it close behind me.

'I'm going to minute this meeting,' decides our daughter, 'on the fridge.'

She tears a sheet of cartridge paper to fit the fridge door and masking tapes it into place. Then she divides the cartridge paper into two columns, marking the one on the left *Edinburgh* and the other *London* in black ink.

'Oh *God*,' says my husband. 'Here we go. Your mother has decided to sell the house.'

He takes his chair at the kitchen table.

'So we need to relocate to London,' I agree, 'to make sure we can still support you both without my salary.'

Our daughter looks at our son, and inscribes the right hand side of the fridge.

'Well, I vote we stay put in Edinburgh,' argues my husband. 'We bought this house for our retirement. If we lose money on it, we'll make ourselves a burden in the future.'

Our daughter makes a note in the left hand column of the fridge.

'If we ask them to pay accommodation costs in Oxford and in London,' I argue back, 'we'll make ourselves a burden *now*.'

'– new hardwood flooring throughout –' my husband is insisting the fridge records.

'– living expenses, travel costs and tuition fees,' I am counting up.

'– fully rewired,' my husband continues 'including state-of-the-art combination boiler –'

'– whereas if we rent a flat in London,' I tell our son, 'then the money we save on your accommodation will pay for hers in Oxford.'

'AOCB?' asks my husband. 'Or are we ready to vote?'

'If you don't mind,' our son tells me, 'I'd rather not vote for the end of my social life. Let's just go for it. Can I take this down or are you keeping it for your portfolio?'

'Do you know,' says our daughter, stepping back, 'that's quite an interesting idea?'

The seven-year archive is stored in a fifth-floor attic. My husband is at the turn of the fourth flight of stairs. His elbows are on its banister, his head hung between them.

'Why are you stopped?'

He straightens his back.

'For a breather. Here, give me those.'

He balances my armload of lever arch files on top of his own, lifts them all up and fastens the topmost with his chin.

'Take two,' he grunts. 'Three's too many for you.'

I manoeuvre two more lever arch files around the attic door. The stairs are so steep I have to sidestep down the top flight. By the time I reach the one below, my interlaced fingers are sliding apart.

On the pavement outside, our son takes my two and our communal six, shoulders them over the tailgate of a hired lorry and leaps in after them.

'Keep going!' grins our daughter as she passes.

She is taking four, two steps at a time.

I scale and rescale the stairs, taking two. My calf muscles lock. I wait for my husband on the landing.

'Does it *have* to come to London?'

'Of course.'

'Are there many more?'

'Every drawing I issued in the last seven years? We've hardly started.'

'I need espresso.'

He looks at his watch.

'No time for nonsense like that,' he says and disappears downstairs.

'I need espresso,' I tell the width of the landing carpet.

My husband climbs back up to it.

'What are you *doing*? I might have stepped on you.'

'I need espresso.'

'For God's *sake,*' he is still fuming, as he fastens the tailgate of the lorry and climbs into its driving seat. 'Make sure you order a double.'

We drink our take-away espresso in the cab. Our daughter lends me her leg-warmers. Our son advises I take down one lever arch file at a time. My husband leads us back up to the attic.

I take down one at a time until the black night sky lightens to charcoal.

'You need another break,' says our son. 'You were bringing ten an hour when we started. Now it's taking you ten minutes a file.'

Our daughter and I lie down to rest. Our son and my husband do a calculation to see whether we can still shift the seven-year archive in time. In the morning parking restrictions will force every lever arch file an extra five hundred yards.

'Will we do it?' asks our daughter, when I waken her.

'They say if we don't take any breaks.'

'Come on then.'

Our son starts lowering files fast in a complicated arrangment of kayak ropes. The schedule has to be recalculated when I panic for twenty minutes he will follow them down the stairwell. He manhandles emptied cabinets down the stairs instead. My husband fends off traffic wardens for an extra half an hour.

'May,' chants our daughter passing her final load over the tailgate. 'June. July. Done.'

We drive in triumph to the café. The café owner stops folding the day's newspapers into his newspaper rack, and offers us one instead.

FILES ON INFECTED BLOOD INADVERTENTLY DESTROYED.

We slump in his café chairs.

My husband wakens after a full night's sleep.

'The house is packed,' we tell him.

'How much sleep have you had?'

'None,' our daughter replies.

My husband locks the lorry's blank tailgate over everything we own. We walk around the corner to the café.

'Here she is,' nods the café owner. 'I've saved your bit of shadow.'

He point to the table furthest from the window.

'Usual?' he asks, rattling a tray of croissants and reloading it into his oven.

We eat the croissants with homemade jam. I drink a last espresso. Tears well in my blistered eyes.

'Second-last,' murmurs my husband, ordering another.

'Still no better?' commiserates the café owner, bringing it to our table. 'What a curse.'

I cannot bear the deception any longer.

'We're leaving,' I tell him. 'We can't afford to stay now I've resigned.'

The café owner pulls his hands out of his oven gloves.

'Now this is a surprise. When are you thinking of leaving then?'

'Now,' I am trying to explain. 'We're leaving now. Our son has flown to London, to collect the keys to a rented basement flat.'

The café owner looks at my husband.

'She couldn't bear to say goodbye again,' he explains.

The café owner gives me a hug. He tells me I am safe enough. The school will not return for another week. The shop door opens. There are a flurry of hellos.

'Not even bread in the house!' the Head of English is mock-complaining. 'How are you, my love?'

Tears spill over my broken lids.

'We're in a rush,' apologises my husband, shaking hands.

He signals to the café owner with a ten pound note and leaves it on the table.

'Goodbye!'

'Goodbye!' cries the café owner over the Head of English's shoulder. 'Goodbye!'

The shop bell rings. We cross the street to avoid the sun. Our daughter runs to catch us up.

'Quick, quick!' I gasp.

My husband unlocks the lorry. Our daughter climbs in the other side. She flips down the cab's sun visors. I pull down the Laura Ashley hat. We drive past the doorstep-in-midair and past the café, past the school and past the turn-off for Dunino, onto the ring-road and past its roadsigns for every place we know.

The night sky in London is not the night sky in Dunino. At night in Dunino the sky is so black that a thousand stars crackle in its silence. In London the night sky is an emulsion of light pollution, emergency sirens and the chatter of a thousand neighbours. Above this chaos, the emulsion coagulates into four white chimneys.

'What are they?'

'They're the chimneys of Battersea Power Station. Now Battersea Power Station stands on the river,' says my husband, 'so that's south, and if we turn our backs to it, then Buckingham Palace is north—'

The white chimneys fade in and out of the night sky with the emergency sirens, until a flash of lightning illuminates them as the columns of a ruined temple.

'Of course it was never a temple!' scoffs my husband. 'And that's not lightning either. It's a train crossing the points as it reaches Victoria Station.'

Another train rumbles unseen towards the station and crosses the points. The ruined temple flashes again.

'All the railway lines to Victoria converge here,' explains my husband. 'So if we face the station, the Queen lives on the *right-hand* side of the tracks and we live—'

'—on the *wrong-hand* side of the tracks?'

'London is a wonderful place!' cries the weaver on the telephone. 'It has *such* significance! My husband's parents had a house there. They used to joke about it. *Not far from the National Gallery,* they used to joke, *on the wrong side of the tracks.*'

'We're on the wrong side of the tracks,' I say. 'We're in a basement flat, on the wrong side of the tracks.'

'I still have all their letters,' the weaver is reminiscing. 'I remember the name of the street.'

I catch my breath.

'That's our street,' I tell her.

'Number eighty eight,' remembers the weaver. 'What? A basement flat in the same street? Which number's basement are you in?'

She has to repeat the question.

'Number eighty eight's,' I croak.

In the National Gallery in Trafalgar Square, there are window blinds.

There are spotlights too, but trained on the pictures and fastened to high ceilings, where the square of the distance diminishes their power. My heart races. I know what will happen now. It is already happening.

Without its constant trigger, my immune response is stalling. Inflammation cools. Swelling subsides. My nasal passages open. The rush of oxygen makes me dizzy. My spine straightens.

By the Renaissance gallery, the dull stare of endurance is fading from my eyes. My hands fly up in awe. My feet dance between oils. My features reassemble into my own face, still without wrinkles because it has not seen the sun in a year. In the dark background of a Caravaggio, I recognise myself.

I miss you, there is time to tell my forgotten expressions, before the halogen lamps in the Gallery Shop extinguish them again.

'Funnily enough, the same thing happened in the Norfolk Music Room in the Victoria and Albert Museum,' I am telling our son. 'It must be the effect of the music. The students are from the Royal College, so the music is the best in the world, a bit too soon.'

He looks up from his revision notes.

'Or was there anything else about the Norfolk Music Room more likely to have an effect on your photosensitive skin?'

'Well, there were fabulous gilt stuccos—'

'Stuccos, eh?' says our son. 'What were the lights like?'

'Oh!' I clasp my hands. 'Candelabra re-wired with tiny bulbs to simulate the dimly lit performances of the period!'

'You don't say?' says our son. 'And did you notice any windowblinds?'

I raise my hands in horror at the thought.

'Certainly not! The Norfolk Music Room is a faithful reconstruction. The curtains are eighteenth century.'

Our son frowns. He turns back to his revision with a shrug.

'Eau-de-nil watered silk!' I tell his girlfriend. 'They once opened onto St James' Square. Of course in the Victoria and Albert Museum they open onto a brick wall, but that's because there's a gallery on the other side.'

'You're better off taking the tube to St Mary's Hospital,' says my husband. 'If you take the bus you'll get stuck in traffic facing the sun.'

'Tube carriages are lit by striplights,' I remind him.

'I know that,' he nods. 'We're not suggesting you spend all day down there. But that's the other advantage of tube travel. It's *fast*.'

I am not convinced that fast is fast enough.

'There are hundreds and hundreds of striplights.' I am fretting to my daughter. 'It's bright as *day* down there.'

Our son shakes his head.

'It's dark down there,' he tells me.

'It's bright as though the sun were shining!' I cry.

'No it *isn't*,' he insists. 'I told you. Your eyes *adapt*. It's a hundred feet below ground and it's dark.'

He looks at our daughter.

'All the same, you'd better go with her. There's not a chance she'll remember to change at Oxford Circus.'

'Hello,' I say.

'Do take a chair,' says St Mary's Hospital. 'What's the problem?'

I see that she knows I have seen the private specialist in Edinburgh. My medical file is open at his letter.

'So in the end,' I explain, 'I did have to resign.'

'I'm reluctant to make a diagnosis of photosensitivity until we've tried a few more months of antibiotics,' says St Mary's Hospital.

My jaw drops. She comes around her desk to inspect it.

'But I can't walk in the sun!'

St Mary's Hospital rolls up my sleeve with one hand, and uncaps a syringe for blood samples with the other.

'It's terribly hot in the sun,' she argues, and sinks the needle into my elbow.

My medical file is already in her out-tray. She puts the phials of my blood in a polythene envelope, writes *previous Hepatitis C* on the corner of its label, and seals it with a firm hand.

In the evening shadows, around our basement flat, undivided townhouses snuggle into their ivy wraps and flash their burglar alarms. Our son appears around the corner.

'Possible eight,' he says without preamble. 'Possible seven. Fucked up the third question.'

His tone is flat. We hurry downstairs. His girlfriend is sitting at the table, interpreting marking schemes on Imperial's examinations website.

'Possible eight, possible seven,' I tell her. 'Not happy with the third question.'

'Did you write a fourth question?' she asks our son.

'Yeah,' he says, unloading his rucksack and rifling through his revision notes. 'But I might have used the wrong equations.'

It takes an hour to work out which were the correct equations. Question four is included as a possible five.

'Can I still do it?' asks our son, peering over his girlfriend's shoulder at her laptop.

'You'll have to pass Optics tomorrow,' she warns him.

The minibus signals to turn out onto Exhibition Road. A dozen kayaks are roped to its roofrack.

'Wait!' shouts our son inside it.

He wrenches open the minibus' sliding door and jumps out.

'So sorry,' apologises our son's girlfriend at the minibus driver's window. 'He must be checking the results board one last time.'

'*For God's sake—*' howl the kayakers inside.

'Oh, here he is,' says our son's girlfriend, before she is swept off her feet.

Our son gets back into the minibus. The kayakers roar in disgust. His girlfriend is jumping for joy on the pavement. The minibus turns into the traffic.

'Go back and tell them!' he shouts to her over it.

'Are mothers expected to wear hats to the Albert Hall?' I ask our son.

'Mine is,' he replies, 'after the hell I went through to get you there.'

The morning of the graduation ceremony dawns hot and sunny. The light reflecting off London's pavements drives my immune system to a frenzy. My face throbs so violently that swollen blood vessels split across my cheekbones. I look like a boxer.

But there is no embarrassment. Our celebration breakfast is as extravagant as my hat, which *The Wolseley of Piccadilly* would not dream of asking a lady to remove.

'Dear God,' says St Mary's Hospital. 'What happened to your face?'

I still have my hand on the door handle. She comes around her desk. Her expression is concerned.

'You walked in the sun?'

'Yesterday,' I say.

I am holding a newspaper over my head. The newspaper is given away in Paddington Station. It has shaded me past busy cafes to the blue plaque which says *Sir Alexander Fleming discovered penicillin on this site*. Behind the blue plaque, architectural extensions have grown and multiplied to the prefabricated office in which St Mary's Hospital is still staring at my nose.

'I'm having that,' she says.

'Having what?'

'Sit down.'

The *Consent to Surgical Procedure* form is already on her desk. She points to the weal across the bridge of my nose with the blunt end of a bic pen.

'That. For the histology lab. Now, don't worry about the biopsy,' she goes on writing *previous Hepatitis C* above my signature. 'Come back at one o'clock and I'll do you in my lunch-hour. We'll review the result at your next appointment.'

At one o'clock there is only one patient left in the waiting room. He turns to smile. My eyes widen.

He has no eyelids. Bits of his lips are missing. He tries to anoint himself with emollient, but most of his fingers have lost their tips.

'You must have been in a terrible fire?' I comfort him.

He looks at me as though I am teasing.

'Just in the sun,' he shrugs.

The coal cellars of London basements are dug into the ground, under the road. My husband says this is because London clay is very strong. His new coal cellar office has three arches. In its furthest vault, the seven-year archive is stored. Over the middle vault, lorries rumble. My husband sits at his desk in the nearest vault with the cellar door open and the bluebell urn to divide it from our basement where I sit, spending a summer hiding from the sun.

The printer clatters into life. Our son leans into the second vault and swipes his portfolio from the printer's paper-tray.

'Thanks.'

'Wait a minute,' cries my husband. 'What are those?'

'What are what?'

'All those stage productions,' marvels my husband.

The printer clatters again. A second sheet drops into the paper tray.

'Look at this!' says my husband, passing the first sheet to me. 'There must be twenty of them!'

'You saw them all,' our son reminds him.

'Yeah I saw them,' my husband agrees, checking the list, 'but I never really *noticed* them. Anytime I noticed you were kayaking?'

'That's the yellow drysuit for you,' says our son. 'Can I borrow your CAD programme?'

'What for?'

'To design a set for a production of *Galileo*.'

He shows my husband his preliminary drawings.

'You'd need a lorry-load of wood,' points out my husband. 'Where would a student production get the money to build a thing like that?'

I slam the coal cellar door behind me.

'It's not the lorry-load of wood I'm worried about,' says my husband. 'It's the postgraduate fees once he's submitted that portfolio.'

'He can't give up his future to pay for what we've lost!'

'I know that, but all we have left is my pension.'

'Well, cash it in.'

'Oh don't be *daft*. My pension? It hasn't matured yet! It's an *investment*.'

'This is a better investment.'

My husband reopens the cellar door for air.

'I'm just pointing out that without my pension we'd have no security—'

'Security?' My laughter grows hysterical. '*Security?*'

'—for the *future*. I didn't say I wouldn't cash it in!'

'Well, that's good,' I snap, 'because in case you hadn't noticed, I haven't got a pension. And I've been living without a *future* for the last twenty years.'

The coal cellar door slams again.

The lorry-load of wood arrives at dawn. Through the window of the basement flat I watch my husband's pyjamas meet the lorry driver's jeans. Our son is tearing on his clothes. He bundles together the drawings on his desk.

'Where's my toolbag?'

'Here,' says his girlfriend.

He slings it over his shoulder.

'Are you coming?'

'Yes,' says his girlfriend.

'Hello?' calls my husband.

We stop in the wings. Our eyes adjust to their gloom.

'Look at that!' my husband swells with pride. 'He's got a couple of ribs up already. *Hello?*'

'Hello!' answers our son's girlfriend from the auditorium.

'Hello?' I am calling as I clamber back out of the wings to find her. 'Where are you?'

'No, I'm wrong,' my husband is still peering upwards. 'He's got *four* up. Four, and – what's the matter?'

'Give me that lunchbox,' I splutter, 'and find yourself a paintbrush.'

'Wait – what's wrong?'

'– painted stage flats all morning –'

'Who?'

'– hasn't had any breakfast –'

'Wait! What are you doing?'

'– *still in her pyjamas* –'

Our son's girlfriend is still in her pyjamas when our son raises the final rib and lights a firmament of stars above the stage. Another waits over Exhibition Road to light our long walk home.

'Put the kettle on!' calls my husband.

'We will!' his girlfriend calls back.

They open a gap between us. I fuss to its empty air.

'Of course we can't interfere. But what if he *is* offered a place? I hope he knows he can ask her to move in?'

'I know where she's moved in,' says my husband.

He points a paintbrush towards my heart.

'Now that you've moved in and you're writing your doctorate in *psychology*,' I tell our son's girlfriend, 'I expect you were wondering why there are so many mirrors?'

'No, I wasn't,' she says.

'I mean,' I rattle on, 'it must seem crazy, all these mirrors. But the simple explanation is—'

'You don't need to explain,' laughs our son's girlfriend.

'—until St Mary's Hospital make a diagnosis, I can't get any treatment so I have to stay—'

'—on guard?' she suggests. 'And so you check for swelling in the mirrors, to relax.'

'Not to look glamorous,' I blush, 'if that's what you were thinking?'

Together we examine my inflamed and anointed reflection in the nearest one.

'Well, sorry to disappoint you—' grins our son's girlfriend.

The showerhead has three settings, but even the gentlest breaks inflamed skin faster than it can wash emollient off it. I wait until everyone else has showered, then clean the bath to bathe in it. In the shallow luke-warm water that is left, the heat of inflammation is conducted away. The throbbing calms. A thousand tiny wounds are soothed.

'Hello?' asks our son.

'Hello,' I drowse.

He pulls his door key from the lock and closes his eyes to cross the passage.

'Hello!' cries our son's girlfriend, pulling her new doorkey from the lock.

'Hello,' I drowse.

Their bedroom door clicks shut behind her. I sit up in the bath. The moment I am dressed I rush in to apologise.

'I always take a bath with the light out because the porcelain reflects it—'

'I can understand that,' says our son's girlfriend.

'—so I have to leave the bathroom door open—'

'—or you wouldn't be able to find the soap,' she nods. 'And you've got used to it, so it doesn't seem odd.'

'But it must seem odd to you!' I wail. 'I haven't got a diagnosis! It must seem crazy!'

Our son turns round from his desk.

'Mum, how long are you going to keep this up? She doesn't think you're crazy.' He turns back to his girlfriend. 'Do you think mum's crazy?'

'I think your situation's crazy,' she comforts me.

'Thank you,' I am sobbing on her shoulder.

'Now go away,' says our son, 'before you drive me crazy.'

'*Galileo* will recommence in two minutes,' repeats the theatre tannoy. 'Act Two of *Galileo*, in two minutes.'

'It's your own fault,' my husband shakes his head. 'You shouldn't have spent Act One so close to that spotlight. We'd better go home.'

'I don't want to go home!'

'Well, you can't go back to your seat,' he says. 'Another hour next to that spot and you'll be going home in an ambulance. We'll have to stand at the back.'

'We can't both stand at the back. He'll think we haven't come!'

'One minute,' warns the theatre tannoy.

My husband walks back to his seat on his own. Silence falls. I know our son is hidden in its darkness but beyond the stage the darkness is so deep that not even a murmur can escape it. The murmur is running into a headset instead.

'There's a woman hiding behind a pillar at the back of the auditorium?'

'Yep,' says the headset, 'that'll be my mum.'

Footlights suddenly illuminate Act Two. The audience gasps. The constellations which spun over Act One of *Galileo* are falling from the sky.

Down, down they are falling, on the ribs of the dome which supported their starry galaxies. At head height, the dome begins to tilt. At forty-five degrees, the ribs become prison bars. There is a dull thud as the prison bars lock onto metal spigots which are waiting for them on the floor.

The constellations which lit Galileo's scientific integrity are rewound into the wings. Vine creepers run out, threading themselves through the long years of his persecution. The murmur is running too, back into the headset.

'There's a man in the front row crying?'

'Yep,' says the headset, 'that'll be my dad.'

'I'm sorry to have to tell you,' says St Mary's Hospital, 'that histology has confirmed a diagnosis of autoimmunity.'

'My own immune system is attacking me?'

'It is attacking your connective tissue,' nods St Mary's Hospital, 'in an autoimmune response. I am afraid so. Yes.'

She picks up her pen.

'It used to be the case that autoimmunity carried a life expectancy of ten years from diagnosis. Untreated, it can lead to heart or kidney failure. But with treatment, we should be able to control it.'

I am trembling.

'Is there any chance that this could be a consequence of Hepatitis C?'

'Autoimmunity is not caused by Hepatitis C,' says St Mary's Hospital. 'You can set your mind at rest about that.'

She deploys the bic pen and writes out a prescription for an antimalarial drug.

'There will be the occasional flare-up—' she is conceding.

'Thank you,' I get up to leave.

'—but barring side-effects you should find you are able to live a more normal life.'

I stop mid-stride.

'What side-effects?'

'Oh!' shrugs St Mary's Hospital. 'The usual. Headache, vomiting, diarrhoea—'

'Are you all right?' cries my husband.

'She's fine,' our daughter elbows him aside. 'Give her a minute.'

'Were you sick?' asks my husband. 'Where are you going?'

Our daughter wraps me in her coat and steers me through the front door.

'For the most expensive espresso we can find.'

'Should I come with you?'

She stops him at the door.

'No need. You may express your concern,' she holds out one hand, 'through the medium of cash.'

I push the espresso bowl aside.

'Drink it,' urges our daughter.

'This can't go on,' I am shaking my head. 'I must have lost half a stone since the weekend.'

'Well, how very Chelsea,' she says. 'Look around you. Most of the women in here are still trying to lose half a stone since the weekend.'

'And it's not a headache,' I am still complaining, 'It's a mind-ache. It's a mental straitjacket. I'm so drugged up I can't string two thoughts together!'

Our daughter lifts her hands in admiration.

'How *very* Chelsea,' she assures me.

I lie in my knickers on a hospital bed. The door swings open. I adjust the blanket St Mary's Hospital has given me.

'Hello,' I say.

There are a couple of dozen quick smiles. One doctor, who is not wearing a white coat and whose hands rest in the trouser pockets of his suit, meets my eyes.

'Hello,' he nods.

He moves to one side of the room and sits on a corner of St Mary's Hospital's desk. His place is taken by a blonde in a very white coat. She bustles to the front of the crowd without introduction.

'Is everyone in?' asks St Mary's Hospital. 'Thank you for coming to see my patient, who has—'

Neither the blonde nor I am listening to the resume of my medical notes. She is inspecting the weal on my nose. I am inspecting the line of navy eyebrow pencil above her spectacles. When her eyes flick to mine, the navy eyebrows arch like tom cats.

'I'm very surprised,' she interrupts 'by the reaction to the antimalarial prescription?'

'—a severe reaction commensurate with the drug's contra-indications—' St Mary's Hospital is explaining to the rest.

'Yes, but my own patient –' the eyebrows crook to argue '– the patient to whom I referred in my comments next door—'

She turns back to fix me with an accusing stare.

'My own patient has taken this drug for *years*.'

I glance round to see whether I am allowed to answer.

'So in your statistical sample of two,' I plead, 'don't I cancel your patient out?'

There is a snort. The doctor in the brown suit slides off the desk and stands up. White coats queue at the door to file out.

The clinic nurse pulls the curtain around the hospital bed. I get dressed in disgrace. The clinic nurse draws the curtain back again. St Mary's Hospital is writing in my medical file.

'Anti-malarial therapy not an option,' she is writing, 'due to rectal bleeding.'

'I don't want to seem ungrateful,' I say, 'or give the impression I'm going to sue, which anyway I can't afford to. But I wonder why you are so certain that this is not a consequence of Hepatitis C?'

'I don't think we will be able to say what has caused your condition,' says St Mary's Hospital.

She pauses, then looks away.

'I don't think we can do that for you.'

On the sunny side of the carriage, a woman and her child are laughing. Through the windows of the train the sun is flashing between trees to make the child sneeze. I am sitting next to my husband on the shadowed side of the carriage.

The train guard announces Oxford.

Sunlight is glinting from its spires. The station platform is bathed in it. The mother and child wrestle with a perambulator at the carriage door. I keep my nerve and my seat until they wrestle it off, then dive for the departure hall before the train sets off again. On the other side of the station, my husband returns with a taxi.

'We're still heading east,' he says. 'The sun's behind you, so look ahead.'

I look ahead. We drive up Hythe Bridge Street. Cyclists over and undertake onto the bridge. Through the open taxi windows the scent of willow and slow moving water mingle to mark a boundary.

'Look ahead!' chides my husband and, to the driver, 'Radcliffe Square.'

The taxi driver drops us at the barrier at the end of Broad Street.

'Off to the Bullingdon Club, are you?' he jokes, looking at my husband's tie.

On the college lawn, knots of cotton shorts and tanned limbs bathe in the sun. Their irregular groupings are punctuated by books. The books lie open on the grass, beneath a chin propped on a fist, or like a prayer mat before crossed legs.

I stop in the shade of the Porter's Lodge.

A page is turned. The stopper of a water bottle is flicked with a thumb. Someone calls our daughter's name.

The farthest knot unravels to a synchronised glance of sunglasses. Our daughter tilts hers over her hair, and waves. A new boyfriend beckons.

I wait in the shade of the Porter's Lodge. Our daughter gets to her feet.

'She can't,' I hear her say.

One by one, as she walks towards me, knots unravel in her wake. Sunglasses stare.

We sit down at a trestle table. The college refectory is fifteenth century with twentieth century striplights.

'Stay under your menu for now,' says our daughter. 'They haven't lit the candles yet.'

A waiter approaches with a taper. The striplights are switched off. I replace the menu card beneath a candlestick. *College Guest Dinner* it glows.

'What does St Mary's Hospital mean it won't be able to say what caused my condition?' I am asking our daughter. 'What does it mean it can't do that for me?'

A spoon is banged against a water glass. We all stand up.

'I'll tell you what it means,' I fume. 'It means there's something they're trying to hide.'

'Well the lawyer says—' interrupts my husband.

'The lawyer!' I scoff. 'The lawyer can't even stop the Government filleting my medical file.'

'Or destroying their own files,' points out our daughter.

'What?' asks my husband.

'*Inadvertently* destroyed, by an over-zealous civil servant,' she reminds him.

'Over-zealous civil servant!' he seethes. 'You would need an over-zealous team of four. Inadvertently working round the clock for a fortnight.'

'There's bound to be a newspaper archive in the Bodleian Library,' soothes our daughter 'I don't suppose anyone remembers where we saw that headline?'

A young man in new spectacles and an old shirt is making his way between tables. Our daughter waves and smiles. The High Table enters after him. A grace is said in Latin. We all sit down.

Our daughter uncorks a bottle of wine. The new boyfriend asks engineering questions, each deduced from my husband's previous reply. He clears candle sticks to right and left.

'So what are you going to do next?' my husband asks him.

'Well,' says the new boyfriend. 'I might try for the Civil Service –'

Our daughter meets my eyes.

'– or I might go in for Law.'

There is a pause. The new boyfriend glances round the table to decipher it. I pour some wine into his glass.

'We're beginning to suspect,' I confide in him, 'they could both do with an overhaul.'

'Party time!' says our daughter.

She hands me her keys and pulls off her college gown.

'Could you drop this in my room?'

'But how will you get back in?'

'I'll ring you,' she calls over the new boyfriend's shoulder.

We make our way through flag-stoned arches to the Lodge. A porter shows us to our daughter's room. I collect empty hangers from a cupboard and start to pick clothes off the floor.

'You've got me worried about a cover up,' says my husband.

'Keep the light off,' I reply.

I make laundry bags of pillowcases and shove in our daughter's shirts.

'Is the Government withholding information?' asks my husband. 'Surely it couldn't be so cruel?'

He rams the contents of the overstuffed pillowcases harder and harder so I can fill them up.

'They can't take much more,' I warn him.

'Neither can I!' he cries. 'If the Government is withholding information, are your doctors withholding it too? How *do* they know all this is not a consequence of Hepatitis C?'

In a photograph frame on our daughter's desk she is still holding hands with our son beneath the apple tree in Dunino. Next to them stands the bottle of wine we didn't drink at dinner.

'I don't know who to trust!' cries my husband. 'You could be dying and I don't know who to trust!'

'Well, we're all going to die,' I comfort him, 'but people who lie and cover up –'

I pick up the bottle. Outside the quadrangle is bathed in moonlight. I kick off my shoes to dance over the college lawn.

'– they already died,' I say.

Our daughter rings at dawn.

'Where have you got to?'

'They're in the laundry,' I hear her ring off.

'The *college* laundry?' wonders the new boyfriend, on the other side of the college laundry door.

'We followed the signs –' I tell him, opening it.

He looks at the glass in my hand.

'– but the tumble dryer put my husband straight to sleep –'

Our daughter grins. She lobs the empty wine bottle into a bin.

'– so I had a top up while I was waiting for the sheets, and one with the wool cycle, and then there was all the ironing –' I am still explaining to the new boyfriend as I attempt the stairs.

'Beautiful evening,' says the chaplain.

He welcomes us with three hymnbooks and a bow. The door closes behind us, shutting out the sun.

The chapel is cool and dim. To the north, trees shade its leaded glass. From the choir stalls, lamplight and anthems splash across a marble floor. The fever of a sunny Oxford weekend washes from my veins. Exhaustion floods into its vacuum. Our wooden pew grows luxurious.

I waken on our daughter's shoulder. Above our heads Dunino Den is grown again. The branches of its trees vault one upon another, opening to canopies of gilt and stucco. From the choirstalls, soprano and tenor voices scale a gilt and stucco crescendo, then tumble back to earth. A final note bounces twice across the marble floor.

'Isn't there a newspaper archive in London?' I ask our daughter.

'The British Library will have a collection.'

We get to our feet. The choir file out in procession. The chaplain sweeps out after them.

'Is that on the Northern Line?'

'Get you,' says our daughter. 'Zipping about on the tube, like a normal person.'

The British Library Newspaper Archive is so far out of central London that the Northern Line leaves the tunnel at Golder's Green. On either side of its track, streets of houses with proper gardens run off into the sun.

I turn east to face away from it. At Brent Cross and Haddon Central, signboards reflect it back. At Colindale a Victorian ironwork canopy runs the length of the platform. Across the road from the station stands a vast brick hangar of post-war construction. It looks like a prison.

I open its door. The British Library Newspaper Archive at Colindale is a library from my childhood. It has high ceilings and sloping desks of polished wood. Its reading lamps are Art Deco, its librarians silent and disapproving.

'I'm looking for a headline I saw in the Scotsman, two summers ago.'

'You haven't a date?'

'No.'

'You need a date if you wish to make a requisition.'

'I can't search through the collection?'

'Only on microfiche.'

'Is that on a computer?'

'No, on a microfiche reading machine.'

He leads the way into the microfiche reading room. It is so dark he falls over a swivel chair.

'It's very old technology,' he explains, 'and depends on our eyes adapting to low levels of illumination.'

I put my cardboard folder on the swivel chair and give him my newly issued library card. He compares its red weal to the one on my nose and gives me four spools.

I load the first spool onto the spindle of the microfiche reading machine and switch it on. Pages of the *Scotsman* follow one another in a vertical progression up and over its screen. The twist of a dial brings them into the horizontal. I sit rewinding our final summer in Scotland. The duty librarian brings four consecutive spools for July.

'Closing at five,' he warns, taking my discarded spools away.

I rewind faster and faster. I do not find the headline that infected blood files are inadvertently destroyed. I find another. When I find it, it spins across the antiquated screen and disappears.

I wonder if I have imagined it. I hold my breath and twist the dial to recall it page by broadsheet page.

LORD OWEN ALLEGES COVER-UP OVER 1757 BLOOD DEATHS.

'One thousand seven hundred and fifty-seven?' cries my husband. 'That's not a *cover-up*. That's a *massacre*.'

'Lord Archer of Sandwell has already chaired a private inquiry to investigate it.'

'Why didn't we know that?'

'Because we're not paying a lawyer to tell us,' I despair, 'and because I can't look at a computer screen. I've lost touch with the twenty-first century. So I need you to look up more reference numbers online.'

'DT1307,' recites my husband in shocked tones.

I scribble the reference numbers in pencil on blank British Library request forms. The duty librarian takes the bundle of forms I pass him and looks at the clock.

'Cutting it fine,' he complains.

'They're all the same date,' I plead.

'23 February 2009?' he asks, reading the reference number for *The Times*.

'Yes.'

He takes the second request form.

'Daily Telegraph, 23 February 2009?'

'Yes.'

'London Evening Standard, 23 Feb—'

He flicks through the rest of the bundle.

'The Sun, The Daily Mail, The Independent.'

'Yes.'

'All 23 February 2009?'

'Yes.'

'Big day, was it?'

Back in the microfiche reading room I load spools onto as many reading machines as I can reach. Lord Winston says it is a very big day. He gives evidence to Lord Archer's inquiry that the contaminated blood scandal is **the worst treatment disaster in the history of the NHS.**

The inquiry finds that a total of five thousand people have been infected. Of these, two thousand are already dead **as a direct consequence of their transfusions**.

The Times takes the official line.

A government's spokesman said, 'We have great sympathy for the patients and families affected by contaminated blood products in the 1970s and 1980s.'

The London Evening Standard retorts:

Ministers have consistently refused funding for a formal public investigation and refused to provide any evidence to this inquiry.

The Sun loses patience.

BLOOD IS ON THEIR HANDS.

I leave the British Library Newspaper Archive and start to count.

Rush-hour in Colindale Tube Station is a relative term. A dozen people queue at the ticket barrier. On the platform, at least two dozen more stroll the Victorian ironwork canopy.

But in the carriage, there is standing room only. I am up to one hundred people before the tube emerges into Euston Station and, by the foot of its escalator in a central London rush-hour, five hundred. Between the station concourse at the top of the escalator and the traffic-jam along Euston Road outside, the first thousand deaths are counted.

Ministers have consistently refused funding for a formal public investigation and refused to provide any evidence to this inquiry.

At Oxford Street I could count at least five hundred more, but I am only crossing it and there is no need, because in the crowded streets between Piccadilly Circus and Whitehall the total number of deaths for which the Government refuses to give evidence is equalled.

We have great sympathy for the patients and families affected

by contaminated blood products in the 1970s and 1980s.

From Whitehall I walk, as any civil servant could have done but didn't, around the Houses of Parliament to Great College Street, where Lord Archer held his inquiry. When I get there I look at my watch. It is a seven minute walk.

How much **great sympathy,** I wonder, does it take to walk seven minutes to give evidence? Had the Government been over-zealous enough to show one quarter of a second of sympathy for each transfusion death, wouldn't it have got here too?

'The government does not accept liability for any of the contaminated transfusions,' says a third reincarnation of the St Andrews lawyer. 'But it is still prepared to pay you ten thousand pounds, in full and final settlement, if you will agree it has none.'

'I don't understand this,' I say. 'If the government isn't liable, why is it offering to pay me anything at all?'

There is a stiff silence. My voice rises.

'And if it *is* liable, why isn't it paying for the salary I have lost?'

'As things stand,' says the St Andrews lawyer, 'we will have to accept that the Government is not liable, I'm afraid. Its own report into the contaminated blood transfusions has exonerated it.'

My husband double clicks on the Government's website. Its own report into the contaminated blood transfusions is uploaded as a printable PDF. Thirty pages roll into the printer's paper tray.

They are titled *Self-sufficiency in Blood Products. 1973-1991.* My husband rolls his eyes.

'Shouldn't that be *Lack of?*' he asks.

His telephone rings. It is a Scottish timber-frame manufacturer. I hold up *(Lack of) Self-sufficiency.*

'Aren't you going to read this with me?'

'I haven't time,' he covers the receiver to reply.

His screen reopens on a CAD drawing. The specification for a new house has been changed. I sit in the shade next to the bluebell urn and read *(Lack of) Self-sufficiency* by myself.

Safe blood is donated by volunteers, who are generally healthy. Unsafe blood is bought or harvested from prison inmates, who are often not. In the 1970s the Government drew up a plan to become self-sufficient in safe blood. But a new blood product was introduced for haemophiliacs. This changed the specification for self-sufficiency. The new product required so much blood that the Department of Health's original plan no longer worked.

My husband pushes his spectacles up his forehead and rubs the bridge of his nose. The plan for the new house is not working either.

'If they must have an extra balcony,' he is telling the Scottish timber-frame manufacturer, 'then there's nothing for it but to redesign the lot.'

The Government first ignores Lord Owen's order to redesign the self-sufficiency plan and then reports the order **inadvertently destroyed**. Yet *Self-Sufficiency in Blood Products* says the contaminated blood scandal is not the Government's fault. It is all the fault of the haemophiliacs who wanted the new blood products.

I open a cardboard folder and put the report inside. My husband replaces his telephone receiver.

'They've been asked to add a balcony,' he says. 'I'll have to work all night to make that safe.'

I hand him back the cardboard folder.

'Why not just wait until the balcony falls off, then blame whoever is standing on it at the time?'

'Lord Owen says there's a cover-up,' I tell the St Andrews lawyer. 'He says his missing papers prove he ordered an emergency reorganisation of the blood supply, and the Government ignored it.'

'Any further question of the Government's liability,' repeats the St Andrews lawyer, 'can only be decided at a Public Inquiry.'

'Then why haven't we had one?'

'Because the Government says **it does not believe any new light would be shed on this issue as a result.**'

I am staring out of the coal cellar office towards the bluebell urn.

'Well, not if they keep shredding the evidence,' I snap.

Beyond Victoria Station, a royal maze protects the palace. Along Cardinal Walk so many designer office blocks stand guard that it is impossible to find Palace Street among them.

'Don't come here on your own,' says my husband.

To the right, a path leads into a mall of shops. Ahead, an empty escalator climbs out of sight.

'Well it can't be up there,' I say, and takes the path to the left.

The path to the left is dark and forbidding. It follows a curve of reinforced glass to a department store's order collection point. Because the glass wall is curved, it forces our reflections to precede us.

'Oh!' says my husband. 'We're here.'

There is no drawbridge but high locked gates, policemen with machine guns and a Red Man at a pedestrian crossing. I press the button to demand an audience.

'Because,' I explain to my husband, 'if the Government won't listen, who else is there to ask?'

We stop at the first high locked gate. The windows of Buckingham Palace are blank. I look at my husband. His expression is blank too.

'I'm not sure the Queen has noticed that we're here,' he says.

I look back at the palace. There are so many windows it is difficult to know which to address. My husband takes my hand.

'Don't cry,' he says.

'Do you think she's here?'

'Well the flag is flying. But it's after midnight. I expect she's asleep.'

We walk along the palace railings the length of the palace forecourt. Its guard boxes are empty. At the far end of the railings an armed policeman steps out of a porter's lodge and glances around Green Park.

'Evening,' says my husband.

'Evening, sir,' says the armed policeman.

Below the canopy of oak branches a diffuse glow is lighting the park.

'There isn't going to be a Public Inquiry, is there?' I ask my husband.

'No there isn't,' he replies.

I blow my nose. The diffuse glow refocuses to the twinkle of a string of gaslights.

'Well, we're not passing this on.' I say. 'Our son and daughter are not paying for a cover-up. Whatever it costs, this is going to stop with us.'

My husband squeezes my hand.

'Feeling better?' he asks. 'Time to go home?'

We turn to walk back again. In the palace's many windows the gaslights are reflected.

'Good night, Your Majesty,' I tell its sleeping queen.

The dental nurse in London picks up my file from reception, reads it and smiles.

'This way,' she says.

She leads me into the dentist's chair, refills its paper cup and switches on the halogen lamp above.

'Sorry about that,' laughs the London dentist, switching the halogen lamp back off.

The nurse murmurs *previous Hepatitis C?* The dentist murmurs back. *Antiviral treatment.* The nurse leaves the file open on a table and tilts me back into the dentist's chair. She leans over my left shoulder to peer into my mouth.

'But how do you see without the lamp?' she asks the dentist.

He peers over my right shoulder.

'With difficulty,' he admits. 'But I'm getting used to it. Upper right molar. Missing. Lower right molar. Missing. Upper right premolar. Missing—'

The dental nurse writes it all down.

'And I'm afraid lower left premolar needs a crown. I could try filling it again but—' the dentist shakes his head at me.

I shake my head back. The London dentist sighs. He knows the story of the contaminated transfusions. He knows that it is going to stop with us.

'Keep the light off,' he tells the nurse. 'Lower left premolar. Extraction. No charge.'

'Good evening,' smiles the white-haired woman.

She heaves the lid from a black Westminster City Council bin. Her little dog backs off to join me on the corner.

'Do you always work at midnight?' I ask.

'It's the best time,' she agrees.

'Because you don't get any hassle?'

'Because the bins are full,' she explains.

She lets go one bin lid to open another. The first shuts with a bang. The little dog growls at my cafetière.

'Sit,' she reproves it.

A third bin is heaved open. The white haired woman pulls a ceramic casserole dish out of it. Under the streetlight the ceramic glaze sparkles.

The little dog runs across the pavement to inspect it.

'Cracked,' says the white-haired woman, 'but still useful.'

An unopened packet of photocopy paper is discovered in a cardboard box.

'Is it useful?' the white-haired woman asks me. 'Will it still go through a photocopier?'

'Not if it's damp,' we agree.

'She says she furnishes whole flats for poor people,' I tell my husband, 'and she says after midnight is the best time for this sort of career because—'

My husband is not listening. He is failing to order office supplies online.

'It's impossible to settle bills in time without your salary,' he tells me. 'We can't even stay in the black with the office supplier.'

He clicks *Print Account Summary* in evidence. Nothing happens. *Refill Paper Tray*, shrugs the A3 printer.

'I can't *refill paper tray*,' complains my husband. 'I haven't got any *paper*.'

'We found an unopened packet downstairs,' I am explaining again.

The cursor on my husband's computer screen hesitates over *Add to Basket*.

'Did you find any ink cartridges?' he asks.

I press my mobile telephone to my ear. In the background our son and his girlfriend are conferring over a Googlemap. In my foreground, three lanes of traffic accelerate towards me.

'*Oh God*,' I mouth, so that the mobile telephone won't relay my panic.

'WHERE ARE YOU?' my husband is yelling.

'I don't know. On a traffic island?'

Traffic lights change green to amber. Taillights disappear beneath the boughs of oak which canopy the end of a park. Sunlight dapples empty tarmac. My traffic island takes on the idyllic isolation of a desert one. I glance towards the distant railings of a palatial townhouse and wonder whether to make a dash for it.

'DON'T MOVE UNTIL WE WORK OUT WHERE YOU ARE!' bellows my husband. 'STAY ON YOUR TRAFFIC ISLAND!'

'She's taken the Victoria Line to Green Park,' says our daughter's voice, 'to test another sunblock. But it hasn't worked, like I told her it wouldn't—'

'—so she's pulled down her hat,' continues our son, 'and missed the pedestrian crossing on the corner.'

'On the corner?' frets my husband. 'What corner?'

'The corner of Buckingham Palace—'

'She's missed *the Palace?*'

'—and then she's walked on up the Mall and tried to cross Park Lane at Marble Arch.'

'ARE YOU AT MARBLE ARCH?' shouts my husband. 'CAN YOU SEE APSLEY HOUSE?'

The cobbles on the desert island are sunk in concrete at five centimetre intervals to deter pedestrians. It is a precarious foothold. I put out my arms for balance and tilt up my hat.

'I can see a big house.'

'TURN TO FACE IT! TURN TO FACE APSLEY HOUSE!'

Another tidal wave of traffic roars out from one side of Marble Arch, swirls around my inconvenient cobbles, sucks the hat off my head and disappears beneath the oaks. Stillness floods back.

'I'm in the sun!' I shout.

'TURN TO FACE APSLEY HOUSE!'

'I'm in the sun!' I scream.

'STAY ON YOUR TRAFFIC ISLAND!' my husband is shouting. 'AND TURN TO FACE—'

Another tidal wave of traffic breaks and roars towards the empty traffic island. The railings of Apsley House slam into my chest. I clutch at my mobile telephone to stop it falling through them.

Instead of the cafetière, my husband brings iced water to the bluebell urn.

'How are you doing?'

I look up.

'Not great,' he winces. 'Your sunblock's melting and sliding off it.'

I wipe some sunblock from my neck and pat if back on my swollen face.

'Wouldn't it be better to come to bed?'

'It's cooler out here.'

There is a silence.

'Could we please give up on the sunblock plan?' begs my husband. 'You're too ill to try to earn a salary again.'

He hands me a letter from St Mary's Hospital. I am referred to St Thomas' Hospital. My husband takes the pot of sunblock from my hands and climbs the steps to put it in the bin. I pick up my glass of iced water to go inside. The little dog runs around the corner and watches through the railings as my husband comes back down.

'Good evening,' smiles the white-haired woman, looking over them.

'Good evening,' I smile back and close the door against her sympathy.

Through the kitchen window, I hear the bin lid bang.

'Oh, look,' says the white-haired woman's voice. 'Here's a pretty pot.'

There is a pause. I imagine her unscrewing the lid.

'But it isn't *useful*,' she tells the little dog.

In my dream, my mother has come down to the sheepfold, to look for me. I am looking for my father, who is catching the evening rise.

'Leave him be!' she calls. 'The midge are out!'

She is standing on the bank of the burn, where the clouds of midge are thickest. I clamber back up the other side. My mother points along the burn, where a thousand feet of fallen scree forces its course to turn, and peppers it with stepping stones.

'Come into the house!' she scolds.

She turns away. I make my way across the scree. Under each mossy boulder, the burn runs thick with peat. Above them, the midge thicken to a pestilence. I slide and scramble and grow hot. Attracted by the heat, they darken to a plague.

There are midge in my eyes, in my ears and lining my tongue. There are so many midge they follow the rules of hydraulics. They flow across my brows and spill down my nose, flooding over each cheekbone and eddying into my hairline. Where they bite, thick weals swell into one another. I reach my mother's house shivering with inflammation, and wake up.

I have fallen asleep without pulling my black-out curtains. Dawn has happened. Our daughter is marching me to the coffee shop.

'I can't really afford espresso without a salary,' I am fretting.

She hands me its paper cup.

'It's false economy to do without,' she says. 'You can't even skivy for the rest of us in a state like that.'

In the dawn, thick weals have swelled across my face, each igniting the immune reaction of the next. They have spilled across my brows and down my nose, throbbing against each cheekbone and draining in dark red pools around my mouth. I am shivering so much that the first sip of espresso spills and burns my lips.

But on the way back to the rented basement I recount my dream to our daughter. And this time I reach my mother's house, still shivering, but with sufficient pain relief to think.

'Can't we at least know what other settlements have been made?'

'I'd have to sue through the Freedom of Information Act to answer that,' replies the St. Andrews lawyer. 'However, within the terms of the current offer the Government has agreed to pay my costs. So that is one option open to you.'

'And how long will it take?'

'Oh, not long. To sue through the Freedom of Information Act? No longer than eighteen months.'

I grind my teeth.

'I understand that it may take eighteen months to sue through the Freedom of Information Act,' says Oxford University. 'But you must understand that our contract is with your daughter. If the money from the sale of your house has run out then, like any of our other students from low-income families, she is eligible to take a student loan.'

'Ah just a minute!' I interrupt. 'We're not a low-income family. We're a middle income family, missing a salary.'

Oxford University laughs.

'But if the Government is refusing to hold a Public Inquiry then technically—'

'Would you be happy,' I interrupt again, 'if the Government took *your* salary and told you to consider yourself a low income family?'

Oxford University hesitates.

'I don't even expect a Public Inquiry to replace my salary,' I try to explain. 'I'm not even sure it ought to. Your other low-income families are probably more deserving. But I won't ask our daughter to pay for a cover-up. So until there is a Public Inquiry the Government is *precluding* her from taking a student loan.'

The hesitation becomes a silence.

'Therefore *I* will pay my daughter's final fee,' I promise, 'as soon as I have settled under the Freedom of Information Act.'

The silence grows resigned. I contemplate a third option, of asking Oxford University for a ten per cent discount and calling it quits, but stop myself in time.

The crypt of the Oxford college has twelfth century columns and, on one side, leaded windows. Faustus is peering through them. One after the other, the audience notices him and starts.

There is a flash of lightning and a soundtrack of rain. In a door in a corner of the crypt, an iron key turns in an iron lock. Faustus enters. The lights come up.

The stage is set as his library. *Lord of the Flies, Pliny* and *The Beginnings of Humankind* are among its several contributions.

'Is that my dressing-gown?' my husband whispers.

Behind us, at the back of the crypt, an unseen door slams shut.

'*Christ,*' swears my husband.

There is a rustle of silk, a hint of perfume and the *click, click* of stiletto heels. Faustus stares past us, straightens and runs his fingers through his hair.

Click, click. Click, click. Click, click.

The heels meet a spotlight at the edge of the stage. Blonde hair reaches the hem of a white lace dress. Lips are painted a scarlet Cupid's bow. The eyelids above them are lowered.

'I thought she was playing a devil?' whispers my husband.

Our daughter looks up.

'Boo,' she says.

'At least it's pouring,' says my husband, 'which saves the expense of a taxi.'

We walk from our daughter's college room over the cobbles of a rain-soaked Radcliffe Square. In the gloom a streetlight flickers into life.

'That very streetlight,' I point it out, 'was the inspiration for the one which lit the way through the wardrobe into Narnia.'

'I wish I could see a way through,' says my husband. 'It's all very well asking for time to pay. But we know the Freedom of Information Act isn't going to make up for your salary.'

The lamp-post stands at the end of St Mary's Passage. I peer past it, towards Oxford High Street. A bus draws up at the kerb.

'Oxford Tube,' I read aloud. 'Oxford *Tube?* Is that a London bus?'

Our daughter peers with me.

'Yeah, it's a direct link. It only takes a couple of hours.'

She sees that we are staring at her.

'Oh God,' says our daughter. 'I could ask the college proctor for permission to commute.'

We press our hands to our faces.

'Four hours a day?' I dread it for her.

She sets her jaw.

'He gave up his college room for me. It's our way through.'

I open my eyes. It is too early for a spring dawn. Through the wall, there is the sound of running water. I pull on coat and boots, and bring a panful of porridge to boil. Our daughter pulls on her coat and wraps a shawl around it.

'Ready?'

The scalding porridge flows into a plastic box. She hugs it like a hot water bottle and puts a spoon in her pocket. In the colonnade behind Victoria station, we stamp our feet to keep them warm. The Oxford Tube pulls in. Its electronic door slides open.

'Morning, angel,' nods the driver.

'Force should be right; or rather, right and wrong,' recites our daughter at a fast walking pace through Paddington Station, *'Between whose endless jar justice -,'*

'You're going to fail this exam.' I am fretting. 'All this commuting! I've never seen you so exhausted – '

- the train now approaching Platform Three –

'*– justice?*' demands our daughter at the ticket barrier, *'justice – what?*'

God,' I gasp, swapping my espresso cup to my left hand and rifling through her notes in my right. 'Which character?'

'Ulysses.'

'Ulysses, right. Uh – uh –*resides – justice resides-*'

'*- resides.*' repeats our daughter, 'I must sleep. You're coming with me.'

'I haven't time to buy a ticket – '

'I'll sleep right through to Banbury,' she threatens 'I'd be as well missing my exam stuck in traffic on the bus.'

- *train now boarding at Platform Three* –

We race Platform Three and leap aboard. A ticket inspector bears down upon our carriage. Our daughter counts how many quotations she still has to memorise, then makes a pillow of them.

'Waken me at Slough,' she says.

'The court has ruled,' says the St Andrews lawyer, 'that you have the right to know what other settlements have been made.'

'You mean we won our Freedom of Information case?'

'You did, yes.'

My husband is weak with relief.

'We must have a settlement as soon as possible. When will we be shown the figures?'

'Oh, the Government is bound to appeal. So, not for another two years. And of course, if they win their appeal, not at all.'

The A3 printer clatters into life again. Excel spreadsheets drop into its paper tray. Our son hands them round.

'Right,' I begin. 'So if we don't put on the heating next winter—'

'I haven't included any winter heating costs,' points out my husband.

'Then in that case,' I say, 'if we cut out clothes, and a holiday—'

'We cut them out last year,' points our son.

'—and tube fares—'

'My travel card ran out a week ago,' says our son, 'and now my shoes need mending, which is going to put some strain on your non-existent clothes budget—'

'Professional insurance?' I read out.

'Must be paid,' said our husband, 'or I can't put out any invoices.'

'What about this column?' I accuse him. 'Have you put professional insurance in twice?'

'Emollient,' sighs my husband.

He scrumples his Excel spreadsheet and lobs it into his wastepaper basket.

'You haven't had a salary for years. We've spent the house and there's nothing left to cut.'

A Chart of Alarming Decline is opening over his computer screen.

'If all this is a consequence of your contaminated transfusion, then so far it has cost us your salary, your pension, our home and most of my pension. And because of that, we have no access to the law, to get any of it back.'

I check whether the sun has left the pavement and fill the cafetière. My husband brings the cardboard folder. We walk through Covent Garden into Holborn and Chancery Lane. Every nook and corner is refurbished to an expensive law firm.

'Here we are,' says my husband.

He hands me a page from the cardboard folder. It is an Appeal to Parliament on behalf of the victims of the contaminated transfusion scandal. One of the expensive law firms has sponsored it. We are using their offices as its backdrop, their doorstep as my stage.

'**We deplore the recourse of successive Governments to the device of Crown immunity**' I begin.

My husband crosses the lane to make an audience of the brick wall of Lincoln's Inn.

'Where's their sense of responsibility?' he agrees.

'**– the resistance to disclosure of documents –**'

'Disgraceful!'

'**– the refusal to hold an inquiry and then disingenuously rely on the fact that there have been no findings of fault against the British Government –**'

'—ought to be ashamed of themselves—'

'And there weren't any findings of fault against the Irish government, yet they awarded damages,' I add.

'I *know* that.'

'I'm just saying.'

'Yes, but get on.'

I clear my throat.

'**– and the suggestion that unless a Government are in some way responsible for a misfortune befalling a group of their citizens, they are under no obligation to relieve it –**'

My husband applauds. I put the Appeal to Parliament back inside the cardboard folder. We walked down the lane towards Lincoln's Inn Fields.

'Of course the Government won't listen to their appeal any more than it would have listened to ours,' reflects my husband, 'so all in all we've probably just saved ourselves fifteen hundred quid.'

'So this is my portfolio,' says our daughter, unzipping its leather case and heaving it onto her bed. 'These are photographs of a ceiling I constructed in evocation of the Fibonacci sequence.'

'That's incredible,' says our son's girlfriend.

'The masking tape manufacturer sponsored me a hundred rolls,' nods our daughter. 'Each whorl contains a metre of masking tape and there were ten metres in every roll, so the complete artwork is made up of one thousand whorls.'

'That's incredible,' repeats our son's girlfriend.

I look at our son, who is not looking at my husband, who is not looking at me.

'She can actually draw beautifully,' I tell our son's girlfriend.

'And these are my photographs of Canova's sculpture *The Dancer*,' continues our daughter. 'It was commissioned by the empress Josephine for her *grande galerie* at Malmaison and is now owned by the Hermitage Museum in St Petersburg. But this summer it formed part of an exhibition in Somerset House. So I went down to get these photographs and then used a rubber to erase large sections of them—'

'That's incredible,' gasps our son's girlfriend.

I look at my husband. He is looking at our son, who is looking at *The* partially-erased *Dancer*.

'She says she'll start drawing again, now that she's finished her degree,' I tell our son's girlfriend.

'And this is a collage put together from the torn envelopes of all the letters mum wrote to me when she had Hepatitis C—' continues our daughter.

'*Dad, Dad!*'

'What?'

'*Ask for your money back*,' stage-whispers our son.

Beyond the bluebell urn, in the coal cellar office, my husband is still at his desk. A streetlight illuminates his exhaustion.

'We can't cope any more,' he is telling our son. 'We need a bigger flat but we can barely afford the rent on this one.'

'You need a break,' our son is telling him. 'Stop worrying about it until you've had some sleep.'

Our son locks the coal cellar office and hangs up its key. His girlfriend brings cups of tea to the kitchen table.

'How can she start drawing again without a studio?' My husband is fretting as he drinks it. 'It's bad enough she's sleeping in the kitchen.'

'I'll make a plan,' I say.

'She'll make a plan,' our daughter agrees.

My husband goes into our bedroom to put on his pyjamas. The bedroom door closes behind him. Our daughter looks at me. I look around the basement flat.

'Give me a *minute*,' I am saying. 'Give me a *minute*.'

I stop at the coal cellar office.

'Don't be daft,' says our daughter. 'What use is a studio without any windows?'

'Then what about the lightwell?'

'The postman would have to step over me,' objects our daughter. 'And what happens when it rains?'

I tap on our son's bedroom door.

'Come in!' calls his girlfriend.

She is cross-legged on the bed, typing up her doctorate. Our son is working at his desk.

'Don't even think about it,' he says.

His girlfriend laughs. She smooths the duvet around her.

'I can share with an easel,' she grins at our daughter.

Our son sighs. He gets up from his desk.

'Let's cut this short,' he says. 'Back up, back up!'

He follows me into the passage.

'There is only one option, mum.'

I nod. He taps on our bedroom door.

'What is it?' calls my husband.

We open the door wide. My husband is lying in bed, the duvet tucked under his chin. Our son clasps his hands together like an opera singer.

'Due to the economic situation,' he begins, 'I'm afraid we're going to have to let you go.'

Our bed is lowered into its new home. It clears the kitchen table by half an inch.

'It was meant to be,' I say.

'No it wasn't,' snaps my husband. 'I was meant to be *in it*. And anyway, the world is constructed to the nearest inch. That's all. It means things fit more often than they should.'

'I hope my black-out curtains fit the kitchen window,' I say, behind an armful of one.

'You're not hanging curtains tonight?' he frowns.

'She can't go to bed if she doesn't,' says our daughter, behind an armful of the other.

My husband's temper is not improved when I stand on the coal-cellar-office chair.

'It's almost midnight,' he grumbles, swiping his tea-mug from the table before I knock it over. 'It's too late for this upheaval.'

Our son and his girlfriend are carrying through our chest of drawers.

'Midnight's not that late,' she laughs.

'Midnight *is* late,' my husband tells her. 'The world is *asleep* at midnight.'

He tugs the newly-hung blackout curtains open, by way of demonstration. Our son grins.

'It's a lightshow,' he tells me. 'They sell the stacks as advertising space.'

'What?' says my husband, turning round.

High against a midnight sky, the four white chimneys of Battersea Power Station are disco-dancing in bubblegum pink.

'Right,' says our daughter. 'There's nothing in the fridge. There must be a drawing I could sell?'

We follow her into the studio-bedroom.

'What's this?' asks my husband, lifting a cardboard tube and prising off its plastic cap.

The half-obliterated photograph of Canova's *Dancer* unrolls across the floor. More photographs and drawings stand in stacks against the wardrobe door. On the bed, our daughter is raising and lowering chalk portraits from one side of a portfolio to the other. Silhouettes of their right-angles rain down upon the duvet.

'Is that your mother?' asks my husband, rolling *The Dancer* back into her cardboard tube.

The chalk cartoon is sitting at a sunny window, drinking coffee between lessons.

'You could sell that,' I tell our daughter. 'It's only a chalk cartoon. We still have the portrait you painted.'

'What portrait?' asks my husband.

We search for it in the Modernist stack, tipping frames from our right hands to our left. A kaleidoscope of acrylic triangles, orange, red and yellow, flashes as we tip.

'Oh look, there's you,' I say.

My husband rolls his eyes.

'And here's me.'

I lift my portrait the right way up and lean it against the bed. Each oil-painted pane of its stained glass window blazes with light and colour.

'Or this one?' I wonder, tipping a pixellated portrait from its stack, 'Where did you paint this?'

Our daughter points to the blackout curtains which are the pixellated portrait's backdrop.

'I must have painted it here,' she says.

We set the sunny chalk cartoon next to the blazing oil portrait, and the pixellated black-out curtains next to that.

'Wait a minute,' says our daughter.

She tilts a stack one after the other against her knees, until she finds a charcoal study of the black-out curtains. Its foreground is unfinished.

'I can't finish it,' says our daughter. 'I can't see you for emollient these days.'

She lifts the charcoal study to the end of the series of portraits and steps back.

'God, look at that.'

'Look at what?'

'*Autoimmunity*,' our daughter titles her studio-bedroom-gallery's display. 'We may not have understood what was happening, but I've painted it all the same.'

In the British Library, *Private Eye* is not stored on microfiche. It is stored in Restricted Access.

Restricted Access is a corner of the Humanities Reading Room. Its designated dozen desks are overlooked by four CCTV cameras and a Restricted Access librarian. She is holding the six copies I am allowed at any one time.

'I'm researching the contaminated blood scandal,' I explain, 'since I can't afford to pay a lawyer to do it for me.'

Restricted Access doesn't comment on that.

'What's the number of your reading desk?' she asks.

'One hundred and twelve,' I reply.

'I don't actually have a proper reference,' I apologise when I return for the next six copies. 'I'm just looking for articles with the word 'blood' in their title'.

Restricted Access doesn't comment.

'Desk number?'

'One hundred and twelve.'

I am searching as fast as I can but it takes longer than I had imagined to skim-read *Private Eye*. Some of the headlines are making me laugh, and I have to decipher their text without the benefit of One Hundred and Twelve's reading lamp.

But the article which reveals that the infected blood files were not inadvertently destroyed, but deliberately withheld until Lord Archer's Inquiry was over, is not funny.

It is titled **A Bloody Miracle.**

Surprise, surprise. Twenty years after Lord Own was told that key documents had been shredded, they have miraculously reappeared on his desk.

'And where are you going with that?' asks Restricted Access.

I point to the far end of the Humanities Reading Room.

'To the photocopying suite.'

All British Library Reading Rooms have photocopying suites. All British Library cards have top-up accounts to pay for them. I proffer mine and raise my cardboard folder in further demonstration.

'Restricted Access material cannot be photocopied without permission.'

'I didn't realize that,' I apologise. 'May I have permission?'

'Desk number?'

'One hundred and twelve.'

I follow Restricted Access across the Reading Room. She photocopies

A Bloody Miracle. I put it in my cardboard folder.

My hands are shaking so much it is a **Bloody Miracle** that **Bloody Disgrace**, **Bloody Whitewash** and all the other articles I have already photocopied do not fall out.

'So that's Dad's office under the road' says our daughter, leading the new boyfriend past the bluebell urn. 'And this is where my parents sleep –'

The new boyfriend stops wiping his feet for fear the doormat is my bedside rug. I put the cafetiere on the kitchen table. A photocopy of *Private Eye's* **It's Still A Bloody Scandal** is lying next to it. The new boyfriend examines it.

'We're studying this case at law school,' he tells me.

I don't say that I wish he wasn't. I don't say that Lord Archer has complained that transfusion victims are forced through courts they cannot afford, to be defeated by Statutes of Limitations which ignore the symptomless progression of the viruses with which they are infected. I don't point to the final paragraph of **It's Still A Bloody Scandal** which states that **To this day, payments are a fraction of those paid in other countries and consign most sufferers to poverty.**

I don't have to.

'And this space is for my easel,' explains our daughter, '—so when you stay over we'll have to share a single bed. And this is my drawer, so that can be your drawer—'

'Use of the shower is by negotiation,' I tell the new boyfriend, 'but as I bathe a lot, to calm the inflammation, all other bathing times belong to me.'

We tap on our son's bedroom door. His girlfriend is sorting her doctorate into chapters on their bed. Our son is working at his desk.

'I need six forty-five,' he says.

'Could I have seven?' asks his girlfriend.

'Seven thirty,' agrees our daughter.

I start chatting to our son's girlfriend. The new boyfriend does his best to fit in, with a request for seven fifteen.

'Are we done?' asks our son.

I am still chatting to his girlfriend. Our son pulls a torch from a drawer, sets it on his desk and switches it to *flash*.

'And finally,' says our daughter, 'if you don't wish her goodnight, she'll worry the emollient has put you off. But don't expect more than a quick hug, because she also worries that, if she gets it on your shirt, it won't wash out.'

'Goodnight,' says the new boyfriend.

To save his shirt, he attempts an air-kiss.

'Don't touch her face!'

The new boyfriend wipes the emollient from his.

'I don't mind,' he smiles to reassure me.

'Yeah, but I do,' I grumble, 'now I have to reapply what you've wiped off.'

The kitchen lamp switches on. I dream of toast and strawberry jam. The kitchen lamp switches off. My dream fades. The door to our son's bedroom clicks shut behind his girlfriend.

At seven thirty, a shaft of light from our daughter's room illuminates the clock.

'Put the lamp on in the kitchen,' says her whisper. 'Mum doesn't mind.'

The bathroom door clicks shut behind her. The newly-showered boyfriend tiptoes past our bed, in silhouette.

'What's he doing?' mutters my husband.

With the lamp kept off to let me sleep, from cupboards unfamiliar, the new boyfriend is attempting porridge with cinnamon and honey. My husband swaps to lie on his other side.

Behind the ruffled tops of the blackout curtains, dawn dazzles. The porridge comes to the boil. Together, they simmer for ten or fifteen minutes. The new boyfriend stirs in silence.

My husband swaps again.

The crockery cupboard is located, the porridge poured, honey spooned and cinnamon sprinkled. The new boyfriend tiptoes back, a bowl of porridge silhouetted in each hand. Not a chink of light escapes my black-out curtains to alert him to the kitchen step.

'Careful!' I sit up to shout, too late.

A High Court judge rules that the Government's refusal to compensate contaminated blood victims for loss of earnings has been, and remains, **infected by error**.

We take the back streets through Victoria with a picnic for the park and wait at traffic lights to cross Pall Mall. A police motorcycle screams to a halt and holds up one hand. On either side taxis brake one upon the next.

'First legal breakthrough in *twenty-two years!*' we cry.

A second police motorcycle accelerates into the empty intersection, skid turns, and puts down one leather booted foot, to claim possession. The first wheels around him, exchanges a word through the microphone fixed to his helmet, and accelerates on to the next intersection.

'*Thank God* we didn't let our children pay!' we congratulate one another.

A silence falls. Around the intersection, people exchange quick glances. A London bus judders to a halt, without resorting to either air horn or insult. The driver is straightening his collar.

'And just in time,' says my husband, 'because we're so far in debt the bank won't lend us any more. I hope the Government doesn't take long to **consider its position in light of the judge's findings**.'

First one blacked-out limousine, then a second, then a third flash between motorcycles through the intersection. A newspaper vendor under a striped tarpaulin gives a mock salute. The police motorcycle spins on its back wheel and accelerates away to overtake the cavalcade. The traffic lights change.

'Do you know who that is?' asks the newspaper vendor. 'That's the new Prime Minister, innit? He don't hang about.'

I stand next to the bluebell urn, facing my husband over the desk. The one o'clock news is playing through the speakers of the coal cellar office computer. A Public Health minister is saying that she is sorry about the contaminated blood scandal. A lorry rumbles overhead.

'Not sorry *for*,' I point out.

My husband does not hear me. He has not heard the Public Health Minister either.

'She's sorry for what happened,' he says.

More cars roll over head.

'No, she isn't,' they drown out my reply.

The Public Health Minister says that no-one knew the risks when the transfusions were contaminated. My husband looks confused.

'They *did* know. Even the old nurse knew!'

Confusion kindles to outrage. He stands up.

'That's why they withheld the evidence!' he shouts at his computer.

The Public Health Minister ignores him. She says that **compensation for contaminated transfusion victims' loss of earnings is unaffordable in the current economic climate.**

'Unaffordable in the current economic climate?' I repeat.

My husband sits back down.

'But if I'm unaffordable for them, how can I be affordable for you?'

My husband does not answer. He puts his head in his hands. I look round his coal cellar office, at his frayed shirt and his second hand computer.

'Are they laughing at you?' I ask.

His hands are over his ears. I snatch them away.

'They're laughing at you,' I say.

'Hey normal person,' rings our daughter, 'which tube platform have you reached now?'

'Colindale. Where are you?'

'I'm with Dad under the road. He says you need more references?'

'Look in the cardboard folder. Some of the articles have links to other publications.'

'Copying them in,' confirms our daughter.

I hear her fingers tap my husband's keyboard, and then the mutter of their conversation.

'All right,' says our daughter. 'We've got links to links to more links. This could take some time. Give me a brief and I'll text you as I find them.'

'Anything which proves they knew the risk when you were born. Because they did know. The old nurse told us it wasn't just AIDS we had to worry about. She said there was Hepatitis and God knows what.'

The Victorian ironwork canopy runs into the station. I run out of it and across the road, at a sprint.

'Lovely weather,' says the British Library Newspaper Archive.

He takes my request forms and sighs.

'Do we have any reference numbers?' he asks.

I click *text message received.*

'SH 791—' I recite.

In the microfiche reading room, there is a queue for reading machines. A research team of economists are trawling for evidence that the press mistake the budget deficit for the national debt. The duty librarian brings my four spools.

'You could try them on this one,' he offers, switching on the most antiquated reading machine of them all. 'But it needs a gentle touch.'

The most antiquated reading machine waits until the duty librarian has left the room, then chews up the first six inches of the first spool. I run after him. He follows me back into the reading room with a pair of scissors and snips the concertinaed section off. Ignoring my alarm, he gives the feeder mechanism of the reading machine a sharp tap with the scissor handles.

'Behave yourself,' he says.

I load a different spool, then another. The articles are hard to find. Some are only a couple of column inches, others are missing because the newspaper archive is incomplete. I load the spool for the most important one. The archive is complete but I cannot find the correct issue. I scroll through the archive's numbered pages, back and forth, each time more slowly than the last.

'Closing at five,' the duty librarian warns the economists.

In the Newspaper Archive stairwell, I keep my back to the window and clamp my mobile telephone to my ear.

'It's not there?' asks our daughter. 'Which one isn't there?'

'The *Sunday Herald*. And there are only ten minutes left to find it. They've turned the lights up so the economists will finish up.'

Her fingers tap my husband's keyboard.

'*Sunday Herald?*'

'*Yes.*'

'23 January 2005?'

'Yes, but it isn't there.'

Our daughter rechecks the link. I hear the hurried mutter of their conversation.

'Are you remembering it's a different newspaper from *The Herald?*'

'What?'

'It's a *Sunday* paper.'

I turn for the stairs.

'Wait, wait! We'll check the reference number—'

'No, I've got it! It's on the damaged spool.'

The economists are leaving the microfiche reading room. The last holds open the door. I grab the scissored spool and check the label. *Sunday Herald* it confirms.

'Please, please,' I am begging the feeder mechanism as the snipped end of microfiche tape slides through it.

The restraining arm snaps into place. I hold my breath and twist the dial. Pages of *Sunday Herald* sail across the screen. I twist in the opposite direction to slow them down. In fits and starts, 23 January 2005 settles into view. *Page one,* I skim-read, *page two, page three.*

The door opens. The light is switched back on.

'The archive is closing,' warns Security.

'Thanks.'

Page four, page five—

NHS knew blood for transfusions was contaminated with Hepatitis.

I press my British Library card to the photocopy ignition pad. The reading machine freeze-frames and clicks. I twist for the other half of the article's double-page spread. The machine freeze-frames and clicks.

Security reappears at the door. I slide the photocopies into the cardboard folder and push in my swivel chair. He escorts me from the building. Outside, the sun is setting over Colindale Tube Station. My mobile telephone rings.

'Did you get it?' asks our daughter.

I wait by the Red Man.

'Yes.'

'What does it say?'

'I don't know. I'm holding it over my face.'

The Red Man gives way to Green.

'Dad says get in the tube,' reports our daughter. 'She's not stupid, dad. She's waiting for the *Green Man.*'

In the tube, I wrap one arm around the safety rail and open the cardboard folder. The *Sunday Herald* reports that the United States stopped using blood bought from prisoners years before our daughter was born. It warned Britain not to use prisoners' blood either. But the advice was ignored. The minutes of a meeting of British Regional Transfusion Directors, dated the year of our daughter's birth, note that many infected bloodpacks still **come from blood donor sessions in Her Majesty's Prisons.**

At Euston Station, I get out and take the escalator into the station concourse.

'You'll have to go back down,' says my husband when I ring him. 'It's still sunny.'

'I know. I came up for air.'

He hears my voice ring hollow.

'You found it?'

'Yes.'

'And they knew?'

'They knew. They definitely knew.'

'I've laid out St Mary's Hospital referral notes,' explains St Thomas Hospital's nurse, 'and the doctor will be along as soon as he is free.'

She stops and reads the notes again.

'Shall I switch the light off?' she asks.

I sit in semi-darkness. Footsteps sweep in the corridor and sweep out of it again. The door opens. A hospital cleaner sticks his head around it, sees the room is in darkness and locks it behind him. I leap from my chair.

'Wait!'

Footsteps sweep back into the corridor. Someone rattles the door-handle. There is confusion. Doors open and bang closed the length of the corridor.

'Where is she?' demands a voice.

'I'm here!'

The cleaner unlocks the door. He looks me up and down.

'The light was out!'

He goes away in a huff. A retinue of registrars comes in, switching the light back on. St Thomas Hospital enters last and switches it off.

We sit down. Someone passes him my medical notes. He reads them, backwards, flicking one page, then another, then another. The registrars wait motionless.

'Have you read all this?' he asks the consultant sharing his desk.

'Yes,' says the consultant.

Another page is flicked, and then another. The registrars wait motionless. St Thomas Hospital closes the medical notes. He puts his fingertips together and looks at me.

'Autoimmunity is not a consequence of Hepatitis C,' he says, 'We will request a second histology report.'

My husband is waiting with umbrellas. He shows me the sleeve of his jacket.

'It's only fog, but I'm soaked through. How did you get on?'

On Westminster Bridge Road, we join the line of black commuter umbrellas heading for the tube station. It weaves its way round colourbursts of tourist umbrellas. The tourists are trying to take photographs of the Houses of Parliament.

'A *second* histology report?' repeats my husband.

We glance at one another, umbrella to umbrella.

'Are they trying to prove you *aren't* autoimmune?'

'I don't know. They're requesting the biopsy plate from St Mary's Hospital so that their own histologist can give a second opinion.'

The line of black commuter umbrellas reaches the bridge, where the colourbursts of tourist umbrellas are most numerous. Lovers queue to take turns against the parapet. Without breaking step, the black umbrellas circumnavigate their gaiety, weaving off the pavement onto the carriageway. Cab-drivers lean on their airhorns in exasperation. My husband's expression matches theirs.

'We're missing something,' I try to joke, 'but every time I look back, everything fogs over.'

'Look back?' repeats my husband. 'That was what they called their survey of all their previous blood donors. A *Look Back* Survey, six years after you were given your transfusion.'

He stops midway across the bridge. His expression darkens.

'Didn't *Self-sufficiency* say that a screening test for blood donors became available three years after you were given it?'

We reach Westminster Station. My husband's expression darkens further.

'Does that mean the *Look Back Survey* only got underway once the statutory limitation for medical negligence claims had run out?'

In the Science Reading Room of the British Library, the red weal across my nose revalidates my British Library card.

'I'm looking for medical papers,' I say.

The Science librarian tells me the British Library does not hold medical papers. It holds expensive subscriptions to the websites of medical institutions which do. He taps the card.

'Which you can access,' he says, 'via any computer in this Reading Room.'

There is an awkward silence. I cannot look at the Reading Room's computers. He cannot stop looking at the red weal.

'Do you have a specific reference?' he breaks first.

'No.'

'What is your subject?'

'I want to check when a screening test for Hepatitis C became available.'

'Shall I get you started?'

He turns from my disfigurement. He fingers fly up and down his keyboard. I watch the light from his computer screen flicker over his face. He prints out half a dozen abstracts.

'There are also several references to the BMJ,' he smiles. 'But I won't print those. The British Medical Journal is held in open access –' he points across the room. '– in boxfiles on those shelves.'

There are the computer screens to be dodged, a wall of windows to avoid and the Reading Room is lit by striplights. But the bookshelves are tall and tightly packed. I zigzag through their shadows, from A to BMJ.

Six shelves of boxfiles of the British Medical Journal is a lot of shade. I start at one end and track down ten years of headlines.

PRESSURE MOUNTS OVER PATIENTS WITH HEPATITIS C.

HUNT BEGINS FOR PATIENTS SUSPECTED OF HAVING HEPATITIS C.

IRELAND ANNOUNCES COMPENSATON FOR HEPATITIS C.

CANADIANS SUE OVER HEPATITIS C INFECTION.

NO COMPENSATION FOR HEPATITIS C PATIENTS IN SCOTLAND.

I look up. A security guard is reading the last one with me.

'What are *you* doing?' he grins.

He helps me replace the boxfiles in date order. I am still apologising as the most recent is slotted into place. The security guard grins again.

'Spotted you on CCTV,' he keeps nodding. 'Who's that? I said. Dunno, he says, but you'd better get her out of here before I set the alarms.'

He leads me through a warren of staff corridors, into a lift shaft and out of it again, through reserved parking lots and onto Midland Road. Monday to Thursday, the British Library closes late.

'But not Friday!' he shakes a finger in farewell.

I ring my husband and recite the Government's disclaimer off by heart.

'Patients received the best medical treatment in the light of medical knowledge at that time. Yet the British Medical Journal says that the United States and France were screening blood for Hepatitis C years before I was contaminated.'

As I walk, I am tilting the cardboard folder of BMJ photocopies against the sun and my husband's expletives.

'There *was* a test,' I tell him, 'but Britain chose not to use it. Our Government officials held out for a cheaper one.'

Above the bed in the light testing laboratory of St Thomas Hospital hangs a daylight simulator.

A laboratory technician puts dark glasses over my eyes and unfolds a large blue sheet. There is a hole in the middle big enough to fit round the matrix of squares she inks across my stomach.

'I'll expose one square at a time,' she reassures me, 'but each one for longer than the last. The tests will take about an hour to complete and of course if we do get a reaction, you're not going to feel very well for a few days after that.'

'But you know you'll get a reaction,' I say. 'You read the second histology report.'

She tapes a stencil over my stomach, pulls the sheet over my face and leaves the room.

The door clicks behind her. The daylight simulator clicks on. I count to thirty. The daylight simulator clicks off. The door clicks open.

'Let me cover that square up—' says the laboratory technician, coming back in.

'I'm just wondering,' I say, 'how can you be so sure all this is not a consequence of Hepatitis C?'

Her fingers catch the edge of the tape. A stencil is lifted away. Another is pressed into place.

Click says the door. *Click* says the daylight simulator. I count to sixty. *Click click.*

'Just cover that one up,' repeats the laboratory technician, coming back in.

'Please—' I say, under the blue sheet.

Click. Click. I count to sixty and give up. Another minute passes. *Click. Click.*

'– cover that up –' she comes back in to chant.

'Please—' I am trembling.

Click, click. I clench my fists. Three minutes crawl past. *Click, click.*

'– cover that up –' sings the laboratory technician to the blue sheet. '– cover that up – cover that up –'

Two of the matrix of blue inked squares are throbbing. My husband pulls back the duvet on our bed.

'And what are those circles on your back?' he asks as I lie down.

'Specific wavelengths.'

'Do they hurt?'

'No.'

'Aren't the squares specific?'

'No, they're different intensities of daylight.'

The matrix of blue inked squares is arranged in four columns and two rows. A third and fourth swells. My head swims. The first is covered in angry hives. My husband copies them onto a piece of paper, cross-hatching for degrees of inflammation.

'What do you think?' he asks our son.

Our son takes the piece of paper. Every square is cross hatched but the last.

'I think they got the test design wrong,' he says. 'Those squares prove she reacts to light. But we knew that. Those blistered ones mean she reacts worse to more light. We knew that too.'

Our son points to the square which didn't react.

'That one shows she doesn't react if the exposure is short enough.

191

The reason she didn't react to any of the test circles on her back could just have been because they didn't shine the specific wavelengths at her for long enough.'

'So putting all that together,' says my husband, 'what exactly have we learned?'

Our son hands back the piece of paper and looks at me.

'Zip diddly?' he suggests.

'Though the laboratory results were inconclusive,' confirms St Thomas Hospital, 'they do show an abnormal reaction to light—'

'—But didn't we know that?' I ask.

'—and I'm sorry to tell you that histology has confirmed St Mary's Hospital's diagnosis.'

'What I want you to tell me,' I say, 'is whether autoimmunity is a consequence of Hepatitis C?'

'Hepatitis C does not cause autoimmunity,' insists St Thomas Hospital, 'You can set your mind at rest about that.'

My mind is not at rest. My mind is running backward and forward, across Westminster Bridge, from St Mary's Hospital to St Thomas Hospital, with my medical file always out of reach.

St Thomas Hospital's mind is elsewhere too. He is staring through the tall arched windows behind me. The windows frame the river Thames. From its further bank, the Houses of Parliament are looming over my shoulder.

'We can *stop* your immune system over-reacting,' he concedes, 'with immunosuppressants. But immunosuppressants would leave you vulnerable to all sorts of infections. Much better to rely on steroid injections to prevent your condition getting to that stage.'

'Steroid injections? Like a bodybuilder?'

St Thomas Hospital shakes his head. Bodybuilders inject steroid into muscle, he explains. He will inject steroids directly into my bloodstream. Whenever light triggers my immune system, the steroids in my bloodstream will counter the resultant inflammation.

'Cover it up, you mean?'

'Contain it,' he allows. 'Your immune system will still be triggered, but the steroids will contain the consequent inflammation.'

'So I don't look ill?'

'Not as much as you do now.'

'I can live a normal life?'

'There may be side effects, of course—'

'Oh let me guess,' I interrupt. 'Sickness? Diarrhoea?'

'And mood swings,' confirms St Thomas Hospital.

He scribbles a treatment plan for steroid injections on a folded card. I take it to the reception desk. The receptionist is shaking loose her hair.

'*And mood swings,*' repeats St Thomas Hospital.

I slip the Appointments Card inside my jacket. The receptionist repins her hair and looks up. I smile. She smiles. My step accelerates onto and down the stairs.

In the children's corridor below, the walls are decorated with mosaics. Bo-Peep puts her hands on her hips. I hurry past. At the far end of the corridor a statue of Queen Victoria glowers. I race for the exits of the hospital shopping mall. From every window, mannequins gesticulate.

The exit doors slide open. Buses and lorries rumble to freedom up Westminster Bridge Road and onto Westminster Bridge. But an Appointments Card is not really shade enough to reach its other side. In the middle of the river, my brow line swells.

'Look what you have done!' I rage at the Houses of Parliament.

On its terrace, government officials do not notice. They are on their tea breaks, turned away, to face the sun.

'What are you hiding?' I howl in the direction of the Department of Health.

I know *where* it is hiding. It is hiding behind the tube station, in Whitehall, with its hands over its ears.

'Which one of you withheld the evidence?' I demand of every face in Westminster Tube Station. 'Was it you? Was it you?'

It is impossible to tell. They all look the same. Same suits, same blank unblemished complexions, same salary scales, same pension rights.

Fifty feet below ground, I am their equal. Eyes blank, complexion unblemished, my jacket hiding the hospital Appointments Card, I leave the Circle Line for the Victoria ahead of them. At Green Park, I get out. They follow me onto the escalator, each one deferential step behind the last.

But light is rushing down the steps towards the ticket barrier. As I climb I have to duck behind the Appointments Card until I can locate the direction of the sun. As soon as we reach ground level, its light bounces off the Royal Academy across the road, in a kaleidoscope of confusion. The suits are all over me in a second, swarming past, hailing taxis in Piccadilly, jay-walking into Mayfair.

I retreat down the hill, into the park, stop, fumble for mirror and emollient, soothe my brow line before it splits, anoint the inflammation that sits like a giant scarlet butterfly over my nose and cheeks.

My head spins. The sun spins faster. Shadows follow its path between the trees. I follow them into the thickest part of the wood, putting down the Appointments Card where they are deepest, and the grass is dampest, to sit on it and cry.

Through the back door of our rented basement lies a garden. It is a London garden, no wider than its wooden table, complete with neighbour's overhanging tree. I sit under the shadow of the tree to sort the photocopies of the *British Medical Journal* into the cardboard folder.

'Were you facing the painted wall?' asks my husband.

He flicks the bedroom light on.

'God, look at your skin.'

He flicks it off again.

'Didn't we tell you not to face the white-washed wall when the sun is on it?'

'It wasn't the wall,' I fret. 'It was the photocopied pages.'

'Didn't we *tell* you not to read in the sun?'

'I didn't read them. I meant to put them into the folder.'

'You didn't leave photocopied pages on the table?'

'*Yes!*' I shout. '*Yes!* I left some pages on a table!'

I step into the bath. My husband follows me into the bathroom with the cardboard folder in one hand and a towel in the other.

'You have got to go back to St Thomas' Hospital, and ask them again about Hepatitis C,' he says.

I close my eyes.

'I have asked them,' I say. 'And you googled it yourself a thousand times.'

I press the towel to my face and stumble out of the bath.

'Every doctor I've asked has said that autoimmunity is not a consequence of Hepatitis C,' I point out. 'And anyway I *recovered* from

Hepatitis C.'

I collapse onto the bed.

'You don't look like you recovered!' he rages. 'You look as ill as you ever did on Interferon—'

We are suddenly still.

Interferon, I am thinking.

'Interferon,' he repeats.

A shiver runs the length of my spine.

'It boosted your immune system to kill off the virus,' says my husband.

Our eyes meet. His are appalled. Mine are opaque with fever.

'It's rammed it into overdrive!' he cries.

He turns on his heel.

'Where are you going?'

'To google autoimmunity and Alpha Interferon.'

I fall back on the pillows.

'Christ!' says his voice from the coal-cellar-office.

He reappears in the doorway to the bedroom. It has taken his search engine so little time to find a match that the cardboard folder is still in his hand.

The inflammation throbs out of control. All night, I fight to regain it, smoothing emollient over my nose and brows and cheekbones, dozing in the exhaustion inflammation brings, wakening to thick dry unyielding skin, running another bath, soaking the heat and the dried emollient out of my face, until it is soft and pliable enough to apply some more.

At dawn, shafts of sunlight drive the inflammation harder. Tears of self-pity run a hot course over it.

'Are you all right?' wakens my husband.

'Do I look all right?' I weep.

I slide from the bed to the floor, on my knees, like a boxer counted out in the ring.

'Where are you going?'

'To run another bath.'

My husband gets out of bed, hurries past, runs the bath for me. Protected from their salt burns by the warm water, my tears run faster.

I am exhausted. But if I sleep, the inflammation will grow hotter. It will accelerate further out of control. I will waken to a mask of thickened, hardened skin, split and riven with dried blood.

So I bite my lip, sink under the water, get out of the bath, smooth on the emollient, draw the black-out curtains closer and take the cafetiere and the cardboard folder to the kitchen table, to search in vain for the answers it suits someone to hide.

We are standing around a battered old car which our son and his kayaking mates have bought for a few hundred pounds. When no-one is looking I am muttering ancient Dunino imprecations over its bonnet. The bonnet is festooned with stickers, sponsoring the battered old car on one of the ten most gruelling road rallies in the world.

The rally will run from one wilderness to another, beset by kind peasants and cruel police, or kind police and cruel peasants. It will run through mountains and deserts, forests and floods. It will run for twelve and a half thousand miles until the battered cars reach Mongolia. If you want to be safe, says the rally website, stay at home.

All around, battered cars are awash with tearful girlfriends.

'You'd better not get lost,' our own son's girlfriend is ticking him off. 'I'm not waiting eight weeks for a no-show.'

'Team photo!' cries our daughter, camera to one eye.

I know that any one of us could stop him, and I know that if any one of us does, it is likely to be me. I am on the brink of it. Our son says something to his girlfriend. She looks at me and nods.

'Right, I'm off to get the best seat,' she says.

She gives our son a hug and walks away.

'Me too,' says our daughter.

She gives our son a hug and follows his girlfriend. I see what they are trying to do.

'Hey mum,' says our son, holding out his arms.

And with nothing but the courage they have lent me, for I have none left of my own, I step forward, cover his team t-shirt in emollient, apologise, look into his eyes long enough to laugh, and follow his girlfriend and our daughter to the best seats.

Goodwood has donated its racetrack for a start-line. Battered old cars are revving towards it. All around, girlfriends and sisters wave and scream. Ours scream with them. They watch our battered old car accelerate away. I am watching, but I cannot see anything. I am screaming, but no sound is coming out.

I am running on empty.

My husband is back in the coal cellar office. His face is as white as a sheet. He takes a small bundle of brown envelopes from the drawer of his desk. Each envelope is marked HM Revenue and Customs.

'I'm sorry,' he tells me. 'I should have told you before this.'

'What's the matter?'

I pick up the first envelope and turn it over to see what is inside. It is sealed.

'What's the matter?' I repeat.

The second envelope is also sealed. I pick up the third, and then the fourth.

'Oh God,' I say. 'You haven't opened them.'

My husband breaks down.

'There wasn't any point,' he sobs. 'If I file a tax return I won't be able to pay it.'

He hasn't opened the fifth or sixth letters either.

'Are these fines?' I ask him. 'Because if they are, they're my fines. My decisions have led to them. And if I could make the same decisions again, I would.'

I tear open the envelopes one by one. As each is discarded, its fine is added to the total of the rest. By the time the sixth envelope is torn, the fine is twelve hundred pounds. And the tax return is still to be filed. Besides the twelve hundred pound fine for not filing it, we owe the Inland Revenue a year of tax.

I break down.

'What the hell are you doing?' shouts my husband.

He has come back to the coal-cellar-office after a couple of hours sleep, to pick up where he left off, racing against the clock to finish a set of racking calculations, while he cuts and pastes tax deductible expenses into an Inland Revenue online tax return.

'I'm just putting the rest in—'

Bewilderment is checking his rage.

'Look at you! Look at your face! Are you trying to make yourself ill?'

I scatter the Inland Revenue fines across his desk.

'They made me ill!' I shout. 'And now they are making me ashamed!'

'We've coped without your salary for *years*,' our daughter keeps repeating. 'We're doing *really* well.'

But I can't walk in the sun, with my head held up, like everybody else. Under cover of night, my husband and I skulk where the shadows are deepest, through the palaces of Whitehall and into the park.

A late frost has stopped the spring. Shoots of croci and daffodils pause, uncertain, in the moonlight. Under a gaslight, I make my decision.

'Settle for *ten grand?*' My husband is incredulous. 'Now that we've discovered this is *all* a consequence of Hepatitis C?'

He throws me an accusing glance.

'You've lost your nerve!'

I have enough left to argue with him, at any rate.

'I'm being sensible. If they won't accept liability for Hepatitis C, how can we make them accept liability for autoimmunity? They won't. They'll fillet my medical file and destroy the evidence. Next time anyone looks, I won't ever have been treated with Alpha Interferon.'

My husband's shoulders slump. The words *surely not?* die on his lips.

'Maybe you're right,' he says.

I take his arm.

'It's only sensible.'

But it's not only that. I walk through the shadows of the park, as frozen in fear as any daffodil shoot. In Buckingham Gate, the armed protection squad are drinking tea in their armoured canteen. I hurry past its reinforced glass windows. I am tired of playing David to the establishment's Goliath.

In Victoria, the first commuters of the day meet us at the pedestrian crossing. They wear new shirts, and newly washed hair. I am tired of my washed-out shawl, my down-at-heel boots, my sticky disfigured face. I am ashamed I have no salary like them.

In the end, I am settling for ten thousand pounds because I am too tired and too ashamed not to.

Dear Sirs,

GILLIAN CLARK OR FYFFE v SCOTTISH NATIONAL BLOOD TRANSFUSION SERVICE AND SECRETARY OF STATE FOR SCOTLAND

I refer to your letter in connection with the above matter.

I would advise you that my colleague who would normally be dealing with this matter has been absent from the office at a long running Public Inquiry.

I apologise for the delay in responding to your letter.

I shall endeavour to get back to you further once I have had the opportunity to familiarise myself with the file in question. No admission of liability is made on the part of my clients or on the part of any employees thereof.

'They've been trying to get me to settle for the last ten years!' I am wailing.

'Most unfortunate timing,' the St Andrews lawyer is saying. 'My opposite number in the Government's Legal Office has got herself caught up in some long running public inquiry.'

'Yes, I read that too, but I need the money now. Can't you settle with someone else?'

The St Andrews lawyer says he will try, but he is not hopeful. The likelihood is that my claim will not be settled until his opposite number returns to her desk.

'I don't believe this,' I groan, 'How long do long-running Public Inquiries run, in general?'

'Oh!' The St Andrews lawyer sounds impressed. 'Some of them run on for *years.*'

Dear Sirs,

I refer you to the Health Minister's statement to the House of Commons in which the Government regretted that compensation for my infected blood transfusion was unaffordable in the current economic climate.

Please find enclosed my husband's tax return. I write to advise you that he is currently unable to forward this payment to you.

*Until this year, and for the majority of the twenty years or so since I received an infected transfusion, my husband has paid for me after tax. We regret to inform you that this is now **unaffordable in the current economic climate.***

'They'll have debt collectors round here in a minute if I send them an email like that,' says my husband.

'Let them come,' I say.

'No, no! We need one of your plans—'

'I'm out of plans.'

'You always come up with a plan!'

I close my eyes.

'You need a future to come up with a plan. And they took mine away.'

Our son is telling our daughter a funny story. It is about three rally drivers in an argument with a border guard.

'– so then they hauled us off for a strip search –'

'*What?*' I cry.

'Oh wheesht,' complains our son. 'They knew we hadn't done anything wrong.'

'But you shouldn't have shouted at them!'

'Why not? They shouted before we did.'

'Because there are some situations,' I am explaining, 'which you simply cannot win. So it is better to back *down*—'

'*WHAT?*' roars our son. 'Back *down?* You never backed down from a fight in your *life*, before you came to London.'

I am shocked.

'You've let London get on top of you,' he accuses me. 'Why aren't we paying our tax? We're not that kind of people.'

Our daughter has come to her bedroom door to listen. He holds up one hand to stop her speaking. I try to meet her eyes, but she looks away, forcing me back to his. My voice rises in frustration.

'Why should we pay it? They haven't paid compensation! It's *so* unfair.'

'Oh get over it,' says our son. 'Since when did you believe that life ought to be *fair?*'

'They withheld the evidence—'

'—so you *got knocked down*,' our son agrees, 'and now you have to *get up again*, remember?'

The injustice is making me light-headed.

'I *can't!*' I yell at him. 'We're *ruined!*'

'*They're never going to keep you down?*'

A lever arch file of bank statements is lying open on the kitchen table. For want of computer access, I have highlighted tax deductible expenses in coloured marker pens. Receipts are cut and pasted with Sellotape and scissors. The tax return is ready for my husband to file online, as soon as we have found a plan to pay it.

My husband blows out his cheeks.

'There is only one plan,' he says. 'We have to tell them we haven't got the money.'

He lifts the lever arch file onto his desk. I lift it back onto the kitchen table.

'My decisions,' I admit. 'My call.'

'Ready?' asks my husband.

'Ready.'

He reads the Inland Revenue Helpline number from the website on his screen, and taps it into my mobile telephone. I press *call*. My heart rate races over a switchback of automated instructions, and accelerates towards an operator.

'Hello?'

'Yes,' I tremble. 'We owe a lot of tax.'

'Just a second—'

'Well, I myself don't owe you any,' I gasp, 'because I had to resign. But my husband has supported me and he owes quite a lot.'

'Just a second—'

'– then you wrote to him,' I nod, 'but he didn't open the letters –'

'Just—'

My heart is hammering so loud my ears hurt.

'– and I'm frightened that you might send him to gaol,' I choke, 'so I am phoning to tell you that I think my husband is a hero, actually—'

My husband is slumped over his desk.

'Just a *second*,' insists the Inland Revenue. 'Let's start again. This is the Inland Revenue. Who are you?'

'It's a long story,' I sob.

I start at the beginning. Our daughter is born. The Inland Revenue listens in silence. I fall asleep at the wheel. The Inland Revenue listens in silence. I open the letter from the Blood Transfusions Service.

'– to tell me the transfusion is contaminated –'

'*Omigod*!' interrupts the Inland Revenue.

'– with the Hepatitis C virus –'

'Oh. My. *God*,' she is chanting. 'Oh. My. *God*.'

It is the only official acknowledgement I have ever received of the havoc wreaked in our lives. I press my mouth to the back of my hand and shake without control.

'We rang the Inland Revenue,' I tell our son, 'and they have given us a year to pay!'

I cannot stop smiling. Our son gives me a hug.

'We'll be really poor now!' I exult to our daughter.

She dances me round in a circle.

'We'll be lucky if we don't end up on the street!'

'Enough,' says our son. 'I'm in a hurry. Can you iron me a shirt?'

I fetch the iron.

'Tell you what,' says our son, 'can you iron two, just in case?'

He hooks their coat hangers over the doorknob.

'Just in case what?' I ask him. 'I thought you were taking your girlfriend to supper for her birthday?'

'I am,' he says.

He gets down on his knees to investigate the bottom of the cupboard. I look at our daughter.

'In a *white shirt?*' she asks him.

Our son reverses out of the cupboard, slams it shut and gets up. He makes a face at our daughter.

'I might even wear a jacket,' he tells her. 'Or I might not. What's it to you? And who's got the shoe brush?'

'Just phoning to ask if you're all at home?' says our son's voice.

I beckon our daughter and the new boyfriend to the kitchen table.

'I did bake a cake. But we thought you'd be back too late?'

'We'll be back in half an hour,' says our son.

'I'll put a candle on it!'

'Cool,' says our son. 'And just to double-check, is everyone at home?'

'Here she comes,' calls our daughter. She doubles back from the window. The door opens.

'*Happy Birthday to you, Happy Birthday to you—*'

Our son's girlfriend steps inside. I throw up my hands. A ring is sparkling on her finger.

'You're engaged!' screams our daughter.

We rush to embrace her. Our son appears in the doorway, laughing.

'Oh my *God*!' squeals our daughter. 'To my *brother*!'

My husband will not hear of engagement presents.

'We have no money to spend on engagement presents,' he insists.

'There will be plenty of time to buy an engagement present once you've paid the tax,' our son placates me.

'Well, we can't postpone the engagement *party*,' I insist. 'The engagement party can't wait. We have to have it *now*.'

'We have no money to spend on engagement parties,' says my husband.

'We really don't,' agrees our son. 'There'll be plenty time for parties when all our debts are paid. We'll have drinks down the pub instead.'

The pub is off Tottenham Court Road. It is a warm summer's evening. College friends and kayakers wave from a lamplit window.

'It's a lovely party!' I tell our son. 'So many of your friends are here! We ought to buy them all champagne.'

'There is no money to spend—'

Our son takes my husband aside.

'You'd better buy the champagne,' he advises him.

'But there's no money—'

'I know you two,' says our son. 'You'll fix this. And one day, when all the debts are paid and you're sitting on your balcony in Paris, she won't shut up that you let this moment pass.'

'I've just been checking my inbox,' complains the Scottish timber-frame manufacturer, 'where your racking calculations are conspicuous by their absence?'

My husband swallows.

'That's because I haven't finished them,' he admits. 'Our first repayment is due to the Inland Revenue. I've had to chase up unpaid invoices—'

My husband's voice falters. The Scottish timber-frame manufacturer always pays his invoices on time. There is that moment of silence which precedes a storm.

'Are you asking whether you can invoice me instead? For racking calculations I haven't even got?'

'– must find a way to pay this tax instalment –' my husband is gulping.

'– terms are *thirty days*,' the Scottish timber-frame manufacturer's voice is rising. 'We are not a bloody *bank*—'

'– if you would accept an invoice,' squeaks my husband, 'you'll have your racking calculations by close of play tomorrow –'

'Close of play? I'm not paying cash on delivery to wait till close of play!' The Scottish timber-frame manufacturer revs into a roar. 'THIS IS YOUR *LAST* CHANCE! I WANT MY RACKING CALCULATIONS, FAST!'

He hangs up. The coal-cellar-office is plunged into silence.

'What did he say?'

'He said yes.'

'By what time?'

'Eight o'clock tomorrow morning.'

The storm breaks. *Oh God!* we are yelling, clearing my husband's desk of unpaid invoices, opening the cellar door for air, taking no calls but only this first of a year of last chances with which the Scottish timber-frame manufacturer will repay all our tax.

I drink a take-away espresso to fortify myself for a sprint into the park. Once the last drop is drained, its paper cup flattens to a sunshade.

'Excuse me! Excuse me!' it ducks through a crowd of tourists.

'*Sorry, lady,*' their camera lenses drawl in reply.

But something is wrong. The crowds are thickening faster than I can thread the paper espresso cup around them. The sprint slows to a walk slows to a crawl.

'Excuse me?'

The sun is almost at its zenith. The crowds thicken to an aluminium crowd barrier.

'I must get to the park,' I tell the policeman on the other side.

He shakes his head and points. Beyond the hubbub, a new guard is on the march along the Mall.

'Twenty minutes,' advises the policeman.

'*Twenty minutes?*'

A brass band strikes up. The crowd reverberates to its beat. The metal crowd barrier reverberates to my panic.

'I won't last twenty minutes,' I explain. 'I *must* get to the park!'

The policeman turns away. I cower between the shoulders of tall strangers. Another policeman arrives on horseback. He scans the crowd and mistakes the cower for a slump. The first policeman is directed to pluck me into the shade of a palace gatepost.

'You're not going to faint on us, are you?' they frown.

I raise my face.

'God,' says the policeman on horseback.

He glances over his shoulder, at the fast-diminishing stretch of tarmac the guard has left to march.

'Let her through,' he raps.

The metal crowd barrier opens. I fling myself towards the nearest oak. Tubas boom. Flashbulbs pop.

'*What* a nightmare,' I recount the Changing of the Guard to our daughter.

A rucksackful of emollient drops to the floor with a thump.

'Why didn't you wait to shop for that tonight?' she remonstrates.

'I was worried I'd run out.'

Our daughter sighs and unloads the rucksack. She stacks two dozen tubs in the coffee-table-trunk.

'*What* a nightmare!' I am recounting their collection to our son. 'It's a relief to be home.'

I open the first tub and slick its emollient over my throbbing brows.

'You don't look relieved,' says our son.

I slide a second slick over the bridge of my nose. Our son frowns.

'You look like you're reacting to artificial light.'

'No, I reacted to the sun—'

'Then why ladle on emollient half an inch thick now?'

I am embarrassed.

'It's not *half an inch*—'

'You look like a meringue,' confirms our daughter.

'I do not—'

'She uses her emollient as a mask,' they agree, 'to block out artificial light.'

'What *are* you talking about?' I ask them, through the emollient's eyeholes.

'I didn't make an appointment,' I confess to St Thomas Hospital. 'I don't want steroid injections. I want someone to tell me what's going on.'

St Thomas Hospital is silent.

'I suppose you know,' I say, 'that a link has been established between Alpha Interferon and autoimmunity? That for the last ten years research studies have identified Alpha Interferon as the *primary cause* of autoimmune disease?'

The silence continues.

'I mean obviously you know,' I seethe, 'given there are medical papers about it all over the internet. And given the whole point of taking Interferon was to ram my immune system up a gear?'

St Thomas Hospital ignores the seethe.

'Whatever has caused your condition,' he says, 'we have to find a way to treat it. If you are not happy about steroid injections, I suggest we defer that decision until we have assessed the effectiveness of your regimen of light avoidance.'

I push back my chair.

'I'm not happy about any of this,' I say. 'Even if I'm wrong, why have none of you ever *mentioned* the link to Alpha Interferon?'

St Thomas Hospital makes a note in my medical file. The stalemate is intolerable. I turn away. Through the window behind me, across the Thames, the Houses of Parliament watch in silence. My face puckers up.

'I am not saying you are wrong,' says St Thomas' Hospital, in a quiet voice.

'I'm not sure how much we're likely to make of the search for the Higgs Boson particle,' remarks our son.

He is talking over my head, to make our daughter laugh. I press on up Exhibition Road towards the Science Museum. Inside, a queue has formed for tickets. With every ticket, an enamelled badge is given away for free.

The enamelled badges say COLLIDER. All over the Science Museum, small boys are taking their badges to heart. It is a relief to stop and spend a few minutes listening to an audiotrack of a scientist spending a few months listening to a computer. I lose patience first.

'So when and if the particles do collide—'

'—that will tell you nothing about what's happening to your face,' finishes our son. 'They're not particles of light, mum. They're particles accelerated close to the *speed* of light.'

No-one could have guessed from the audiotrack that anything was happening close to the speed of light. The scientist gets so fed up sitting around Geneva that she rings her mum.

The audiotrack explains that nothing in our universe can be faster than the speed of light.

'What?' I say.

'I told you you wouldn't understand,' says our son. 'Oh here we go.'

In the audio reconstruction, the scientist pushes back her chair.

'Hallo?' says the scientist's mum.

'Mum, we found it!' the scientist replies.

The audio reconstruction announces its own credits and reopens six months earlier, at the start of its electronic loop.

'Any the wiser?' asks our son.

We find my husband agog by Stephenson's Rocket and dodge collisions all the way back onto Exhibition Road. My husband leads us into the tunnel to the tube station. Crowds are hurrying through its tiled arches.

'There's no reason why lightbulbs shouldn't trigger a reaction,' my husband is explaining to me. 'Lightbulbs emit lots of different wavelengths. The trouble is we don't know which one is to blame.'

'Do all lightbulbs do that?' I ask our son.

'LED bulbs emit a narrower range,' he replies, 'so statistically they're less likely to set you off.'

I stop walking.

'Then why don't we get some of those?' frowns my husband, colliding into me.

'Because they're not commercially available,' explains our son, colliding into him.

We are tidying the coal cellar office. It is to become, says my husband, a paperless office, once he has found time to scan all the documents I am wedging in his pending tray. I glance under the second arch and into the third, where the engineering archive is still wedged into forty cardboard packing cases.

'One step at a time,' says my husband, following the glance. 'What's that you've got there?'

It is the letter from the lawyer.

'Pending tray,' nods my husband.

'It's too full.'

He places an empty photocopier paper box next to it. I unfold the letter from the lawyer, to make it ready for scanning. The copy of the letter from the Government Legal Office is inside.

It is the letter which starts with my name, hinges on a v for versus, and ends Secretary of State for Scotland. Through the emollient mask, my eyes narrow.

I would advise you that my colleague – the junior lawyer who wrote the letter cannot be bothered to let me know which one – *who would normally be dealing with this matter* – I suppose lawsuits for contaminated transfusions do seem normal to junior lawyers. This junior lawyer was probably not yet qualified when I raised this one. I look up long enough to wonder whether he was even *born?* – *has been absent from the office at a long running Public Inquiry.*

I put the letter in the Pending Paper Box and fold my arms. I am wondering how standard is that last line? Is it the one the junior lawyer uses for all public inquiries? Or was it invented specially for this Public Inquiry? Is that why Public Inquiry has capital letters?

I unfold my arms, and take the letter back out of the paper box. If the standard line is talking about a particular Public Inquiry, does the absent 'colleague' have some particular expertise to offer it? I read the line again – *my colleague who would normally be dealing with this matter* –

My fingers tap my husband's desk.

A colleague, working as a lawyer for the Government, with a particular expertise in contaminated transfusions, is so vital to a Public Inquiry into Something that she cannot be spared to accept my surrender?

I tap the desk again.

'Do you have to do that?' asks my husband from the other side of his computer screen.

'What was the name of the Government lawyer whose letters used to be copied to us?,' I ask him.

'God, I can't remember,' he scoffs.

'Well, you've got more chance than me.'

He hazards half a guess.

'Google it.'

'What? I can't google half a name.'

I pick up the letter.

'Google what you can remember with Scottish Public Inquiry and today's date.'

'That's ridiculous—'

'Go *on*.'

My husband clicks and double-clicks. His eyes widen as his search engine finds a match.

'Scottish Public Inquiry—' he starts to read aloud.

His expression changes. It is obvious what the Public Inquiry is about.

'And our lawyer didn't tell us?' he cries. 'Whose side is he on?'

I pick up the page he prints and read it aloud for myself.

The Penrose Inquiry

This is the website for the Scottish Public Inquiry into Hepatitis C infection from NHS treatment in Scotland with blood and blood products.

'All right,' says our daughter, brushing toast crumbs from my husband's keyboard and realigning it. 'Fire away.'

'Dear Sirs,

I have until today been unaware of the Penrose Inquiry, partly due to the side effects of my treatment for a contaminated transfusion, which prevent me looking at a computer screen, partly because the loss of my salary forced me to move with my family to London before the Scottish Inquiry was set up, and partly because the Penrose Inquiry has never been mentioned by you in any of our correspondence—'

'*—are you in fact acting for the Government, or are you just plain stupid?*' continues my husband.

'Shut up, Dad,' complains our daughter, deleting to *plain stupid*, and nodding to tell me she is ready.

'*Now that I have heard of this Inquiry,*' I continue, '*I am no longer happy to continue negotiations until Lord Penrose has reported.*'

'When is he supposed to report?' asks our daughter.

'Later this year,' says my husband. 'Not that it will make any difference.'

He takes the mouse from our daughter's hand and clicks for the Penrose Inquiry website.

'Terms of reference,' he reads. 'To identify any lessons and implications for the future, and make recommendations. In other words, still no compensation.'

I press my hands to my heart.

'This isn't about compensation any more,' I tell my husband. 'This is about the truth. This is about not living with the *insult* of their lies.'

Our daughter's fingers are flying over the keyboard.

'Good,' she looks up to nod. 'Strong.'

'I know I'm cutting it fine,' I apologise, 'but is there time to bring myself up to date with Lord Penrose's Public Inquiry?'

The duty librarian is not looking at the clock. He is looking at the calendar.

The Newspaper Archive at Colindale is about to close. Its outdated microfiche reading machines have been declared obsolete. The entire collection is to be transported to a special new storage facility in Yorkshire, where it will be tended by robots.

'Robots?'

The duty librarian thinks the robots will be great. They will hover until I make a requisition, he explains to me. Then they will track it down and read the page I want with their own robotic eyes.

'– and scan it straight to our new Newspaper Archive Reading Room on Euston Road,' explains the duty librarian. 'It's a very exciting development, and long overdue. The images will be clearer, able to be cut and pasted –'

A cold hand clutches at my heart.

'Images?' I dread.

'Oh yes,' says the duty librarian. 'We've caught up with the twenty-first century. All newspapers will now be available in digital form, via any computer in—'

'How long have I got?' I interrupt him.

'What?'

'I mean, how much longer is the collection to remain here?'

'Closing at the end of the year,' says the duty librarian.

He remembers what he is about and looks from his calendar to his clock.

'Cutting it fine,' he chides me.

But by the time the first spool for the *Scotsman* has announced the Penrose Inquiry, there are fears of another whitewash. The *Herald* reports that doctors have been allowed to give evidence unchallenged, even though victims despair over their false assurances that the transfusions were safe.

The *Herald* even reports that once again hundred of files have been destroyed, lost to the Penrose Inquiry because the Government shredded them 'in line with normal records management processes.' Yet many were shredded *after* the Penrose Inquiry had been called. Can it be 'normal records management' to destroy documents likely to be the subject of litigation? I load the final spool, but it is too late to ask. The deadline for submissions to the Penrose Inquiry is passed.

My shoulders droop. I pick the photocopy of its first announcement from the printer tray and scrumple it into the wastepaper basket.

The dial to rewind the last spool clicks right, then left. The end of the tape is released from the feeder mechanism. I put the spool back in its cardboard box, push back my swivel chair and push my hands through my hair. There are no spools left to search. And yet the Penrose Inquiry began with such high hopes!

I cannot bear to leave the Newspaper Archive at Colindale with none. Even creased, dog-eared and a quarter of a century late, the Penrose Inquiry is the only hope left. I fish its scrumpled promise out of the wastepaper basket and smooth it into the cardboard folder.

Inquiry into infected blood scandal will 'name names' of those to blame.

'All Hepatitis C correspondence you ever received is archived like everything else,' says my husband, following me round the bluebell urn, 'but you're too late to submit new evidence.'

'I'm submitting it anyway. How can Lord Penrose find out the truth, if he doesn't have all the evidence?'

My husband shakes his head for Lord Penrose's chances, and unlocks the door to the coal-cellar-office. I duck under its first arch.

'So what's all my Hepatitis correspondence catalogued under?'

'Under the road,' nods my husband, ducking to follow me in.

We start at one end. Each packing box of seven-year archive holds a dozen files. The files' names are scrawled in black marker pen on its cardboard sides. One by one, taking an end each, we lift the boxes clear of the third arch, check their black scrawls, and store them under the second arch. The cardboard box with HepC scrawled in black marker pen is the second last of all.

My husband opens the first lever arch file on top of the pile of boxes under the second vault. I put my elbows on the top box and stand on tiptoe, but it is too high for me to see. I pull another box across the cellar floor to make a step.

'I can't believe,' my husband is saying, 'that after all those years we don't have documentary evidence of your Interferon injections. Don't stand on that. You'll fall through the box.'

'You must find a letter,' I say, standing on it. 'I can't write to Lord Penrose without evidence. One letter from a doctor is all we need. Isn't there one from the Royal Infirmary of Edinburgh?'

'Not so far,' he replies, lifting page after page over the lever arch. 'This is all legal stuff.'

'We'll be lucky to find one,' I am fretting. 'Hospitals didn't write to patients about their treatment in those days.'

'But they wrote to your GP,' argues my husband. He stops searching and looks round to make the point. 'These letters to your GP must still exist somewhere.'

'In my *filleted medical file?*' I suggest.

'Oh God,' says my husband, and turns back to search.

'Lawyer, lawyer, expert opinion from barrister, lawyer –' he lifts the pages one by one, up over the curve of the lever arch and down its other side. 'But it won't be filleted yet, will it? How would the Government have known to destroy evidence of Interferon treatment?'

'They wouldn't,' I agree. 'Though once I tell Lord Penrose it has led to autoimmunity, it isn't going to take them long to work it out.'

'– lawyer, lawyer –' frets my husband, searching faster.

He stops and flicks the lever arch open.

The letter he raises from it is dated before the millennium. It is sent by a clinical fellow to the research team who treated me. She writes to confirm that my liver function tests have remained normal, though she is still waiting for the post-Interferon virology report.

I fall through the box.

Our daughter removes a coffee cup and realigns the keyboard on my husband's desk.

'Is it your letter to Lord Penrose that I'm to email?'

'Yes please.'

'Did you type it yourself?'

'Yes I did.'

She hesitates.

'Is that why the screen was switched off?'

DEAR LORD Penrose,,

Further to your Piblic Inquiry, please find encolosed the following documentaiton.

1.   Correspondecne with my lawyer, regarding this later submission to our inquiry and the long term side of effects of treament with Alpahr INterferon follwing tranfsuons of Hepiticis C CONTMAINatied blodd in October 1988.

2   A diagonise of autoimmune idease from St Thomas HOpsital LOndon.

2.   Meidcal Paperes linking autoimmune idease with Alpha Interferon.

3. Referene to my resignation on grounds of light sensistivity.

5. Photogrpahsts of light sensivitive reaciton.

5. SNBTS admission of contaminated tnrasfusion.

My husband prints an email and passes it across the kitchen table. The final payment for our daughter's final term at Oxford University has finally been made. Our daughter takes the email from my hand and gives it back to my husband.

'Not now,' she says. 'I'm having enough trouble with her as it is.'

My husband laughs.

I am not allowed to laugh, nor speak, nor quiver with frustration. I am allowed to sit at the kitchen table, reading a page I have already read, next to a cup of coffee grown cold, twenty minutes at a time, with five minute breaks.

'Break.'

I uncross my legs and clap my hands.

'You'll be allowed to graduate! When's the next one?'

'I don't know.'

'We'll take a picnic,' I dream, 'and hire punts. How much does it cost to hire a punt?'

Our daughter is lifting pieces of charcoal out of a cardboard box and holding them up behind my black-out curtains, to see what grade they are. She chooses the softest and puts the rest back in the box.

'More than we can afford after paying a fee like that,' she says.

In my daydream, we take to the river in two punts. Our son poles one, the new boyfriend poles the other. Their poles flash up and down, throwing up lacework shawls of pale green water.

'It's not a race!' I remonstrate, flicking droplets from my best frock.

Our son's pole breaks the river's surface harder. In the other punt, his girlfriend and our daughter laugh.

'Go faster!' they exhort the new boyfriend. 'Go faster!'

'Sit still!' my husband warns them.

Another lacework of pale green water unfolds in midair.

'Sit still!'

The shawl of water and my graduation daydream collapse together.

'Sit still!' our daughter is repeating.

'What?'

'Sit *still*.'

I blink.

'Oh great,' she continues. 'So now the eyelid's wrong.'

I blink again. Our daughter puts down her stick of charcoal.

'Sorry,' I recollect myself.

There is a pointed silence. I recross my legs. Our daughter picks up the piece of charcoal.

'And anyway,' she says, 'I don't want to graduate until *I* think I'm good enough.'

Our son slams the door behind him and drops one shoulder. A rucksack slides down his arm and lands on the floor with a thud. He straightens and looks from one to the other of us.

'What's up?'

I raise one palm, above the bookcase, towards my portrait's frame.

'Bloody hell!'

Our son takes a closer look.

'Did you draw that?' he asks our daughter.

'Yes, I did', she says.

'*Bloody hell*,' our son is repeating to my husband. 'I thought it was a photograph.'

'Do you mind?' I ask the new boyfriend.

'What?' he says.

They are crowded around my husband's computer, watching a three minute film of Imperial College throwing itself over waterfalls again. Our daughter glances up and yanks the new boyfriend's arm.

'She's watching it in the mirror.'

'What?' he says.

The new boyfriend glances up into the mirror, encounters my expression and steps aside. Another bright plastic kayak, its occupant obscured by foaming torrents, rushes towards the waterfall, bounces briefly clear of its rocky precipice and disappears.

'There he goes!' enthuses our son. 'And here I come!'

'Sorry,' says the new boyfriend, still looking in the mirror.

The three minute film clip flashes up our son's kayak, tumbles into the next rapid and cuts out underwater. I sink into a chair.

'That was great!' my husband is applauding.

Our son is looking up the trip schedule on the kayak club website.

'I can't do the next one,' he says. 'I've got a wedding plan to make.'

'Publication of Lord Penrose' report is postponed,' my husband reads aloud.

'That's Public Inquiries for you,' replies our son.

He takes my husband's mouse and closes the twelve *Terms of Reference* on the Penrose Inquiry website. In its place, he opens a spreadsheet he has written himself.

'*Wedding to-do list,*' he reads. '*Finish degrees, get jobs, find flat.* You see Lord Penrose' mistake? He didn't keep his short.'

'Right,' decides our son's girlfriend. 'My viva isn't for another week. I'll spend it learning to knit.'

She rings her mum.

'How do you knit?'

'Well,' says our son's girlfriend's mum, 'you start by casting on the first stitch – '

' – and then, the more proficient you become, the more intricate knitting patterns you can attempt,' continues the knitting yarn shop. 'But here is a simple pattern for a scarf –'

Our son's girlfriend examines it.

'Hmm,' she decides. 'Too complicated. I'll make mine up as I go along. What wool have you got?'

The knitting yarn shop frowns.

'Well, that depends on your pattern. For fine work, we recommend a four ply. But if you just want to knit up something fast, you might prefer these double knitting yarns –'

Our son's girlfriend feels one strand.

'Haven't you got anything faster than that?'

The knitting yarn shop coughs.

'Well, for a really fast knit, I'd recommend one of our chunky range –'

'What's the fastest you've got?' asks our son's girlfriend.

Back home, she unwraps the parcel to show our daughter.

Super Double Chunky reads the yarn's label.

'*Yay!*' they grin.

According to the shower's schedule, doors click open and click closed. Our son's silhouette swipes a lunch-box from the fridge, and an apple from the bowl.

'Go back to sleep,' he says.

The door to the street clicks closed. His footsteps clatter past the window to the pavement and fade towards the tube station. In her best suit and a double chunky scarf, his girlfriend's silhouette pours cereal in a bowl.

'Good luck!' I whisper.

'Thanks,' she whispers back.

'Her revisions could take months,' I tell my husband, buttoning up my shirt, 'so the *soonest* they can marry is the summer after next – '

His mobile telephone beeps.

'No revisions,' he reads.

I reach for mine to doublecheck.

'No revisions? She's ticked one out of three and I've only just got dressed?'

'Mind your face,' says our son, coming into the kitchen and switching on its lamp.

I put down the iron and hide behind his new black shirt.

'Have you got *another* show tonight?'

'Certainly do,' he says, opening the cupboard.

'Now you're trying to tick that to-do list,' I accuse him. 'But getting a career off the ground *isn't* something you can rush.'

Our son pulls his graduation suit from the cupboard and switches the kitchen lamp back off. He folds the suit into a kitbag, crawls under the kitchen table, inspects the toe-caps of my husband's black shoes, and stuffs them in the kitbag too.

I put my hands on my head.

'You're wearing your graduation suit *backstage*?'

'No time to change after this show,' says our son. 'Got to make it along the Portrait Gallery fast enough to meet the Queen.'

'I expect you're thinking of getting married next summer?' I concede. 'Everyone wants a summer wedding, don't they? Well, not me obviously, because I can't face the sun. Not really, not at the height of summer. I mean, not even long enough for a photograph—'

'It's a winter wedding,' says our son.

'What?'

He pours two cups of tea from the kettle I have boiled.

'A winter wedding. We've decided to get married this winter.'

'*This* winter? But you haven't found a flat!'

'Since when did that stop you?' he grins.

I refill the kettle in a daze. Our son puts off the kitchen lamp with one hand and finishes the milk with the other.

'But – but – don't you have to plan further ahead for a London wedding?'

'I'm not getting married in *London*. Why would I get married here? I'm getting married in the school chapel.'

His bedroom door closes after him. I rush into the studio-bedroom-gallery.

'It's a winter wedding!'

'I know,' smiles our daughter.

'They're looking for a flat!'

'I know,' she smiles.

'And they're getting married *in the school chapel!*'

'I know,' she smiles. 'Would you mind not crying so near the easel?'

I am sitting on a bedroom floor. There are no black out curtains over the bedroom's windows, but through the trees, beyond the streetlamp, the sky is black.

It is long past midnight. I am sitting on the floor because there is no chair to sit on, nor bed, nor desk. No chair, no bed, no desk, no books, no films, no skating boots, no dry-bags of kayaking equipment waiting to explode in the bath –

'Are you all right?' asks my husband.

I shake my head. He comes in and sits down beside me.

'Don't make me cry,' I warn him.

My husband nods and holds out a printed page instead.

Dear Ms Fyffe,
I have read all the papers you sent to us, and I have discussed them with Lord Penrose. May I begin by expressing our sympathy for all that you have gone through? Lord Penrose is now at the stage of writing up his Final Report, so statement taking has ended. We have, however, taken note of your photosensitivity and the link to Interferon. I would like to thank you for sharing this information with us.

I look up.

'You got through!' says my husband.

'What?'

'Well, it wasn't a foregone conclusion. Quite the opposite. The deadline for submissions had already passed.'

'Yes, but it says "statement taking has ended.'

'You got through anyway.'

'I didn't get to make a statement.'

My husband takes the email back and reads it aloud.

'*We have however taken note… of the link to Interferon.* A statement is only a means to an end. You make a statement in person or you make a written submission – the point it, yours got through. They've taken the information on board.'

'So when is the truth going to come out?'

He shakes his head.

'There's been another delay.'

'Another delay?'

'It says so on the Penrose Inquiry website. Someone must be fighting a legal battle to stop it coming out at all.'

He gets to his feet, and helps me to mine. I take back the email and search it for hope from the top.

We would like to thank you for sharing this information with us. We would like to thank you for sharing this information with us. We would—

'Hey, come on,' says my husband in a gentler voice.

He puts his arm around my shoulders.

The door to the coal-cellar-office opens.

'She's here,' calls my husband.

He steps inside.

'Oh not *again.*'

The contents of the cardboard folder are spilled over his desk.

'You have got to let go of this,' he insists as he shuffles them together. 'This Penrose business has only upset you. I told you the truth will never come out. Here, give me that.'

He holds out his hand for my printed copy of *(lack of) Self-Sufficiency.*

'No, wait—'

'Give it here!'

'No, wait! Look at this appendix.'

My husband groans. He sits down. I flatten the appendix on his desk between us. In the year of our daughter's birth, it notes **the UK was still not self-sufficient in blood products and could only be expected to become self-sufficient in a couple of years.**

'So why did they lie to me that the blood was safe?'

My husband puts his head in his hands. I fold the appendix back in the cardboard folder, put it under my arm and dash round the bluebell urn.

'Where are you going?' he cries.

He comes out of the coal-cellar-office and squints up its steps to the railings. The sunlight shining through them dazzles him.

'Are you mad?' shouts my husband.

'Yes!' I shout back. 'Yes! I don't care about their contaminated transfusions. Their lies are driving me *mad!'*

'Today may be your last chance ever to find out,' agrees the duty librarian at the Newspaper Archive at Colindale, 'but this is not a proper reference. You've only given me a date.'

He points to the request form. It is blank save for the date of our daughter's birth.

'Shall I give you one of your usual suspects?' he asks. '*Telegraph? Independent? Times? Guardian?*'

I wipe my eyes.

'*Guardian*,' says the duty librarian, and writes it in the space on the form.

I load the spool for the *Guardian* onto a microfiche reading machine. But I know it is pointless to search without a reference. I put my hands over my face. Tilted just out of the vertical, the screen dial allows the broadsheet pages to drift on. I sit in silence and watch the month of our daughter's birth go past. The spool unwinds to a *Guardian* letters page.

The Blood Transfusion Service writes to confirm, in the same month she is born, that safe blood donated by volunteers is sent to private hospitals.

In the week that follows, other letters arrive on the *Guardian* letter page. Some are from volunteers who do not know that their safe donations are being rerouted from NHS patients to wealthier ones.

'**When blood supply difficulties occur**,' the Blood Transfusion Service writes back to reassure them, '**priority will be given to NHS patients.**'

I open the cardboard folder, take out the appendix to *Self-Sufficiency in Blood Products* and lay it next to the screen of the microfiche reading machine. But *Self-Sufficiency in Blood Products* is adamant.

UK was still not self-sufficient in blood products, and could only be expected to become sufficient within a couple of years.

When blood supply difficulties occur, contradicts the Blood Transfusion Service's letter to the *Guardian* Letters Page, **priority will be given to NHS patients.**

I put my hand to my mouth. The statements are dated within three weeks of one another.

While it poisons NHS patients with high-risk blood it has harvested from prison inmates, the Government is claiming to have insurmountable supply difficulties. But in the same three weeks, when the Government sends safe donated blood to private hospitals, it is claiming to have no supply difficulties at all.

In the same three weeks, in October 1988, our daughter is born.

I hold my British Library card to the photocopier pad, and print the *Guardian* letters page. But the fingers which hold the card, and collect the photocopy from the microfiche reading machine are not my old, ill, debt-ridden fingers. They are the fingers of a young woman. She is educated, ambitious, blessed with a son and an unborn daughter, and in love.

She leaves the Newspaper Archive and take the tube from Colindale to Euston Station, then walks in the shade of London's busy streets towards Trafalgar Square.

'Where are you?' shouts my husband. 'Why aren't you answering your phone?'

'They were sending safe donations to private hospitals. Even though they knew self-sufficiency was not possible for another two years, the Government diverted safe donations to private hospitals.'

I hold the setting sun behind the cardboard folder until I reach the National Portrait Gallery. High on his column, overlooking the *great sympathy* of Whitehall, Lord Nelson slouches on one leg, discomfited.

In the twentieth century gallery, everyone whom the young woman used to know is waiting. The exhibition begins with her grandparents' generation. Winston Churchill glowers through cigar smoke. Aneurin Bevan's point is cast in bronze. Thatcher sits in imitation of a post-war queen. Blair stares in shock and awe. And somewhere between the entrance and the exit, it becomes all right to lie.

It becomes all right to tell a young mother that blood is safe, when you know that it is not. It is all right, even when safe blood is diverted from the young mother's bedside, and replaced with bloodpacks harvested from prisons, because Britain is not yet self-sufficient, and somebody must have it, and the Government will withhold the evidence, to save its pensions and ennoblements, while it steals her future to sell to someone else.

We meet our daughter at Green Park Tube Station. My shoes are leaking, and my coat soaked through.

'She was in the park,' my husband is fuming.

In Green Park Tube Station, the rush-hour is at its height. My husband's fury is only audible in snatches.

'– *and* she's in a funny mood –'

I tap my Oystercard against the ticket barrier.

'What?' yells our daughter, tapping hers.

'– a funny *mood* –'

The ticket barrier registers my husband's Oystercard empty. He turns to fight his way back to the ticket machines. Our daughter looks at me.

She has rechecked the Penrose Inquiry website since my telephone call. There has been yet another delay. Yet another batch of warning letters have been sent. Yet more legal battles are being fought to stop the truth coming out.

'How can these people live with themselves?' seethes our daughter. 'How could they make *us* live their lie?'

We step onto the escalator. My husband is weaving back towards the ticket barrier. I start to cry. He races the left hand side of the escalator to catch us up.

'– in a funny *mood* –'

Our daughter turns back to comfort him.

'No, she isn't, Dad.'

We leave the tube at an unfamiliar station and follow rush hour traffic down an unfamiliar street. Our daughter presses the button on an unfamiliar entry phone. Inside, the stair is carpeted, reducing our distress to a nervous hush. At the top of its first flight, a door is thrown open.

'Hey!'

In a daze, I take in the chair, the bed, and the desk. The chair, the bed, the desk, the books, the films, the skating boots, the dry-bags of kayaking equipment waiting to explode in the bath. And beyond them, between London and its streetlit sky, a balcony sown with flowers.

In the closing scene of my favourite film, Maggie Smith is walking through a garden of flowers. She has worked out the identity of the bomber. The detective inspector is impressed, but the gardener is not happy that the bomber has escaped. Maggie Smith picks a camellia and waves it towards the view.

'*If he has, we'll forgive him,*' she says.

'*Forgive him!*'

'*We all need forgiveness, Quinty,*' Maggie Smith replies.

'Forgiveness?' asks the new boyfriend. 'Who said that?'

Our daughter looks up.

'Who said what?'

'Somebody just said something about forgiveness.'

Our daughter has heard the soundtrack of my favourite film so many times that it no longer registers. She listens for a moment.

'Oh that. Mum's watching a film.'

She follows the new boyfriend's eyes to the blanked computer screen.

'With the screen switched off,' she nods.

I am embarrassed.

'Only films I've seen before, of course,' I say.

The new boyfriend can't help pointing out this method has not much of a future.

'*But for now,*' laughs Maggie Smith, '*I'm as happy as it's possible to be.*'

Our daughter brings a bowl of pasta. She sits down at the kitchen table next to me and stops, one forkful held aloft, when she realises my husband is staring at it.

'What?' she says 'I *like* plain pasta.'

'She likes plain pasta,' I explain.

'No she doesn't,' says my husband. 'Not any more than I like it.'

'But we're going to eat it,' I vow. 'And cut every budget we can find so we can save up for the wedding.'

My husband prints out The Chart of Alarming Decline and puts it on the kitchen table. Then he prints out the tax repayment budget and puts it alongside. We put our heads together.

'Apart from plain pasta,' my husband frowns, 'I can't see any budget left to cut.'

I meet our daughter's eyes. The budget left to cut is obvious. Our daughter wipes her last forkful of plain pasta around the bowl.

'Here we go again,' she says, and pops it in her mouth.

'Come on,' says our daughter, 'and keep your head down.'

The exits from Victoria Station swell with commuters. Booted heels, stilettoed heels and a soft shoe shuffle make a percussion of the rush hour. There is no chat. There is no time for chat.

The commuters swarm into Victoria's piazza. Traffic brakes and bakes in the sun, pinned down at pedestrian crossings. With none to stand against them, the army of commuters redoubles its pace. We step into its flow and accelerate into the light.

Victoria Street dazzles. Outside its theatres, liveried doormen blink out of their element. At the other end, Big Ben chimes six o'clock.

The crowd is on mobile telephones, finishing the business of the day. *When I see you in Frankfurt… couldn't live with margins as narrow as that… try to fix a follow-up appointment.* Liveried doormen discipline their queues. *Ladies and gentlemen, please! This is a public thoroughfare!*

The shadowed entrance to Cardinal Walk races up on my left. We swap lanes, and swap again to meet it.

Safe in its shade, our daughter looks at her watch. Ninety seconds, from one side of Victoria to the other. In a shop window, the layer of emollient is still visible on my reflection. There is enough left over for Palace Street and, with our backs to the sun along Pall Mall, the vennels of St James.

'We've found a smaller flat at half the rent!' we tell my husband.

'There's no point travelling to the end of tube lines for a cheap rent,' he repeats. 'We've been through this. You lose as much in tube fares as you gain—'

'It's a garret in St James.'

'In *St James?*'

'Oh all right,' I huff, 'St James-ish.'

The garret in Soho has a crooked stair and a straightforward landlord.

'Fact is,' he says, 'it's not worth the expense of doing it up.'

Our son has come to look it over in his lunch-hour.

'What do you think?' I ask him.

He is trying to keep a straight face.

'On the small side,' he manages, opening the door to a cupboard. 'Oh! Surprise kitchen.'

The garret has been divided into two rooms. Its surprise kitchen is in a corner of the room looking over the street. In the corner of the room looking over the yard stands a shower cubical, perfect for stretching paper and rinsing brushes. The yard is surrounded by offices, and squashed full of their air conditioning units. Our son pulls his head back in the window and straightens with care, so as not to bang it on the ceiling. He grins at my husband.

In the room overlooking the street, we hang the lanterns my husband wired to light school Guest Night. To keep us warm in winter, the walls are lined with the books I have forgotten I have read. To keep us cool in summer, a milk jug of water makes a fountain of the bluebell urn. That first night, the butter-coloured moon hangs so close to the garret window I could stretch out my hand and touch it.

Next morning, I waken to roof-tops, and the bowed heads of two roosting demolition cranes.

'Isn't this perfect?' I have time to ask my husband. 'Why on earth was it so cheap?'

He is engrossed in a CAD drawing and slow to raise his head. The demolition cranes beat him to it. I watch in awe.

In one synchronised hydraulic yawn, they unfold above the Soho skyline then dive back down to tear jack-hammered lumps from it.

My husband looks at me across the coffee-table-trunk.

'Wha-at?' he bawls.

'Shall I roll it for you?' asks the Art Shop, 'or can you carry it as a flat sheet?'

The sheet of paper stretched over the Art Shop's cutting desk is cold-pressed and thick as linen. The Art Shop's halogen spotlights are reflecting so much light from its surface that, without the mask of emollient to protect me, I have to keep my hands over my face.

'We'll take it rolled,' says our daughter.

The Art Shop fetches a sheet of plain brown paper to roll it round. Our daughter pulls my hands apart.

'You can come out now,' she says.

Our daughter unrolls the thick-as-linen paper and cuts it into wedding invitations. Each is printed with an inscription in an Art Nouveau font and embossed on a wooden pattern. The embossing is hand-painted last.

She holds one up and switches on the kitchen lamp.

'What do you think?'

I slick on more emollient to examine it. As an artwork, it is executed to perfection. My heart stops.

'I know,' laughs our daughter. 'I'm so excited too!'

She sees I am rereading the inscription and tries to gauge the emollient mask's expression.

'I haven't made a mistake, have I?'

She twists the wedding invitation to doublecheck the inscription for herself.

'What's the matter with it?'

'Well – shouldn't her name come before his?'

In the light of the kitchen lamp the embossed and hand painted wedding invitation gleams on for a further second.

'Fuck!'

Our daughter scrumples it into the wastepaper basket.

'Nearly wrote myself off as bridesmaid!' she straightens up to grin.

'Can ye no ring back in the morning, sir?'

'The trouble is,' explains my husband, 'that our son and his girlfriend have posted all their wedding invitations. In the morning, their friends will book online and put your hotel prices up.'

The hotel in Edinburgh is the townhouse from where Shackleton once planned his Antarctic expeditions. Its night porter can appreciate the meticulous planning of my husband's late night call. He pads from Shakleton's study, still lined with the glass-fronted wooden cabinets of his library, to the hotel reception, where night porters are supposed to sit.

'A north-facing room with thick curtains?' he repeats.

'Thank you,' my husband replies. 'I know it's an odd request but we need to know which room number to book online.'

I hold my breath.

'Aye well,' continues the night porter. 'North-facing, with thick curtains? And would it be ensuite ye're after? Then ye might book forty-six.'

I race the stair of the Soho garret, tear off my coat and show my husband our son's text. He looks at the clock.

'He must have had a show,' he says.

I have brought a grocery bag from the corner shop.

'Put that bottle of beer in the fridge.'

My husband removes his reading glasses and opens the fridge. Inside, two pints of milk and half a pound of butter are lasting out till Tuesday.

'There isn't even time for it to chill!'

I am opening a packet of our son's girlfriend's favourite chocolate bars.

'Are there tea-bags?'

He puts his reading glasses back on to count them.

'She won't want tea,' he is complaining. 'She'll be asleep in her bed by now. She's getting married in a fortnight!'

I put the chocolate bars back in their packet.

'But if she does come,' I wonder, 'should I offer her our bed?'

I open the coffee-table-trunk to find clean sheets instead.

'What?' says our son.

He looks at the clean sheets in the coffee-table-trunk. Then he looks at our daughter and rolls his eyes.

'Don't be daft, mum. I'm only here for ten minutes. I've brought you a present.'

The present is in a cardboard box. The label on the top says LED.

'They're light-emitting diodes,' our son tells my husband. 'LED bulbs,' he translates for me.

It is a wonderful present. The LED bulbs are short and fat, specially ordered to fit the Guest Night lanterns and only just commercially available.

'And what does LED stand for?' I ask.

My husband laughs so long he has to clean his spectacles on his sleeve before he can tap out their acronym.

'Light. Emitting. Diode,' he taps. *'Cost. Of. Order. £63. Cost. Per. Unit—'*

The laughter drains from his expression. Our son grabs his chair and pushes it beneath the first Guest Night lantern.

'How much?' cries my husband.

Each time our son moves the chair beneath another Guest Night lantern, my husband holds it steady. In the glow from each succeeding Light Emitting Diode I can read in his expression the running total of their sum.

I wash off the mask of emollient.

A sheet of paper lies over the kitchen table, cold-pressed and thick as linen. It is waiting to be cut into menu cards. From its surface the light from the LED bulbs reflects back in my face. In my many mirrors, for as many minutes, our reflections hold their breath.

Nothing happens.

St Thomas Hospital hands me a copy of his report. Together, we walk back through his deserted clinic towards the tall windows which overlook the Thames and the Houses of Parliament. To be on the safe side, I turn my back on them.

Previous Hepatitis C, reads the report, *acquired from blood transfusion. Responded to antiviral treatment. Current diagnosis: autoimmunity, well controlled by rigorous light avoidance.*

I raise my eyes. St Thomas' Hospital is smiling. I am smiling too.

'Oh, hallo son,' an English voice rings up to say. 'Just wondered if you saw the rugby, by any chance?'

Our son groans. The English voice laughs.

'Listen, I've just reread your wedding invitation. When it says *Scottish dancing*—'

'Yeah?' says our son.

'– does that mean *sword* dancing?'

Our son winks at his girlfriend.

'Yeah,' he says.

The polished brass sign requests that visitors press for appointment.

'Exciting!' grins our son's girlfriend, pressing for hers.

'If only these were your special bulbs!' says her mum. 'Here, hold up your poetry book and I'll find us a dark corner. We'll stay here by the door, thanks,' she refuses to leave my side.

In the fitting rooms of the bridal shop, every silk lace cuff, every fine tulle bustle and scalloped hem is halogen-spotlit. The emollient mask melts at once. I wipe its tears out of my eyes.

'I can't really cope with this,' I laugh.

The curtains of the fitting room are flung aside. We gasp. The dressmaker tucks and pins and smiles for our delight. Our son's girlfriend swears us to secrecy. The curtains whisk shut.

Her mum's composure melts at once. She wipes her tears out of her eyes.

'I can't really cope with this,' she laughs.

'A *tartan* tie?' asks the English grandfather. 'Why would I want to wear a tartan tie?'

The English grandmother is bent over her sewing machine.

'Nobody asked whether you want to wear it,' she says. 'You're wearing it, and that's that.'

The catalogue in the dress shop in St James is big enough to double as a parasol. Before I put it up, it reminds me that if I buy a coat to wear to our son's wedding then the dress shop will note down the place and date of it, to make sure it does not sell the same coat to any other guest.

The coat I am wearing is silk, with matching shoes. The catalogue itself is wearing silver tassels. They tremble as it tilts back down to inform me that the silk coat costs seven hundred pounds, and the matching shoes three hundred.

'I think I'll leave them,' I decide in pantomime. 'I expect it will be too cold for silk, in Edinburgh.'

We scurry into Piccadilly Arcade and out onto Jermyn Street. I put my hand over my eyes.

'You've no ideas what you're doing,' says our daughter. 'You'd better let me find you something to wear to the wedding.'

I follow her into the shade of the park.

'We mustn't spend any money,' I am saying, 'but it can't be from a charity shop. I am The Groom's Mother.'

'You are indeed,' says our daughter walking fast into Victoria.

We reach the first charity shop. A volunteer is hanging a silk coat in its window.

'Just ignore that,' I tell our daughter, walking on

She stops. I am forced to backtrack a few paces.

'I am not trying that on,' I insist. 'I am The Groom's *Mother*.'

Our daughter looks the silk coat up and down.

'Italian,' she says. 'Looks like your size. Minimalist, so you couldn't wear jewellery. But that's good, because you haven't got any.'

In the LED light from the Guest Night lanterns, the charity shop coat is matched with the Laura Ashley hat. Our daughter puts it back on top of my wardrobe.

'I haven't any other hat,' I say.

'Well, you can't wear that one. The brim is frayed. And you do have another hat.'

She lifts down a straw bowler. It is the hat I wore to our son's christening. By coincidence, the charity shop coat and the bowler's ribbon are an exact colour match.

'Minimalist,' approves our daughter.

'She can't wear that,' argues my husband. 'It hasn't got a brim.'

'She doesn't want a brim for a wedding,' says our daughter. 'She'd spoil the photographs.'

'Not as much as she'll spoil them without one,' he replies.

Our daughter is feeding menu cards through my husband's printer on a backing of photocopy paper, so that the printer is fooled that thick-as-linen is only thin. When the photocopier is not fooled, the menu cards come out squint. Then it is my job to argue with my husband until he prints them all again.

'I haven't *time* to print them all again,' he keeps complaining. 'What about these racking calculations I'm supposed to be scanning in?'

Our daughter takes the first right-angled menu card into the room overlooking the yard and washes it with watercolour paint. I take it back to the room overlooking the street. By coincidence, the bowler's trim, the charity shop coat and the painted menu card are the same exact colour match.

I try them on together. Our daughter rolls her eyes.

'Minimalist,' I defend myself.

The final thick-as-linen menu card is edging, millimetre by millimetre, into the printer's tray. My husband is peering at his computer screen.

'I don't understand this,' he peers, scrolling up and down.

Whirr, grumbles the printer. *Whirr. Whirr.*

'I *know* I scanned *West Elevation House Type C* –'

Whirrr. Whiccup!

'– but for some reason –'

Beep. Beep.

'– it isn't showing up?'

Our daughter lifts the final thick-as-linen menu card out of the printer's tray and holds it up.

'Would this be it?' she asks.

'No you cannot take your menu card to chapel,' says our son. 'People do not take menu cards to chapel.'

'But my hat hasn't got a brim—'

'Well hold up a hymnbook then,' he says.

Our son has come to double check the specification of the LED bulbs. He is standing on my husband's chair, unscrewing a Guest Night lantern. When one arm gets too tired he swaps it for the other and gives the first a shake.

'And what if *my* arm gets tired?'

Our son peers at the LED bulb's inscription, screws it back into its Guest Night lantern and sighs.

'I don't know!' he says 'Ask one of the ushers to hold a hymnbook for you.'

He returns my husband's chair, winks at our daughter and goes away. I run to the top of the crooked stair. The door at the bottom of it bangs shut.

But what if there isn't an usher handy? And even if there is, which one should I choose? The physics usher who understands light? Or the schoolfriend usher who knows his way around? Or is the theatrical usher more likely to be practised at this sort of thing?

Our son's girlfriend has written out her wedding speech in sparkly gold ink.

'In my day,' I tell her as we do the washing up, 'no girl would dare to make a wedding speech! I never heard of such a thing! What are you going to say?'

Our son's girlfriend is going to say that on her wedding day, she is supposed to get a new family. But it doesn't feel that way to her—

'*Oh!*' I choke.

Inside me, lemonade bottles of happiness are fizzing over.

'It's a wonderful speech! Even the last bit –' my eyes are filling up '– of course in my day no girl would dare to say it, but—'

'What last bit?' asks our son's girlfriend, scrubbing clean a casserole dish.

'You know. That last bit. That you can't wait to get hold of him—'

Our son's girlfriend stops scrubbing and frowns. Her expression clears.

'*Grow old* with him,' she says. 'I can't wait to *grow old* with him.'

She rinses the casserole dish to hide her smile.

'Oh, *grow old* with him?' I am blushing. 'Oh yes, of course. *Grow old* with him.'

At the bottom of the crooked stair the door bangs shut after the postman.

My husband shakes his head.

'There's no point hoping that means we can buy train tickets. No-one pays by cheque any more.'

I know that no-one pays by cheque any more. I have given up rushing down the crooked stair to see whether anyone has paid at all. My husband can check that at his desk, every morning, via Online Banking.

'Nope,' he shakes his head again.

No-one ever pays in December. Everyone knows that for the twelve days of Christmas no-one is going to pay *them*. So there is no question of buying train tickets to Edinburgh, no matter that at the stroke of midnight their Super Advanced saving is about to disappear, transformed to Off Peak return, and all to the tune of another, unaffordable, three hundred pounds.

'I reckon you could do it,' says my brother, 'but not in a fortnight. It would take you three weeks, minimum, to walk to Edinburgh.'

'Is your house on the way?'

My brother tucks his mobile telephone between his shoulder and his ear, to scroll up the map of England open on his screen.

'Yeah,' he says. 'I'm Camp Nine.'

'It's not the cost of the train tickets that's worrying me,' my husband is complaining to the Scottish timber-frame manufacturer. 'It's yet another week off with no invoicing.'

The Scottish timber-frame manufacturer cannot believe his ears. A *week* off? For a *wedding!* When a morning off would more than cover it?

'Right,' he decides. 'This is your *last* last chance. If she must spend the week before the wedding in Edinburgh, you will have to bear the expense of a hired car –'

He ignores my husband's convulsions.

'– to get yourself to this office every morning AND FINISH MY RACKING CALCULATIONS!'

My husband adjusts the angle of the hired car's side mirror, signals, and manoeuvres into the traffic. It sweeps us onto Tottenham Court Road and to the North.

'*Seven hours* behind schedule,' he is fretting. 'It'll take all night to drive to Edinburgh. And that's not counting stops for the driver—'

'*Stop!*'

'What? Not *now*—'

I clap my hand over my eyes.

'I didn't get the confetti.'

At the *stop!* my husband has decelerated into a bus lane. With relief he accelerates back out of it again.

'You shouldn't shout *stop!* like that. I thought it was important.'

'It *is* important!'

He laughs. I appeal to our daughter.

'We must go back to Peter Jones.'

My husband only laughs the louder.

'*Peter Jones!*' he repeats, searching the rear view mirror for her mirth.

'Nowhere else stocks confetti in December,' says her reflection. 'I checked online.'

We drive back through Hyde Park. I pull down the hired car's sunvisors against the headlights of the oncoming traffic's jam.

'At least we aren't stuck in that,' I console my husband.

'We will be,' he snarls, 'when we set off again, *eight* hours late.'

In the vanity mirror on the back of my sunvisor, our daughter meets my eyes.

'It is getting late, mum. Won't Peter Jones be closed?'

'Not in December,' I say. 'It's Christmas opening hours.'

'Are you sure?'

My husband changes down a gear to listen, stalls in second, and is swept into the no-exit traffic lanes of Victoria.

'*For God's sake!*' he complains.

'Pretty sure,' I reply.

Our daughter looks at her watch and shakes her head.

'It's too late, even for Christmas opening hours.'

'Too late!' confirms my husband, in a rage.

The no-exit traffic lane spills us into Eaton Square. On its farther side, a tower of tinselled glass rises above the trees. My husband signals to turn back the way we came.

'Will you ever learn,' he is still raging, 'not to push your luck too far?'

In the rage, he misses the turn-off and has to follow a taxi round Sloane Square. At the tinselled tower's foot, a uniformed doorman doffs his hat.

'I don't believe this,' says our daughter.

I jump out at the traffic lights. The uniformed doorman steps forward, hat in hand, to close the hired car door.

'Good evening, madam! Welcome to our Special Christmas Event!'

He pulls wide Peter Jones' plate glass door. I step inside. On the first floor balcony, an orchestra strikes up *God Rest Ye Merry Gentlemen*.

'Care for a glass of prosecco?' asks an elf.

Back out on the merry-go-round of Sloane Square our daughter waves each time the traffic lights force my husband to an extra spin. In the end he picks me up on a double yellow line.

'Is one of those paper cups for me?' she grins, catching my packets of confetti.

I pass her prosecco into the backseat.

'You could have had one too,' I toast my husband. 'But Santa said, since you're driving, better not.'

Through the windscreen, motorway signs offer The West, or Keep In Lane for The North. We signal The North, and dip our headlights as The West crosses their beams and disappears. An articulated lorry falls behind in the inside lane. Bereft of its headlights, The North stretches into blackness.

'I can't sew ribbons on wedding favours in the dark,' protests our daughter.

'And I can't I drive four hundred miles with the interior light switched on!' my husband is adamant.

'But I said I'd deliver them as soon as we arrived—'

'I'll sew them on,' I tell our daughter. 'I can sew ribbons in the dark. I had to do everything in the dark until I got my LED bulbs.'

Our daughter drains her prosecco and falls asleep on the backseat. I drain mine and make a pillow of my coat.

'You haven't learned how to thread needles in the dark,' observes my husband.

'What?'

'Thread needles.' He changes down a gear to overtake, then changes up again. 'You can't thread needles in the dark.'

The hired car threads its way in silence through another mile of darkness to The North. I pull my husband's coat over my shoulder.

'I'll think of a plan,' I reassure him, 'once we're further up the road.'

'How much further up the road?' he persists.

He dips his headlights for oncoming traffic and glances at the dashboard's clock.

'Because if it takes five minutes to stitch one ribbon,' he goes on, 'you're running late.'

'Ullo?' says our son. 'Did I wake you?'

'Yeah,' says our daughter.

'Sorry about that. What bus do I get back from Fleet Street?'

'Uh?'

'What number bus?'

'I don't know!'

'Well, look up Transport for London's website!'

Our daughter squints at the dashboard clock.

'Can't you look it up yourself?'

'I've tried that,' says our son, 'but I've had too much to drink.'

Our daughter sits up on the backseat and pushes her hair out of her eyes.

'How on earth did you end up on your own?' she grows concerned.

'I got lost.'

'Are you still lost?'

'No, *of course* not.'

Our son knows he is not lost. Above his head, an enamelled street sign confirms his position. *Fleet Street.*

Our daughter hands me needle after needle, timing her dozes according to their length of thread. The needles turn in and out, in and out. On the backseat, the box of ribboned favours is filling up.

'There are birchwoods on the border,' I remember. 'We can sleep in one of those.'

We reach the birchwoods before dawn. The wheels of the hired car jolt over the ruts in the mud track running through them. Our daughter wakens up.

'Where is this?'

She rubs the condensation from the rear passenger window. My husband handbrakes and switches off the ignition. Silvered trunks close in all round.

'You're on guard,' I tell her. 'We mustn't sleep longer than two hours, or we'll hit the Edinburgh rush hour.'

She nods. My passenger seat reclines to meet my husband's levelled snore.

'Ullo?'

'Are you all right?' asks our daughter.

'Yeah, I'm fine,' says our son. 'Only I just remembered. I'm in Brighton.'

'Do you think we should?' I ask my husband.

'I don't know,' he replies.

In the rear-view mirror, my eyes meet our daughter's.

'I think you should,' she says.

'Even though it's not ours?'

'You won't be happy till we have.'

We drive up the cobbled lane past the door-in-mid-air.

'They've kept my curtains!'

'Good to know,' approves our daughter. 'You won't have to sew replacements when I buy it back.'

'Do you see that old couple trying to lift a wheelchair out of their car?' says the best man's girlfriend. 'Why don't you give them a hand?'

The best man doubles back into the hotel car park.

'Can I give you a hand with that?'

The old lady explains the trouble is the best man will only do it all wrong. She manhandles the wheelchair onto the tarmac by herself.

'Stand back, son,' the old man warns.

The old lady holds the wheelchair steady. The old man launches himself towards it.

'Oomf,' he says.

They make their way together towards the hotel entrance.

'Are you here for Christmas?'

'No, we're here for our grandson's wedding,' the old couple tell the best man.

'The jury's out on the new boyfriend,' reports my husband to our son.

'Very funny,' says our daughter.

The new boyfriend is not doing well. His law school has timetabled an examination in London hours before the wedding in Edinburgh. My husband rebooks his train without expression.

'Borrowed a kilt,' he is overheard recounting to our son, 'and fastened it with a safety pin!'

Our son laughs.

'Would you leave my boyfriend alone?' protests our daughter.

My husband waits until our daughter isn't looking, mouths *through both layers?* and shakes his head.

The bridesmaid is nonplussed.

'You melted the *cake?*'

'I didn't know the radiator was switched on,' apologises our son.

The bridesmaid takes a moment to pull herself together.

'All right,' she says. 'Never mind. Give me the plastic cake container and I'll bake you another.'

'Um—' says our son.

'*For God's sake!*' howls the bridesmaid. '*You melted my plastic cake container?*'

'Now at this point,' says the school chaplain, 'I will ask whether anyone knows of any impediment et cetera et cetera –' he flicks a couple of pages ahead in his copy of the marriage service '– and assuming there aren't any unforeseen interruptions—'

'Hang on!' says our son's girlfriend.

She is looking at her phone.

The ushers' kiltpins have been sent to the wrong address. They are not waiting in a hotel reception in Edinburgh. They are still in London, in the sorting office off Victoria Street. Consternation breaks out. The kiltpins are our son's present to his ushers. He has no more money to buy another present. The wedding rehearsal descends into chaos.

'Does anyone know of a guest who is still in London?' shouts the best man.

Our daughter holds up her hand.

'My boyfriend is still in London,' she says.

Our son and his girlfriend exchange glances. They are both thinking the same thing. They are thinking that the new boyfriend is too kindly and well-mannered to take on the sorting office off Victoria Street.

My husband and I do not exchange glances. I have already read his expression and refused to countenance it. My husband's expression says that the new boyfriend will no doubt substitute a box of safety pins. The new boyfriend does not even understand how a kiltpin *works*. If only the new boyfriend were not a lawyer, but an *engineer!*

Our daughter presses the new boyfriend's number on her mobile telephone. The other bridesmaids crowd around her. In the sorting office off Victoria Street, an argument gets underway.

'Yes, but there's no legal requirement for twenty four hours' notice,' the new boyfriend is saying. 'That's just your internal mail management system. You can make an exception for a wedding and give them to me now.'

'How long has he got?' I ask my husband.

Now look here,' the new boyfriend is telling the sorting office. 'I don't care about your queue. I am not leaving for this wedding without my kiltpins!'

'He won't be leaving for it at all unless he catches a tube in the next five minutes,' replies my husband.

'So either you hand them over,' the new boyfriend threatens, 'or I'll still be holding up your queue when you close in half an hour!'

The argument fades to the steady beat of trainers running along Victoria Street. Our daughter turns to the bridesmaids in delight.

'He's got them!' she cries.

HOORAY! the ushers roar.

Our son's girlfriend shakes the sleet from her coat.

'Get you lot!' she grins.

Her sister-bridesmaid waves a powder puff in acknowledgment.

'You'd better get yourselves sorted out,' continues our son's girlfriend. 'The drinks party starts in half an hour.'

Powder puff and make-up remover pads whirl into the air. Chignons are shaken until they tumble back to curls. One by one, five coat hangers of ethereal insubstantiality are hung over a wardrobe door.

'Taxi's here!' shouts our son's girlfriend. 'Are you all ready? Shall I open the door?'

'Right,' says the best man. 'Who's doing the reading?'

From the ushers' choirstall, the theatrical usher raises his hand.

'Have you practised it?' asks the best man.

'Yeah,' says the theatrical usher.

'Do you want to give it a go now?'

The theatrical usher gets to his feet and climbs up to the lectern. The choirstall of ushers gazes up at him. The theatrical usher gazes out, over the empty chapel.

'I may have to give the drinks a miss,' he announces.

The littlest cousin has a new tartan frockcoat. She knows how to hand jive to *Surfin' Safari*. My sisters and brothers, their children and lovers, move as one.

'That's a nice anorak,' says our son's girlfriend.

'Glad you like it,' says the sister-bridesmaid. 'If this keeps up, I'll be wearing it tomorrow.'

'Dietary requirements,' reads the best man. 'Who put *medium to large?*'

On the morning of our son's wedding I am up before dawn.

'And where do you think you're going?' asks our daughter.

She is silhouetted in the doorway of the hotel bedroom. I have to hop to keep my balance until I get my leg back out of my trousers. Our daughter glances across the duvet to check it still defines the sleeping form of my husband.

'Sneaking out for espresso while Dad's asleep?'

'I'm not *sneaking*. I specially got up early to run to the café before the sun comes up.'

Our daughter opens the curtain. Save for its lamplit windows, Edinburgh lies in darkness. Above it, over the North Sea, a charcoal sky is smudging to pink.

'You're too late,' she says, closing it again. 'There's no point me spending the morning in a beauty parlour to come back here and find you a suppurating mess.'

I sit back down on the edge of the bed.

'And now I'm sorry for you,' she seethes, 'which means that *I'll* have to get the bloody espresso.'

'Not if you haven't got time,' I say. 'Don't make yourself late for the others.'

'Oh yeah,' says our daughter, grabbing my purse.

I get back into bed. The pink sky lightens to gold. The door opens again. Our daughter is carrying a paper espresso cup in one hand and a paper parcel in the other.

'You and your charity shops,' she complains. 'I am *not* happy about this.'

She puts the espresso on the bedside table and the paper parcel on the bed.

'You've got me at it now. Ten quid in the window, but he let me have them for eight pounds fifty because he hadn't opened the till. So I spent your change.'

She sees my expression.

'Same size,' she nods. 'Same colour.'

I scrabble for the parcel.

'The matching shoes!'

My husband wakens up. Our daughter has her hand on the door handle.

'Happy now?'

I am ecstatic.

'She's all yours,' our daughter is telling my husband. 'See you at the church.'

I drink my espresso and hold my nerve. At the last minute, my husband runs my bath and puts out the bathroom light. Under the water, a week of inflammation is soothed away. The emollient mask slides over my face. The minimalist coat slips around my shoulders. I step into the matching shoes.

'You look lovely,' says my husband, 'so keep your head down till we get there.'

'Till we get there?'

He is laughing,

'You won't need your menu card. At least, not at the wedding breakfast. They've changed the bulbs!'

Hotel stairs run into hotel steps. I run into the taxi he has called. The taxi's carpet glides like a magic one. On either side there is a flicker of school gates. We stop in a crunch of handbrake on gravel.

Ushers rush to make an escort of their shadows. Their kiltpins flash at the turn of the chapel stairs.

'You won't need a hymn book either,' they smile.

The stone sills of the chapel's stained glass windows are lined with candles. With every step toward our pew, their candlelight grows sparklier. The kayaking usher laughs and dabs his eyes.

Our son stands up. Our daughter is smoothing clouds of tulle and lace beyond the chapel door. The choir is singing the first notes of the *The First Nowell.*

And the future is rolling out the way it used to roll, up the aisle of the chapel to where a bride is waiting, and on and on forever.

Acknowledgements

My heartfelt thanks to Jenny Brown for her outstanding commitment. My thanks are also due to Sara Maitland, for her editorial insight and to Amy Smith, whose secretarial skills and integrity replace my access to a computer.

I would also like to thank Adrian Searle, Robbie Guillory and Fiona Brownlee at Freight Books for giving LifeBlood its chance, the British Library Newspaper Archive, Scott Gordon, the Francis Head Bequest and the waiters and waitresses of *le Pain Quotidien* and *Carluccio's*.

Those who read LifeBlood will understand how much I owe my family, whose courage and unfailing responsibility are its story.

FREIGHT BOOKS

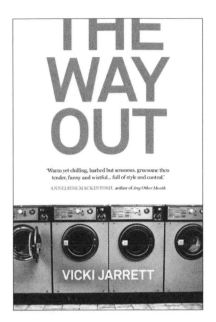

'The stories in The Way Out are warm yet chilling, barbed but sensuous, gruesome then tender, funny and wistful. In her fairytale-like accounts of men, women, children and arseholes, Jarrett serves up a platter of dilemmas, desires and disappointments – occasionally with a big dollop of mustard on the side. This is a collection full of style and control.'

Anneliese Mackintosh,
author of *Any Other Mouth*

The Way Out
Vicki Jarrett

RRP **£8.99**
Release Date **16th March 2015**

A girl on a paper round gets more than she bargained for. A couple feels the strain when the money runs out. Life plays out in the bingo hall and at the bus stop. Welcome to a world of chip shops, offices, call centres and run-down homes.

In this remarkable debut collection of stories from an acclaimed new voice,

the lives of women at the margins are explored; people living on the edge of relationships, the economy and society. Jarrett's unforgettable characters dream of escape from jobs, relationships and lives but, most of all, from the consequences of failure and success.

The Way Out is heart-breaking, tender, devastatingly honest and brimming with black comedy.

FREIGHT BOOKS

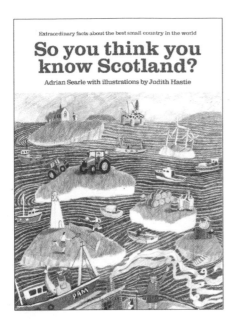

So you think you Know Scotland?

Adrian Searle and Judith Hastie

RRP **£8.99**
Release Date **11th May 2015**

Did you know Morris dancing was just as popular in Scotland as it was in England from the 15th to the 17th century until it was banned by the Church of Scotland? Did you know 11 percent of all Nobel prizes have been awarded to Scotsmen? Did you know Scotland has the highest proportion of redheads in the world?

Sometimes those places that seem most familiar to us are actually more alien that we think. Take a journey with us through the weird, wonderful and downright bizarre facts of Scottish life, culture and heritage. With stunning full colour illustrations by award-winning artist Judith Hastie, we guarantee that you will be surprised and maybe even a little shocked by what you learn about those neighbours you thought you knew.

**FREIGHT
BOOKS**

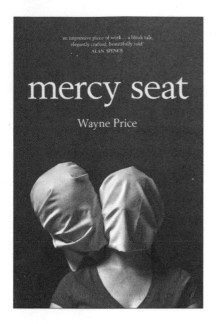

an impressive piece of work ... a bleak tale,
elegantly crafted, beautifully told'
ALAN SPENCE

mercy seat

Wayne Price

'Wayne Price gifts us this black pearl
of a novel. In Mercy Seat, the pressing
responsibilities of straightened young
parenthood are gorgeously depicted
with Price's usual calm finesse. Yet this
is a world taut with seismic menace,
where heaven's weak stars are all
affixed against our better human
wishes.'

Alan Warner, author of *Morven
Callar, The Stars in the Bright Sky*
and *Dead Man's Pedal*

Mercy Seat
Wayne Price

**Shortlisted for Scottish First
Book Award, Winner Brit Writers
Award, Listed for Frank O'Connor
Short Story Award**

RRP **£8.99**
Release Date **23rd February 2015**

Mercy Seat is a compelling story of
desire, loss and regret set against the
rugged coast of west Wales.
Luke, a boy on the brink of manhood,
drifts to a remote seaside town but
can only replace his lonely childhood
with responsibilities – marriage and
fatherhood – for which he is perilously
unprepared.

The arrival of Christine, his wife's
estranged sister, draws Luke into the
unspoken, destructive mystery at the
heart of the two women's relationship. As
his understanding of himself and others
begins to unravel, he must make
a choice that will haunt his life forever.

FREIGHT BOOKS

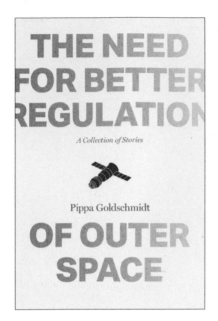

The Need for Better Regulation of Outer Space

Pippa Goldschmidt

RRP **£8.99**

Release Date **11th May 2015**

Pippa Goldschmidt, author of the acclaimed novel *The Falling Sky*, brings together an outstanding collection of short stories on the theme of science and its impact on all our lives. In turns witty, accessible, fascinating and deeply moving, Goldschmidt demonstrates her mastery of the short form as well as her ability to draw out scientific themes with humane and compelling insight.

Goldschmidt allows us to spy on Bertolt Brecht, as he rewrites his play *Life of Galileo* with Charles Laughton after the bombings of Hiroshima and Nagasaki. She introduces us to Albert Einstein as he deals with the loss of his first child, Liesel. We meet Robert Oppenheimer scheming against his tutor, Professor Patrick Blackett, at Cambridge University, having fallen in love with Blackett's wife.

FREIGHT BOOKS

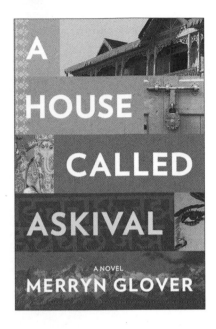

'It wrestles with battles for independence both personal and national, and with the shocking fallout, in families and in countries, that ensue wherever power struggles take place. I was transported to the monsoons of Mussoorie, a hill station in the Northern State of Uttarakhand… Glover gives us an epic and raging sweep of history through many eyes, for there are no victors.'

Northwords Now

A House Called Askival
Merryn Glover

RRP **£8.99**
Release Date **25th May 2015**

James Connor is a man who, burdened with guilt following a tragic event in his youth, has dedicated his life to serving India. Ruth Connor is his estranged daughter who, as a teenager, always knew she came second to her parents' missionary vocation and rebelled, with equally tragic consequences.

After 24 years away, Ruth finally returns to Askival, the family home in Mussoorie, a remote hill station in the Northern State of Uttarakhand, to tend to her dying father. There she must face the past and confront her own burden of guilt if she is to cross the chasm that has grown between them.

In this extraordinary and assured debut, Merryn Glover draws on her own upbringing as a child of missionary parents in Uttarakhand to create this sensitive, complex, moving and epic journey through the sights, sounds and often violent history of India from Partition to the present day.

FREIGHT BOOKS

Fishnet
Kirstin Innes

RRP **£8.99**
Release Date **6th April 2015**

Twenty year old Rona Leonard walks out of her sister Fiona's flat and disappears.

Six years on, worn down by a tedious job, child care and the aching absence in her life, Fiona's mundane existence is blown apart by the revelation that, before she disappeared, Rona had been working as a prostitute. Driven to discover the truth, Fiona embarks on an obsessive quest to investigate the sex industry that claimed her sister. As she is drawn into a dangerous and complex world, Fiona makes shocking discoveries that challenge everything she believed, and will ultimately change her life forever. Bittersweet, sensual and rich, *Fishnet* takes a clear-eyed, meticulously researched, controversial look at the sex industry and the lives of sex workers, questioning our perception of contemporary femininity.